The · Master · Musicians

STRAVINSKY

Series edited by Stanley Sadie

The Master Musicians Series

Titles available in paperback

Bach *Malcolm Boyd*
Bartók *Paul Griffiths*
Beethoven *Denis Matthews*
Berlioz *Hugh Macdonald*
Britten *Michael Kennedy*
Dufay *David Fallows*
Grieg *John Horton*
Haydn *Rosemary Hughes*
Liszt *Derek Watson*
Mahler *Michael Kennedy*
Mendelssohn *Philip Radcliffe*
Monteverdi *Denis Arnold*

Rossini *Richard Osborne*
Schoenberg *Malcolm MacDonald*
Schubert *John Reed*
Schumann *Joan Chissell*
Sibelius *Robert Layton*
Richard Strauss *Michael Kennedy*
Tchaikovsky *Edward Garden*
Verdi *Julian Budden*
Vivaldi *Michael Talbot*
Wagner *Barry Millington*

Titles available in hardback

Bach *Malcolm Boyd*
Brahms *Malcolm MacDonald*
Liszt *Derek Watson*

Stravinsky *Paul Griffiths*
Vivaldi *Michael Talbot*
Wagner *Barry Millington*

In preparation

Elgar *Robert Anderson*
Handel *Donald Burrows*

A list of all Dent books on music is obtainable from the publishers:

J. M. Dent & Sons Ltd
The Orion Publishing Group
Orion House
5 Upper St Martin's Lane
London WC2H 9EA

The · Master · Musicians

STRAVINSKY

Paul Griffiths

J. M. Dent & Sons Ltd
London

© Text, Paul Griffiths 1992

First published 1992

Typeset at The Spartan Press Ltd,
Lymington, Hants

Made and printed in Great Britain by
Butler & Tanner Ltd, Frome and London for
J. M. Dent & Sons Ltd
The Orion Publishing Group
Orion House
5 Upper St Martin's Lane
London WC2H 9EA

ISBN: 0 460 86063 1

*for Robin, Marina, Lara
and Sacha Cleminson*

Acknowledgments

A book like this has many debts: some to previous writers on Stravinsky (especially to Robert Craft, Eric Walter White, Stephen Walsh, Pieter C. van den Toorn, Louis Andriessen and Elmer Schönberger, Richard Taruskin, Simon Karlinsky, Louis Cyr, Milton Babbitt, Alexander Goehr, Mikhail Druskin and Pierre Boulez), some to performers of Stravinsky (and here I would mention the composer himself – a strangely doubtful guide, in musical as in verbal self-reflections – again Pierre Boulez, Simon Rattle, David Atherton and the London Sinfonietta, Oliver Knussen, Philip Langridge, Robert Tear, Cathy Berberian, Peter Eötvös, James O'Donnell and the Choir of Westminster Cathedral, Elaine Bonazzi, Leonard Bernstein and the Royal Ballet). But my gratitude has to be greatest to those who have been through these pages before you, and who have not only corrected me but allowed me to pass off their knowledge, wisdom and sensitivity as my own. Stephen Walsh – though engaged on Stravinsky projects of his own, including a much needed and passionately awaited biography – not only read the typescript but earlier was unfailingly helpful, prompt and friendly in response to my postcards and phone calls. He made the writing so much easier. As for Ingrid Grimes, well, she made the rewriting so much harder, and I am no less thankful for that. Not a page here (except maybe this one) but has been improved by her uprooting of errors and inelegances, her persistence in pressing me to clarify what was confused, and her taste for active verbs. I must also thank Julia Kellerman and Stanley Sadie, who commissioned and encouraged me.

For the preparation of the music examples I am grateful to Steven Carr, and for permission to reproduce them to Boosey & Hawkes Ltd (Exx. 3b, 4–7, 10–15, 17 and 21–30), Schott & Co Ltd (Exx. 3a, 16 and 18–20), Chester Music Ltd (Exx. 8–9), Richard Schauer (Ex. 2) and Faber Music Ltd (Ex. 1).

P.G.

Preface

Игорь Стравинский , Igor Strawinski, Igor Stravinsky, by nationality Russian, French and American, by affection Venetian, Spanish and Swiss, by his own creation pre-literate and modern, Hellenist and Hebraist, Christian and pagan. Stravinsky's variety is no doubt one component to his stature as the outstanding composer of the twentieth century, through fully two-thirds of which he was actively creating and re-creating. But of course that variety is a problem for an introduction such as this, a double problem of organization and orthography. So far as the former is concerned, it seemed inevitable to deal with the works chronologically; apart from the first and the last, each chapter begins with a short consecutive account of Stravinsky's doings during a certain portion of his life – more in the nature of chronicle than biography – then goes on to consider the works and other aspects of his musical existence.

But consistency in matters of language, transliteration and time is more difficult. Until the Revolution, Russia followed the Julian calendar, which was eleven days behind the Gregorian in the nineteenth century and twelve days behind after 1900. Julian, or 'Old Style', dates are indicated here by an asterisk, with a question mark interposed where there is doubt which calendar applies. On the language front, I have generally followed the *New Grove* practice of giving titles in the original where that was English/American or French/Swiss (hence *Histoire du soldat*) but in English where the original was Russian (hence *The Nightingale*), though with some misgivings. There is, in particular, an ambiguity in the notion of 'original title': does one mean what the composer wrote on the score (which may have changed in different versions), or what appeared on the first edition, or what was printed on playbills and programmes for the first performance? Also, in the world of ballet, where French is the lingua franca, forms in French may always have had greater currency among those who presented and saw the original performances, so that *L'oiseau de feu* and *Le sacre du printemps* could claim greater authenticity than their Russian equivalents. *Zvezdoliki* owes its most common English name, *The King of the Stars*, to the intermediate French form *Le roi des étoiles*; a direct translation of the title would have to be something like 'Star-Faced', which misses the effulgence of the Russian and has unfortunate connotations of gangsterdom. It seems better to keep to the Russian, and the exceptionalness is not unwarranted by the work. *Les noces*, as a title, obstinately remains in English usage, and I have not tried to stand in its way. Similarly *Renard* remains the usual form, and here there is the added justification that a translation of the Russian title, *Tale*, would be colourless and confusing.

The same problem is even more acute in the case of the names of people, partly because, in a book filled with émigrés, those names change through time, and partly because two forms might well have equal validity. It is a moot point, for instance, whether a well-born Russian girl of the late nineteenth century would have considered herself an Ekaterina or a Cathérine. In most such cases of doubt I have simply preferred an English form of the name, but not in the dedication.

Lower Heyford
18 March 1992

Contents

Illustrations

Between pages 130 and 131

1 Scene in Fyodor Stravinsky's library, early 1890s (© *Theodore Stravinsky*)

2 The family at Morges, 1915 (© *Theodore Stravinsky*)

3 The composer at work in Les Diablerets, 1917 (© *Theodore Stravinsky*)

4 Drawing of the composer by Picasso, dated 24 May 1920 (© *DACS, 1992*)

5 Draft of the opening of the Piano Sonata, 1924 (*By permission of the Paul Sacher Foundation, Basel*)

6 Serge Lifar and Alice Nikitina in the first production of *Apollo*, 1928 (*From the collection of the Theatre Museum. By courtesy of the Board of Trustees of the Victoria & Albert Museum*)

7 The composer as gentleman, 1930s (*M. Andre Schaeffner*)

8 Tatiana Leskova, Marina Svetlova, Tamara Toumanova, Roman Jasinsky and Paul Patroff in *Balustrade*, New York, 1941 (*From the collection of the Theatre Museum. By courtesy of the Board of Trustees of the Victoria & Albert Museum*)

9 Nicholas Megallanes and Maria Tallchief in the first production of *Orpheus*, New York, 1948 (© *New York City Ballet. Photo from the collection of the Theatre Museum. By courtesy of the Board of Trustees of the Victoria & Albert Museum*)

10 The composer in his Los Angeles studio (© *Boosey & Hawkes*)

11 Page from the draft of the Variations, with the composer's annotation of serial transpositions, 1963 (*By permission of the Paul Sacher Foundation, Basel*)

12 Rehearsing *Fireworks* at the Royal Festival Hall, London, during the 1960s (© *Laelia Goehr*)

1

Childhood

Igor Fyodorovich Stravinsky was born on 5 June 1882* in Oranienbaum (renamed Lomonosov in 1940), a place which had been an imperial residence in the eighteenth century and was now a summer resort: a small town of parks and palaces, with a port on to the Gulf of Finland and a railway to St Petersburg, forty kilometres to the east. After the birth the family returned to their apartment in the city, near the Mariinsky Theatre at 66 Krukov Canal, and Stravinsky did not revisit his birthplace until 1962, nor did he again during his childhood see the sea. His father, Fyodor Ignat'yevich (1843–1902), was a leading bass at the Mariinsky, where he created roles in operas by Rimsky-Korsakov and Tchaikovsky; his mother was Anna Kirillovna, née Kholodovsky (1854–1939). Of their four children, all boys, Stravinsky was the third, following Roman (1874–97) and Yuri (1879–1941). The last son, Gury, was born just over two years later.

During the summer of Gury's birth Stravinsky was in the country, a hundred and fifty kilometres to the south east of St Petersburg. The first musical memories he later recorded may date from this holiday, which was followed by other country summers. In 1885 he made the first of several visits to Pavlovka in the Samara government, the estate of his uncle Alexander Yelachich and aunt Sophie, one of his mother's sisters: this entailed a long journey by road and on the Volga. Later the young musician was to find support in his uncle, who also had his town house in St Petersburg, and whom he remembered as a man of progressive political and artistic sympathies. Then in 1891 he stayed with another of his mother's sisters, Catherine, on her estate at Pechisky in the western Ukraine. Here he met his cousin Catherine Nossenko (1881–1939), later his wife, and from here he visited the fair at Yarmolintsi. Some time when he was nine, too, he began piano lessons.

In the autumn of 1893, when he was eleven, he was taken to a gala golden jubilee performance of Glinka's *Ruslan and Lyudmila* at the Mariinsky, with his father on stage as Farlaf. Among the crowd he caught sight of Tchaikovsky. But this is unlikely to have been his first visit to the theatre: his autobiography mentions *A Life for the Tsar* as the first opera he saw, though at an age when he was already able to have played through the vocal score, and there are also references to *The Sleeping Beauty* (first performed at the Mariinsky in January 1890) and a Serov opera – perhaps *Judith*, in which his father was noted for his portrayal of Holofernes (he appears to have been a powerfully dramatic performer, in both serious and comic roles: Rangoni and Varlaam were his parts in *Boris Godunov*).

In the summer of 1895 Stravinsky's parents took him with them to the spa town of Homburg; it seems he was useful to them as an interpreter (he had a German nanny, Berthe). The next year he spent his first holiday at Ustilug in Volhynia, close to the present Ukraine–Poland border, where yet another of his mother's sisters, Marie, and her husband Gabriel Nossenko (the parents of Catherine) had an estate. This was to be his usual summer destination until the outbreak of the First World War: he and Catherine were given their own establishment there after their marriage. During the summer of 1897, however, he was again with his parents in Homburg; his brother Roman died at Pechisky while they were away. The following year, at the age of sixteen, he wrote a Tarantella for piano, his first surviving composition (it is dated 14 October 1898*). Three years after that he began law studies at the university in St Petersburg.

So the years of childhood passed – remembered later, though, in conflicting ways. For though childhood may be the time of most subjection for the individual, it becomes for that individual as autobiographer the age of greatest freedom. The autobiographer is the sole authority; events are unhooked from dates; impressions are more important than facts; time is subjective. So it very definitely is with Stravinsky, whose autobiography,[1] innocent of dates before 1902, begins rather in the manner of a medieval *vita*, with two anecdotes to show the adult prefigured in the infant. Both are concerned with music, and specifically with peasant singing: a man of enormous size entertains children grouped around him ('I can see it now', the memoirist assures us) with a two-syllable song rhythmically accompanied by armpit raspberries; women sing as they return from work in the evening, and the future composer is praised for being able to memorize their song. In the context of Stravinsky's narrative it is

---

[1]*Chroniques de ma vie* (Paris, 1935–6). But, as so often, Stravinsky's literary voice is admixed with that of a collaborator, in this case Walter Nouvel, an old St Petersburg friend. Reference to the book here is to the 1975 English translation published as *An Autobiography*.

significant that these are both rural, summertime experiences. So much more striking, then, can be the contrast: 'Winter was quite another story – town.'

Here the attractions were different: concerts, and opportunities to play and discuss music with an older friend, Ivan Pokrovsky;[2] visits to the Mariinsky Theatre and the freedom of his father's library of vocal scores; 'the morning vision of the Imperial sleighs of Alexander III, the giant Emperor, and his giant coachman,'[3] both perhaps seeming particulary gigantic to an adolescent who was conscious of his shortness. All contributed to an attachment to St Petersburg that lived on, and perhaps contributed, when Russia was closed to him, to his affection for another city of canals: Venice.

But he describes his parents as cold or even malicious, and, like many of his time and class, he formed his closest relationships with servants (the butler and of course Berthe, who came to take care of his own children in Switzerland and died there in 1917)[4] and siblings (his younger brother Gury much more than the others). Also, he was no scholar. A 1908 letter[5] records that he started at the St Petersburg School No. 27 when he was eleven, going on from there to the Gurevich School, but neither institution is mentioned in his autobiography. Nor did he ever have much to say about his early musical education, other than to acknowledge his debts to Pokrovsky and to two piano mistresses, A. P. Snyetkova and L. A. Kashperova. Quite possibly there was not much to be said, for there seems no reason to suppose he had any training in theory and composition before meeting Rimsky-Korsakov in 1902: the two teachers he mentions in the same 1908 curriculum vitae, Fyodor Akimenko and Vasily Kalafati, were both pupils of Rimsky in the early years of the century, and in his autobiography he referred to Rimsky's early advice to him to 'continue my studies in harmony and counterpoint with one or other of his pupils'.[6] Before that he had, in his own words, 'ripened in ignorance'.

So the picture that emerges from Stravinsky's own testimonies, early and late, is of a boy who was born into a professional musical household, but for whom, being ignorant of musical science, what his father sang from the stage of the Mariinsky would have been as inapprehensible as a fat peasant's rudimentary folksong – and perhaps as immediate. Nor, apparently, is there any reason to alter this view in response to his single extant childhood composition, the unpublished

[2]*An Autobiography*, pp. 9–11.   [3]1921 letter to *The Times*, reprinted in White: p. 573.
[4]See *Memories*, p. 20.   [5]*SPD*, pp. 21–2.
[6]*An Autobiography*, p. 15.

Tarantella.[7] And yet a photograph of the same period[8] shows him sitting in his room with portraits of the masters – Bach, Beethoven, Wagner, Schumann, Berlioz, Musorgsky – stuck to the wall behind him. And yet, too, his memoirs always insist on his early vocation. He wanted to compose; he did not necessarily want to take the obvious educational route, which he could surely have done in his own reading, even in the face of parental opposition to a musical career. In his musical mind he stayed in the country, and waited before submitting himself to the town's order and discipline.

This may have been the action of a dilettante, as Robert Craft has suggested.[9] However, the tenor of his teenage Ustilug letters to his parents[10] – in which music features no more prominently than sketching, theatricals or hulling raspberries – may have as much to do with the intended recipients as with the facts, and the problem of interpreting his creative latency is the greater because these brief extracts are our only direct access to Stravinsky before his twentieth year. One can surmise that without that period of inaction, that ripening in ignorance, he could not have taken a position so resolutely askew to tradition, could not have learned to speak conventional musical languages as if they were foreign to him, however fluent his achievement, could not have kept his music to a different rhythm from that of continuous rational progress. Yet it is hard to know how much this could have been deliberate, how much an accident of personality.

When talking about the creative process, Stravinsky consistently shifted attention from the motivation to the act, from the intention to the achievement, from the why to the what: he liked to present himself as a machine for making music. And this same abhorrence of the psychological marks his autobiographical reminiscences and his letters, so that despite all the wealth of evidence he remains, as a personality, remote. It is not just that all his public utterances about himself were, to a greater or lesser extent, ghosted by others – though they all were. Nor is it just that his recollections of different periods contradict each other – though they often do. It has much more to do with an absence of introspection, which leaves us with a Stravinsky who, despite all the memoirs and photographs and films and interviews, is more like a character in a Nabokov novel than one from Tolstoy: a little unreal, a little constructed. His life story is one of facts, of responding to opportunities, of thought expressed only in action; and it is in facts, opportunities, actions that he will be traced in what

[7]See Charles M. Joseph: *Stravinsky and the Piano* (Ann Arbor, 1983).
[8]In *SPD*, p. 41.   [9]Ibid., p. 19.   [10]Ibid., pp. 19–20.

follows. The larger congruences are not there, and we have the authority of one as close to Stravinsky as Robert Craft[11] for remarkable changes in his character, especially between the stiff, urbane, dispassionate personage of the inter-war years and the later smiling, world-embracing figure.

It would be tempting to see this particular change as reflected in the journey his music took in the decade after the Second World War, but it could equally be the other way around, that what and how he was composing affected the face he showed to the world. The music came first, as surely it came first in affecting his memories. This, too, makes them weak delineators of his inner life, when so obviously the aim of the memoirist is to offer a rather too pat explanation of what he was doing, or was to do, at the beat-up upright piano where he composed. For instance, his reminiscences of the Yarmolintsi fair[12] seem designed for quotation a propos *Petrushka*. Nor can there be much mistaking what was in his mind when Craft asked him what he had loved most about Russia, and he replied: 'The violent Russian spring that seemed to begin in an hour and was like the whole earth cracking. That was the most wonderful event of every year of my childhood.'[13]

[11]See *Glimpses*, pp. ix–x.   [12]See White, p. 22.   [13]*Memories*, p. 30.

2

Apprenticeship

Stravinsky's origins as a composer were obscure during his lifetime, when his creative history began suddenly and splendidly with the Symphony in E flat of 1905–7. But since his death the published record has been pushed back to start with a Pushkin song, *Storm Cloud* (dated 25 January 1902*), and a piano Scherzo of the same year. Also in 1902, accompanying his parents again during the summer to a German spa (Bad Wildungen), he paid a call on Rimsky-Korsakov in Heidelberg: he had an entrée in that Rimsky's son Vladimir was a student companion of his. The next year, in Pavlovka, he started a piano sonata in F sharp minor, and on his way back to St Petersburg he again called on Rimsky. By 6 March 1904* he was clearly absorbed into Rimsky's circle, for on that day his cantata for his teacher's sixtieth birthday was performed in the latter's apartment. Then in the summer, once more at Pavlovka, he finished the sonata, which was played at Rimsky's on 9 February 1905* by Nicolas Richter.

A bigger project followed: a symphony, begun in the summer of 1905 at Ustilug, where Stravinsky was also formally engaged to his cousin Catherine. After their marriage, on 11 January 1906,* they spent a honeymoon in Imatra, now just over the border into Finland, where Stravinsky worked on the orchestral Pushkin song cycle *The Faun and the Shepherdess*, which he dedicated to his wife. In May he graduated from the university, and the following February the first of his four children, Theodore, was born. Now his music began to be heard beyond the Rimsky circle within which his songs and piano works had been performed in 1904–6. A song, the first of two to poems by Sergey Gorodetzky, was given at one of the Evenings of Contemporary Music in St Petersburg (27 July 1907?*), and the symphony, whose middle movements had received a private performance by the court orchestra in the spring of 1907, and whose orchestration had been completed in the summer, was played in full and in public at one of the Belyayev Concerts, again in St Petersburg (22 January 1908?*), under Felix Blumenfeld. Blumenfeld also conducted the first performance of *The Faun*, though accounts differ as to whether this was at the same concert or another on 16 February?*.

Stravinsky's next orchestral work, the *Scherzo fantastique* begun in Ustilug in the summer of 1907, was finished in the spring of 1908 and dispatched to Rimsky, but returned on account of the addressee's decease, whereupon Stravinsky embarked on a *Chant funèbre* for wind instruments in memory of his teacher. This was during the summer, again at Ustilug, where he also worked at four studies for piano, the second Gorodetzky song, and a new orchestral piece, *Fireworks*. In November he started his first stage work, the opera *The Nightingale*, adapted from the Hans Christian Andersen story in collaboration with another member of the Rimsky circle, the writer and musician Stepan Mitusov. The following February his *Scherzo fantastique* and *Fireworks* were introduced by Alexander Ziloti at a concert in St Petersburg which Dyagilev may have attended, and his *tombeau* for Rimsky had its first and only performance under Blumenfeld at the conservatory.

Coming so close to the time of his father's death (on 21 November 1902*), Stravinsky's association with the Rimsky-Korsakov circle had provided him, on his own account,[1] with a new family, and perhaps a more welcoming one. Many of his works of the next few years were dedicated to members of the group: the Scherzo, Sonata and second study to the pianist Nicolas Richter, the Symphony to Rimsky himself, the Pastorale to his daughter Nadezhda, *Fireworks* to her and her husband, Maximilian Shteynberg, the last two studies to the Rimsky sons Andrey (later honoured with the dedication of *The Firebird*) and Vladimir, and the first study to Stepan Mitusov, who was soon to write the libretto of *The Nightingale*. At the same time other friends, including Pokrovsky and Nouvel, were establishing the Evenings of Contemporary Music, where he had his first public performances: of the Sonata as well as the 1907 Gorodetzky song. As he wrote thirty years later: 'It is needless to speak of the importance of these two groups in my artistic and intellectual evolution, and how much they strengthened the development of my creative faculty.'[2]

But the evolution and the development had quite some way to go. If *Storm Cloud* and the Scherzo are representative of what he had to show Rimsky in 1902, it is surprising he was admitted to the circle at all – particularly in the light of his characteristically waspish recollection that Rimsky was 'unkind only to admirers of

---

[1]*Memories*, p. 54.   [2]*An Autobiography*, p. 17.

no, the saturating influence here is Skryabin (e.g. his own F# minor Piano Sonata, which Griffiths perhaps does not know); v. the sharpened fourths, the harmony marked *, the duplet cross-rhythm in compound time even in Ex 1

Stravinsky

Tchaikovsky's,[3] since Tchaikovsky's is precisely the influence most conspicuous in these 1902 pieces and still in the Sonata of 1903–4. Stravinsky could well have been grateful that all three compositions disappeared until after his death: certainly his statement that the sonata 'was, I suppose, an inept imitation of late Beethoven'[4] is, wilfully or not, wide of the mark. The piece, though composed under the direction of Rimsky and presumably Kalafati, has passages of incoherence, and if it suggests the man who would be writing *Petrushka* just seven years later, it does so only by pointing up his problems with traditional musical continuity. For example, in the slow movement, after repeated efforts to provide a smooth harmonic conveyance for his awkward idea, Stravinsky plunges into a radical denuding that could fit into his music of the 1920s or 1930s but here sounds merely amiss:

no, this is silly — it won't sound like that, but will blur in the pedal into a gentle, sonorous murmuring, which is presumably the effect intended

Ex. 1
Piano Sonata in F sharp minor: III

Such moments substantiate Alexander Goehr's argument that Stravinsky created a musical language out of his 'faults': 'Stiffness of relationship of voices, repetitiveness and inexpressive tags of melody – a disadvantage in traditional music – come into their own now, as virtues.'[5] This was his essential difference from his close contemporaries Webern and Berg, who also arrived at their teacher as gentlemen amateurs in terms of creative skills, but whose juvenilia were proficient.

In that respect, Stravinsky's gaining of proficiency in his next work, the Symphony in E flat, might be regarded as a retrograde step, though that would be a harsh way to judge a piece of such youthful ebullience and amiability. Also, the work demonstrates another crucial feature of

[3] *Memories*, p. 54.   [4] Ibid., p. 28.
[5] *The Stravinsky Festival* (programme book, London, 1981), p. 4.

8

the mature composer: his ability to copy. What is lacking, of course, is any self-consciousness in the copying. Much later Stravinsky was to say that the only cloud at the first performance had been the approval of Glazunov,[6] but in the piece itself there is no such irony: the symphony goes in emulation of Glazunov in its solid standard form and Russian melos, departing only for occasional thefts from Tchaikovsky, and just possibly too – though these are extensions to the basic style rather than contradictions of it – for off-beat accents (in the scherzo, placed second, and the introduction to the finale) that could with a lot of hindsight be described as incipiently Stravinskian. The overwhelming debt to Glazunov is not at all surprising. Seventeen years older than Stravinsky and likewise a Rimsky pupil, he was the most dazzling new composer in St Petersburg: quite unlike Stravinsky in this respect, he had made his public début with his own first symphony when he was sixteen, and was by now on to his eighth, besides having written a large quantity of concertos, overtures, suites, dances and chamber music. During Stravinsky's boyhood and youth there can hardly have been a St Petersburg concert in which he was not represented, and in a late reminiscence Stravinsky reported that he had transcribed a Glazunov quartet for piano 'in my fifteenth year', taking the result to Rimsky, who had not been impressed.[7] A decade later it must still have seemed that imitating Glazunov was the way to win Rimsky's approval.

Stravinsky designated the Symphony his op. 1, in a sequence of opus numbers he maintained until the Verlaine songs of 1910; but it was more an end than a beginning. It was, for one thing, his last fully assured and largely consistent big piece before *The Firebird*: what happened in the interim was a turmoil of responding to new influences, particularly from French music, which presumably he was hearing at the Evenings of Contemporary Music. According to his own statement,[8] his teacher Rimsky was the first to detect Debussy behind the whole-tone usages of his op. 2, the orchestral song triptych *The Faun and the Shepherdess*, though the contrast here between a robust folksong style for mythical human personages (in this case the fifteen-year-old Shepherdess) and a slippery chromatic manner for magic beings (the Faun) is one with a long history in Russian music, not least Rimsky's, and a notable future in *The Firebird*. The brilliance of the orchestration is also as much Rimskian as French. Presumably the choice of Pushkin's precocious piece of Arcadian eroticism was for the benefit of the dedicatee, Stravinsky's new wife, but at the same

---

[6]*Memories*, p. 59.   [7]See *Dialogues*, p. 131.   [8]*Memories*, p. 59.

time, as later with *The Nightingale*, the text happily makes possible a musical growth that can seem inevitable with hindsight: Stravinsky always had luck in turning accidents to his advantage. Thus a very Tchaikovskian style seems perfectly appropriate to the first song, which is a lingering portrait of the Shepherdess as she settles herself to sleep in a forest glade. The Faun only enters in the second song, and with him a much more sophisticated harmonic–orchestral manner, as well as tensile syncopations in the vocal line when the poem first sights him. The final song, teasingly ending just at the point where the Faun in chase is about to capture the Shepherdess, invites the kind of sudden, even peremptory resolution that was to be as much a feature of Stravinsky's later output (cf. *The Nightingale* and *Oedipus rex*, for example) as his more celebrated long apotheoses.

There may also be a touch of Musorgsky in the irregular phrasing and declamation of this work, as again in the two Gorodetzky songs (the only published songs, until his last, which Stravinsky did not at some time score), of which the first contains an early sprinkling of bell sounds. But the Pastorale is quite different. It is not clear whether Stravinsky could have taken the vocalise idea from some French source: the examples by Fauré and Ravel are works of the same year, and in any event there seems no immediate precedent for what is most essential in this piece, which is its unloosing of small motifs from any progress through time. Ideas are simply copied and changed, in a process which, once started, could continue indefinitely, so that the final cadence seems a bit of a fraud. Stravinsky's later arrangement, for voice and reed quartet, sharpens the independence of the lines in the accompaniment, and prepares for the pipe ensembles of *The Rite of Spring*.

His more immediate orchestral composition, the *Scherzo fantastique*, is an oddly malformed piece, and once again his later judgement of it appears disingenuous: 'I see now that I did take something from Rimsky's Bumblebee (nos. 49–50 in the score), but the *Scherzo* owes much more to Mendelssohn by way of Tchaikovsky than to Rimsky-Korsakov.'[9] Leaving aside the very debatable relation between the contributions of Rimsky and Mendelssohn, what goes unnoticed here is the substantial debt to Wagner, amounting to trespass on the copyright of *Die Meistersinger*, in the central slow section. One can understand why Stravinsky should have wanted, half a century later, to ignore what he owed to the composer – maybe even the very work – now long most foreign to him, but this Wagnerian

[9]*Conversations*, p. 41.

10

episode is interesting at least in pointing up his problems. Unwilling to tack his music to the regular forward movement of tonal harmony, he seemed to have only two alternatives: ostinatos à la Rimsky, or Wagnerian sequences. He forgot, too, how this piece had come into being, disowning the programme printed in the score about the life of the hive, and also disowning the ballet version produced at the Paris Opéra in 1917 as *Les abeilles*. However, his letters to Rimsky, keeping his teacher abreast of this work during the summer of 1907, make it quite clear that the *Scherzo* was launched by Maeterlinck's book *La vie des abeilles*.[10] Taking 'something from Rimsky's Bumblebee' was by no means fortuitous.

But there is still some buzz of it in his immediately succeeding orchestral piece, *Fireworks*, along with an almost literal quotation from Dukas's *L'apprenti sorcier* (but Dukas had got there through Rimsky, who in turn had owed something to Berlioz, in a switchback of Franco-Russian exchanges that would be continued with Stravinsky's gifts to Poulenc, Milhaud, Messiaen and Boulez), and with Wagnerian touches again in the sequential use of diminished-seventh formations. This is, though, a more compact piece, and its episodic structure is justified not only by the title but by what justifies the title: the orchestral panache. The Rimsky–Glinka magic of multicoloured quick figurations, usually outlining symmetrical and therefore harmonically static divisions of the octave (the diminished-seventh chord, the whole-tone scale, the octotonic scale of alternating major and minor seconds), is conspicuous, but there is also an extraordinary short passage of glowing even-note trajectories for woodwind and percussive sounds (flutes, bassoon, bass clarinet, celesta, pizzicato violins and cellos) that seems to look forward to Stravinsky's later and leaner orchestral style, while other things suggest *The Firebird* in ovular form.

This is the usual way of seeing Stravinsky's early works, like all artists' juvenilia, as steps from dependence to independence. But the journey is complicated in Stravinsky's case by the fact that its destination was not a style but an attitude towards style. Also, although the gaucheness of his pre-*Firebird* compositions makes it hard to avoid the evolutionary metaphor, it need not have been clear to him, of course, that he was travelling a path from *Ruslan* to *Petrushka*; and the Four Studies for piano, apparently written straight after *Fireworks*, emphasize other directions too, other possible Stravinskys. One of them might have become an adept of Skryabin, whose presence here in the first study may have been provoked by the reawakened interest accompanying his return to Russia in 1908 after six years abroad. However, in the second and fourth studies Stravinsky is suddenly himself – or rather, he is the self who was then projected, though with so many displacements, through the music of the next sixty years. These are the first pieces not clamouring for influences to be spotted; they are also perhaps the first pieces of Western music since the Baroque in which rubato is ruled out. Stravinsky later made pianola versions of all four studies, but these two are pianola music already, mechanically phrased and organized, asking for mechanical, staccato performance. The ostinatos, syncopations, cross metres and loose connections between treble and bass in the second study, for instance, suggest that Stravinsky hardly needed to discover ragtime a decade later:

Ex. 2
Piano Study no. 2

While there is a harmonic progression here, going on from G major to A minor and so back to the original D major, the movement halts at the end of each bar, partly because the tonality is confused by diminished-seventh and octotonic ideas that have now become fully structural, but surely also because each bar is stamped so much as a unit. This is digital music, coming in chunks which can be repeated

12

But this is wilfully, perversely to ignore or misinterpret received 'piano étude' gestures — exhaustively-driven regular figuration, cross-rhythms — traceable back through Skryabin to Chopin and earlier. More interesting here are the shifts in implied inner parts that blur across the bar-lines in a manner reminiscent of Rakhmaninov's virtuoso textures (see *s in Ex 2).

indefinitely or alternated or switched. Each moment does not necessarily entail the next; they just follow one another. Here already is one of the central lessons of Stravinsky's music.

As for those larger moments that are the complete works, what might have been the next step is missing, since the *Chant funèbre* is lost. Stravinsky's own recollection in the 1930s was of a piece in which 'all the solo instruments of the orchestra filed past the tomb of the master in succession, each laying down its own melody as its wreath against a deep background of tremolo murmurings simulating the vibrations of bass voices singing in chorus'.[11] This is a tantalizing aural glimpse, but of course one needs to be careful here. The case of the 1903–4 Sonata has already shown how Stravinsky's memories of old works could be wildly misleading, and these 'vibrations of bass voices' may have more to do with the recent Symphony of Psalms than with a work written a quarter of a century before. However, the idea of instruments as actors in a drama – one of Stravinsky's most original and fruitful notions – may indeed have been adumbrated here, since he was on the point of beginning, if he had not already begun, *The Nightingale*, an opera in which instrumental voices would take major roles. Before that would be completed, though, his life was to turn in a quite new direction through his meeting – which may already have taken place as he sat at the first performance of the *Chant funèbre* – with Dyagilev.

[11]*An Autobiography*, p. 24.

3

The Firebird

The initial result of Stravinsky's meeting with Dyagilev, whether or not the occasion was the first performance of the *Scherzo fantastique* and *Fireworks*, was a commission to reorchestrate two Chopin pieces for a production of *Les sylphides* to be danced in the first Ballets Russes season in Paris, in June 1909. Following the success of this visit (which Stravinsky did not accompany: he was in Ustilug, finishing the first act of *The Nightingale*), Dyagilev decided to create a new ballet for the next year, his 1909 repertory having consisted entirely of productions already seen at the Mariinsky. The subject was to be a Russian folktale about a firebird; the composer was to be, according to varying accounts, either Nikolay Tcherepnin or Anatol Lyadov or, at different times in the meandering history of the commission, both: both were prominent St Petersburg composers, and Tcherepnin's ballet *Le pavillon d'Armide* had gone to Paris as part of the 1909 selection. But certainly by November 1909, when the first notes of the score were written, the hand guiding them was Stravinsky's.

Meanwhile he had fulfilled another commission, orchestrating two settings of Mephistopheles' 'Song of the Flea' from *Faust*, by Beethoven and by Musorgsky, for a Goethe concert given by Ziloti in St Petersburg on 28 November 1909*. After that there was nothing to distract him from *The Firebird*, though in the spring of 1910, as he was finishing the score, something else came into view: 'I saw in imagination a solemn pagan rite: sage elders, seated in a circle, watched a young girl dance herself to death. They were sacrificing her to propitiate the god of spring.'[1] *The Firebird* was finished on 18 May?*, and later in the month Stravinsky left for Paris, where the first performance took place at the Opéra on 25 June. As usual, Dyagilev engaged a French conductor, Gabriel Pierné, but the production team was entirely Russian. The choreographer was Michel Fokine, who had been responsible for *Les sylphides* and *Le pavillon d'Armide*, and who was indeed the chief engineer of Dyagilev's

---

[1]*An Autobiography*, p. 31.

successes between 1909 and 1912. The lavishness and exoticism of the spectacle (lavishness and exoticism were very much the stock-in-trade of the early Ballets Russes, the reason for their rapturous reception) were completed by Léon Bakst's designs for the costumes of the Firebird and the Tsarevna, and the company was led by three of the Mariinsky's principal artists: Fokine and his wife, Vera Fokina, as the Tsarevich and the Tsarevna, and Tamara Karsavina as the Firebird.

The firebird, of course, is the phoenix, a prominent symbol of regeneration at this time of ferment in all the arts in Russia: Konstantin Balmont, three of whose poems Stravinsky was soon to set, took it as the title for a collection he published in 1907. For the Dyagilev company, too, the firebird was an emblem of newness: this was their first ballet created from scratch. And though the subject was not of Stravinsky's choosing (never again would that be the case), it provided a suitable occasion for a creative birth, even if what appears in the score is less the rising phoenix than the flames of the old Rimsky student, along with Promethean fire borrowed from Skryabin.

The story was adapted by Fokine from Russian folklore. As the work opens, the Tsarevich is wandering at night in Kashchey's magic garden in pursuit of the Firebird, whom he catches, but releases in return for one of her feathers. Thirteen enchanted princesses appear. They dance a *khorovod*, or round dance, but are obliged to return to Kashchey's castle at sunrise. When the Tsarevich goes after them, the magic carillon awakens the monsters guarding the castle, and they capture him. Kashchey comes on the scene: a hideous ogre. The princesses intercede on the Tsarevich's behalf, but nothing helps until he remembers the Firebird's feather and waves it in the air. The Firebird comes back and casts a spell on Kashchey's subjects, who execute their 'Infernal Dance' and then are charmed by her lullaby. She also reveals to the Tsarevich how he may dispose of Kashchey by breaking the egg which is the embodiment of his soul. Once this has been done the captive princesses, and the warriors who had been turned to stone for trespassing into the magician's domain, can all join in thanksgiving.

To create this story Stravinsky used combustibles not only from Rimsky and Skryabin but also from the earlier pieces of his own that had won him the commission. For instance, the opening of *Fireworks*, with its resolute diatonic motifs forging through a whirl of figuration, could have provided a clue to the portrayal of the hero prince taking a folksong path to catch the firebird, as she brilliantly prevaricates between tonalities and orchestral groupings in her rapid, lustrous patterns. *Fireworks* also foreshadowed, or forelit, the glissades of harmonics on violins and cellos in the introduction that provided *The Firebird* with its most celebrated orchestral innovation[2] – and this is still a world where special effects are proudly presented, a world of glamour and display. But the miscalculations of the preceding works – the open steals from Dukas, the Wagnerism of the *Scherzo*, the rumbustious tutti of *Fireworks* – are nowhere repeated. *The Firebird* comes with a sudden bolt in accomplishment.

Just as remarkable, though, is the leap Stravinsky took after it, requiring from him some rapid revisionism. As White points out,[3] the more lyrical tempo markings ('Sostenuto mystico') were soon ousted, and the suggestion that the several suites represent successive self-criticisms – beginning in 1911, the year after the ballet – originates with the composer himself.[4] These self-criticisms were all the more decisive, given that he never conducted the complete score in the concert hall[5] and that he intended the final, 1945 suite to be used for ballet productions,[6] as it was by Balanchine in 1950. What he immediately deleted, and never restored, was the Skryabinesque music for the thirteen princesses pressingly repeating a yearning motif. He also cut out the passages of pantomime, perhaps more because these were not so musically self-sufficient rather than because of any distaste for this kind of music (after all, there is plenty of pantomime in *Petrushka*). Other passages to go in the 1911 suite were the Firebird's lullaby and the finale of rejoicing when Kashchey has been destroyed. However, Stravinsky made versions of these with reduced wind,[7] and then put them back at the end of his 1919 suite, which altogether pares down the *Firebird* orchestra for less lavish times. But his biggest cut, again never rescinded, was of a great chunk from the middle of the score, including the daybreak signalled by offstage trumpets and the score's most extraordinary invention, the magic carillon made up of a crowd of overlapping ostinatos in exhilarated rootless octotony. Like the second Piano Study, this is machine music, but now as potentially endless as change ringing, which it evokes in its principal pattern, coloured by glockenspiel, celesta and piano.

There is more campanology at the end of the score, in a passage which can be readily seen as the first of Stravinsky's apotheoses,

---

[2]But Louis Andriessen and Elmer Schönberger, in *The Apollonian Clockwork* (Oxford, 1989), p. 236, identify the effect as Ravel's and provide more evidence for Stravinsky's forgetting of what he owed to Ravel and Skryabin (one might add Musorgsky to the list), a forgetting necessary perhaps not only to his self-esteem but also to his self-definition once he had become a different composer from the one who wrote *The Firebird*.

[3]p. 188. [4]See *Expositions*, p. 132. [5]See *SSC II*, p. 219.
[6]See *SPD*, pp. 377–8. [7]Ibid., pp. 58–9.

bringing a ceasing of motion into slow repetitive pattern, as later in *Les noces*, or the Symphonies of Wind Instruments, or the Symphony of Psalms, or, right at the end, the Requiem Canticles. Other presages of later Stravinsky crop up, too, in the sections retained through all the reworkings: the quick, even, staccato movement of the scherzo, for example, or the emphatic syncopated pulsation of the 'Infernal Dance', which could almost find a place in *The Rite of Spring*, except that it is still phrased in utterly regular two-bar units. But while full of Stravinsky to come, *The Firebird* also carries the weight of Rimsky-Korsakov, Borodin and Musorgsky past. The savagery of the 'Infernal Dance' is that of malignant power in the 'Polovtsian Dances', for example; the Firebird herself borrows Rimsky's plumage; the frank diatonic–chromatic contrast is his, as has been noted; the bell sounds echo on from 'The Great Gate of Kiev'; and the scherzo refers back to other pictures from that exhibition, such as 'Tuileries'. The 1919 and 1945 suites are trimmer than the original ballet, maybe primmer too, but the music is still in an Imperial Russia the composer was soon to leave, artistically and in fact.

4

Petrushka

Soon after the première of *The Firebird* Stravinsky returned to Ustilug to collect his family – there were now two children, with a third on the way – and bring them with him to France. In July they holidayed at La Baule, a coastal resort in the south-east corner of Brittany, where he set two Verlaine poems in Russian translation for his brother Gury, who was following their father's profession as a singer. Apparently he began to orchestrate them immediately, though the definitive orchestral version was not completed until 1951. He also began work on what it seemed at the time would be his next major composition, again for Dyagilev: *The Rite of Spring*. This time his collaborator was not Fokine but Nicolas Roerich, whose concerns as artist and anthropologist were with the ancient peoples of Russia (whether the original idea came from Roerich, or from Dyagilev, or from Stravinsky's vision of the preceding spring is hard to say: it is perhaps enough that the execution of the idea took place fully in what Stravinsky was to compose during the next two years). In a letter to Roerich, written from La Baule on 9 August 1910, Stravinsky revealed that he had begun sketching *The Rite*. Later in the month, however, he and his family moved to Chardon Jogny, near Vevey, and from there to Lausanne, where he started work on something else: *Petrushka*.

On 23 September Catherine Stravinsky gave birth to their third child, who was named Sviatoslav Soulima in a reminiscence of the family's descent from the Polish counts Soulima-Stravinsky. Shortly afterwards they all moved into the Hôtel Châtelard in Clarens, also on the Lake of Geneva, and a favourite resting place during the next five years; it was in this town that *The Rite* was largely composed. In October, however, and until the following April, the family transferred to Beaulieu, near Nice. Quite why the decision should have been made to remain in the West is not clear, though Stravinsky was following a gentleman's, and especially a Russian gentleman's, tradition in settling on the Swiss Riviera, his home until 1920. His only long stays in Russia after *The Firebird* were in returns to the old pattern of spending composing summers in Ustilug, which he did in 1911, 1912 and 1913.

There was a shorter visit in January 1911 when he went to spend Christmas in St Petersburg, planning *Petrushka* with those who would be involved in the stage production. Then in April, when his family returned to Russia, he went with the Ballets Russes to Rome, and there completed his new score for the company while staying at the Albergo d'Italia and surveying the sights in the company of Alexandre Benois, his co-scenarist and designer. Finished on 26 May, the work was first performed just eighteen days later at the Théâtre du Châtelet in Paris, with Pierre Monteux conducting. The choreography was again by Fokine, and the main female role, of the Ballerina hopelessly loved by the puppet Petrushka, was again taken by Karsavina. But the star part was Vaslav Nijinsky's.

Stravinsky never said much about the process of composing *The Firebird*, except to record his appreciation of Fokine's exact requirements.[1] But *Petrushka* became the occasion of one of his most celebrated stories of creative happenstance. Before going on to the already imminent *Rite of Spring*, so he said, 'I wanted to refresh myself by composing an orchestral piece in which the piano would play the most important part . . . In composing the music, I had in mind a distinct picture of a puppet, suddenly endowed with life.'[2] After this, by his own account, came the title, and later still the realization that he had the makings of a ballet score, this change of plan prompted by a visit from Dyagilev that must have been in September or October, since he records it as having taken place in Switzerland. Hence this chronology: first the intention to write an orchestral piece in the abstract, then the illustrative idea, then the naming, then the proposal to give the illustrative idea an embodiment on stage. But whatever the actual course of events, Stravinsky's recollection of it in this way serves to emphasize the fact that *Petrushka* was to have a life, bifurcated like so much else about this work, both in the concert hall and in the theatre. The anecdote would support its being seen as primarily a musical work, not the justly timed accompaniment to a dance, and certainly not primarily a vehicle for the brilliant, wayward Nijinsky.

This speaks of a protective artistic pride, the pride of one whose *Firebird* had brought him to the notice of Proust, Debussy and a host of other French celebrities. Perhaps it was the success that induced him

---

[1]*Expositions*, p. 129.   [2]*An Autobiography*, p. 31.

to stay in the West; perhaps it was an awareness that he was outgrowing the Russian style – the Russian export style, as he acutely observed later[3] – which had brought him that success. But already at this date, before the Revolution had made it inevitable, there was a distancing from Russia: the two Verlaine songs, though setting Russian translations, signal that determination by their very existence, as well as by their Debussyisms, which seem not yet digested, seem gulped down, having to mix with Russian folksong strains and ostinatos in music that is quite uncharacteristically lugubrious. Looking at this opus when it was done, Stravinsky might have concluded that he was not after all to become a French composer. It was, rather, in the space between France and Russia that he would situate himself, and *Petrushka*.

The ballet is in four scenes, of which the first, 'The Shrove-Tide Fair', achieves its mechanical character by means of mechanical rhythms, sharp cuts from one kind of music to another, and textures created by accumulations of repeating motifs: this is the impersonal bustle of city life. After a while the focus moves in to the Showman, who, in the 'Tour de passe-passe', charms his dolls with his flute, heard alone, and they step down, seemingly alive. They join in a vigorous Russian Dance. In the second scene Petrushka, one of the dolls, is alone in his cell, raging with sorrow, with love for the puppet Ballerina, and with violent despair. The third scene shows the Blackamoor, third member of the puppet trio, seducing the Ballerina. They dance a waltz, while Petrushka grows increasingly jealous until he bursts in and is brutally ejected, whereupon the scene returns to the fair. This time there is a sequence of dance episodes interrupted by the puppets. Petrushka is killed by the Blackamoor, and the crowd dissolves, leaving only the Showman to see his creature's grinning ghost.

The Russianness of *Petrushka* was keenly felt by Stravinsky even while it was being composed. As he wrote back to Andrey Rimsky-Korsakov after his return to Beaulieu in January 1911: 'My last visit to Petersburg did me much good, and the final scene is shaping up excitingly . . . quick tempos, concertinas, major keys . . . smells of Russian food – *shchi* – and of sweat and glistening leather boots. Oh what excitement!'[4] Once again, too, as in *The Firebird*, he used Russian folksongs. But the treatment is entirely different. Ex. 3a is the opening of the princesses' *khorovod* from *The Firebird*; with its warm string harmonization, in F sharp minor, it

[3]*Expositions*, p. 129.   [4]*SPD*, p. 67.

20

Ex. 3
(a) *The Firebird*: The Princesses' Khorovod

(b) *Petrushka*: Wet-Nurses' Dance

could, as Stephen Walsh remarks,[5] be by Borodin. But Ex. 3b certainly could not. The tune is not dissimilar, but against the backcloth of F major harmony it retains its C Mixolydian identity, and the same frame accommodates other alien lines: an ostinato for trumpets, clarinets and bassoons (just bassoons, and legato, in the original version: an instance of Stravinsky making the 1945 revision keep up with his now crisper orchestral style); another ostinato for the oboe group, but in units of six, not four, beats; and a return of the signal on flutes from the very beginning of the work. There are, of course, consistent features here in the pulse and the notes of the F major scale, but the metrical and harmonic interpretations of those features in the separate lines are quite different, to the extent that one line, that of the flutes, can be shifted to another position in the next two bars. All it needs for the musical machine to function is that the cogs of pulse interlock.

Earlier pieces, notably the second piano study and the magic carillon music from *The Firebird*, had pointed the way, but the scale of musical engineering in *Petrushka* is startlingly new, and perhaps another measure of the self-confidence Stravinsky had gained from his first ballet. It is his next Dyagilev score, *The Rite of Spring*, that has been remembered as embodying one of the great revolutions of twentieth-century music, but the change has already come in *Petrushka*. For one thing, the enmeshing of harmonically and metrically contradictory lines, as in Ex. 3b, eliminates the single coherent viewpoint most characteristic of Western music since the Renaissance. Attack on that comes too from the unprovoked chopping between dissimilar textures, as found particularly in the first scene, and the way in which sections of a melody can be separated or repeated at will. By such means the music emphasizes the separateness of the element from the whole; the elements coexist only here, in the score, and not in some idealized composing voice or listening ear. There is no composing voice; no imaginary narrator is telling us about the fair. Indeed, the fair is only a metaphor for the liberated celebration going on in the orchestra: the music is not a depiction of the fair, but rather the fair on stage is a visual equivalent for the identities and freedoms suddenly given to motifs within a score, to instruments and groups within an orchestra.

There are, though, imitations of the fair's instruments: not only the concertinas of Stravinsky's letter are brought in (notably on reeds and horns at fig. 169 in the revised version), but also two hurdy-gurdies (in

[5]In his *The Music of Stravinsky* (London, 1988), p. 21.

the long passage beginning at fig. 18) and a barrel organ (for the waltz danced by the Ballerina and the Moor, to Petrushka's incensement, in the third scene). It is significant that these are all mechanical instruments: they can be fitted to the regular pulse of the score, and to its habit of cutting melodies into incomplete phrases. But they are also all examples of musical low life, to be included with others (the double bassoon at fig. 57 and elsewhere seems to be remembering the robust peasant of Stravinsky's earliest musical memory) alongside the extreme sophistication of the passage that comes straight after the first rude bassoon noises, the 'Tour de passe-passe', where Stravinsky gives the Showman some aural magic to help his trick along. The fair inside the music is a place where all contraries can be found, including most prominently the paradox of a mechanical populace, in the outer scenes, and human, feeling puppets.

The existence of two fairs – one behind the proscenium, in which the *corps de ballet* is the Showman's audience, and one in front, in which the audience is the audience – seems to have caused Stravinsky some momentary difficulty, for he wrote to Benois to suggest that the drumroll which attracts the stage crowd to the 'Tour de passe-passe' should not be repeated before the second and third scenes, because 'Petrushka's actions and the Moor's, on the other hand, are not a presentation for the stage crowd but are for us'.[6] But finally the drumrolls were repeated, and again to introduce the last scene, because everything that happens in the score is for the benefit of the audience in the theatre. It is their attention that the music so vociferously claims by such devices as the drumrolls or the appellant flute signals at the very start (this idea of the signal opening, the beginning announcing itself as a beginning, was to feature again in Stravinsky's music, and was not lost on Varèse). There is no frame within a frame: everything is within the one frame. Everything is acting out its function.

The self-consciousness of *Petrushka* comes from the way it is made: these are events and gestures that are existing only for themselves, not elicited and necessitated by any symphonic continuity, any composing voice. The difference can be seen quite clearly in Ex. 3. Where the *Firebird* round dance is voiced by the music, projected as the single subject, the folktune in *Petrushka* is one of several objects. And though the collage assembly sharpens the character of each object, makes it stand out for itself, the effect is also to make the choice of objects rather arbitrary. Just as they can be shifted in relation to one another,

[6] *SPD*, p. 70.

so they can be exchanged. One could even make a similar collage with entirely different objects – say, the clichés of musical chinoiserie – and call it 'The Nightingale', or with the trademarks of the Brandenburgs and call it 'Concerto in E flat', or with those of Schoenberg's chamber music and call it 'Septet'.

One of the effects of the drumrolls is to emphasize how Petrushka's agonies are just as much constructed. As already mentioned, this is a work in which human beings behave like dolls while puppets have emotions, but the emotions are painted in starkly individual brushstrokes, like expressions on masks indicative of pathos or malevolent power. The second scene, where Petrushka is alone in his cell, is made up from generally shorter units, but the nature of the music is the same. The war of feelings is objectified as a war of instrumental gestures, as Stravinsky made clear in his description of what was the first part of the score to be written: the puppet–piano is seen as 'exasperating the patience of the orchestra with diabolical cascades of arpeggios. The orchestra in turn retaliates with menacing trumpet blasts. The outcome is a terrific noise which reaches its climax and ends in the sorrowful and querulous collapse of the poor puppet.'[7] And of course the identification between the puppet and the piano is by no means complete: what has always been regarded as Petrushka's theme, based on simultaneous arpeggios of C major and F sharp major, belongs in this scene to a pair of clarinets, and the 'sorrowful and querulous collapse' must surely be the Andantino in which the piano is merely accompanying a solo flute. It is not so much a battle between puppet–piano and orchestra as an orchestral battle through which the features of the puppet are drawn. If the piano here represents anyone, it is the composer. He made no secret of the fact that he nearly always composed at the piano; he also wrote piano parts which resist interpretative flexibility of tempo, rhythm and dynamics. The piano in *Petrushka*, as in later scores, is the sound of Stravinsky composing the piece.

This does not, of course, in any way imply that Stravinsky is Petrushka. The Romantic self-implacement of the artist in the work's principal figure, taken to an edgy extreme by Schoenberg a year later in his *Petrushka*, *Pierrot lunaire*, is thoroughly alien to Stravinsky's thought, and to the objective, openly constructed manner in which that thought was displayed. And though there is an obvious temptation to see *Petrushka* as an allegory of the Ballets Russes, with Dyagilev as Showman holding a hazardous control over his artist–

[7] *An Autobiography*, p. 31.

puppets, the essential Showman here is the composer. The Showman on stage, after Petrushka has been killed by the Moor, reassures the crowd that the victim was only a thing of painted wood. In the same way, Stravinsky is telling his audience all the time that what they are hearing is a contraption of notes, colours and rhythms. Petrushka's resurrection, coming at the end but still inside the work, throws back the question.

5

The Rite of Spring

The summer after *Petrushka* Stravinsky spent again in Ustilug with his family, and, exactly as he had the year before, turned from ballet to poetry. He set two brief lyrics by Balmont as songs with piano accompaniment, and began a heavyweight but compact work for male chorus and orchestra conveying another Balmont poem, *Zvezdoliki*, a vision of the risen Christ. Continuous work on the interrupted *Rite of Spring* started only after his return to Clarens in September 1911: there seems some doubt as to whether he remained there at work through the autumn and winter, or went back, however briefly, to Ustilug in November.[1] It was, though, in Clarens between September 1911 and the spring of 1912 that *The Rite* was largely composed. The first part was finished on 7 January, and Stravinsky went on to the second, taking a break the next month in order to be with the Ballets Russes in Vienna. Some time in March Dyagilev decided not to present *The Rite* in his next Paris season, scheduled for the early summer as in each of the preceding three years, his reason being, as Stravinsky wrote to Benois, that 'Fokine is too busy with other ballets'.[2] Nijinsky's involvement as choreographer, therefore, must have come later.

During March and April Stravinsky paid two visits to Dyagilev in Monte Carlo, and played what he had written of the new score, which seems to have included the first part (orchestrated by early March) and the concluding 'Sacrificial Dance'. A letter of 19 March to Roerich, saying that the first part 'will represent about three-fourths of the whole',[3] suggests that the intervening sections of the second part were not at this stage planned. The postponement from 1912 to 1913 may therefore not only have slowed Stravinsky's progress on the work but given him space to extend it.

The early part of the summer was taken up with accompanying the Ballets Russes. Stravinsky was at the first performances in Paris of *L'après-midi d'un faune* (29 May), as choreographed and danced by

[1]A letter to Florent Schmitt is headed 'Ustilug/November 2, 1911' in *SSC II*, p. 104, but there seems no time for a return to Russia in the chronology given in *SPD*, p. 83.
[2]*SPD*, p. 85.   [3]Ibid., pp. 84–5.

Nijinsky, and of the major 'other ballet' that had absorbed Fokine's attention, *Daphnis et Chloé* (8 June), danced to Ravel's score. The day after *Daphnis* came a pregnant moment: Stravinsky and Debussy at Bellevue played through the duet version of *The Rite*. However, the relationship between the two composers, other than at the keyboard, seems to have been obstructed by awe on Stravinsky's side and amusement on Debussy's: Stravinsky was meeting a man whose music he had known since the Evenings of Contemporary Music in St Petersburg, and the piece that Nijinsky had just scandalously danced was now nearly twenty years old, while Debussy's correspondence suggests that his evident admiration for Stravinsky – the only composer to make any impression on his mature music – was mixed with self-protecting irony. Stravinsky was closer to French colleagues of his own generation: Ravel, Florent Schmitt and Maurice Delage, the dedicatees of the Three Japanese Lyrics he was to compose the next winter.

Meanwhile, after making his first visit to England for the London première of *The Firebird* (18 June), he went once more for the summer to Ustilug, where he finished *Zvezdoliki*, and from where he went on a trip with Dyagilev to Bayreuth (for *Parsifal* on 20 August) and Lugano. In October he returned to Clarens, where he wrote the piano version of the first Japanese Lyric (finished on 19 October), and completed *The Rite* in sketch score (on 17 November). Three days later he left for Berlin, to attend Ballets Russes performances of *The Firebird* and *Petrushka*, and to make another significant encounter, with Schoenberg: he was at a performance of *Pierrot lunaire* that Schoenberg conducted on 8 December. Back in Clarens he turned the Japanese Lyrics a little towards *Pierrot* by giving them an accompaniment for flutes, clarinets, string quartet and piano, completing the second song for that combination on 21 December and eight days later finishing an instrumentation of the first for the same ensemble. The final member of the set was completed in Clarens on 22 January, between visits with the Ballets Russes to Budapest (*The Firebird*, 4 January) and Vienna (*Petrushka*, 15 January), and to Covent Garden (*Petrushka*, 4 February), where Stravinsky also attended performances of *Elektra*.

Once more back in Clarens he finished *The Rite* on 8 March 1913, though additions and revisions, partly in the light of rehearsals, continued – indeed, the revisions went on until the publication of the last edition during the composer's lifetime, in 1967. More immediately, in March and April 1913, he and Ravel worked together on another task for Dyagilev, a performing version of *Khovanshchina*.

Then to Paris, to rehearse *The Rite* in company with the conductor Monteux, the choreographer Nijinsky and the designer–sage Roerich, and to be present in the Théâtre des Champs-Elysées for the opening night: 29 May.

A furore, of course. The first night of *The Rite of Spring*, echoing for half a century and more in the recollections of those who were present (not least the composer, who recorded his own reminiscences for television back in the Théâtre des Champs-Elysées in 1965), provided twentieth-century modernism with an heroic moment to equal the opening of *Hernani* in the same city in 1830. For those who had been in on the conception, this angry birth cannot have been a surprise. On 7 March 1912, by which date much of the score had been written, Stravinsky wrote to Andrey Rimsky-Korsakov: 'It is as if twenty and not two years had passed since *The Firebird* was composed.'[4] Even before that – writing to Roerich on 26 September 1911, when he had only just begun the composition – he remarked that: 'The music is coming out very fresh and new.'[5] (This same letter gives other rare glimpses of the work in genesis. Stravinsky mentions that he has 'sketched the Introduction for "dudki" [reed pipes]', and indeed the first nineteen bars of the finished score are entirely, except for one accompanying horn figure, for reed instruments. There is a hint, too, of visual images prompting the way the music moves: 'The picture of the old woman in squirrel fur sticks in my mind . . . I see her running in front of the group, sometimes stopping it and interrupting the rhythmic flow.' Since this old woman was to enter at fig. 15, the reference must be to the following swirls interrupting the 'Dances of the Young Girls'. Finally, Stravinsky is already 'convinced that the action must be danced, not pantomimed': there was to be only one – though crucial – invitation to mime in the music, in the four bars marked 'The Sage' unleashing the 'Dance of the Earth'.)

The newness of *The Rite* was recognized not only by the public, who may have been keyed up to make another protest just a fortnight after the opening of *Jeux*, but also in the press,[6] where, whether the final judgement was for or against, the music was immediately characterized as being at once primitive and radically new. Stravinsky had been placed hitherto in the company of his Russian predecessors, of Debussy and of Ravel; now his colleagues were Bartók and Schoenberg. The level of dissonance was an approach to barbaric

---

[4]*SPD*, p. 84.   [5]*SPD*, p. 83.

[6]See *Igor Stravinsky: Le sacre du printemps: Dossier de presse/Press-Book*, ed. François Lesure (Geneva, 1980).

noise and at the same time a pushing at musical frontiers. As Debussy put it in a letter written on the day of the first performance to André Caplet,[7] the irony characteristically glancing: 'Le sacre du printemps is extraordinarily wild . . . As you might say, it's primitive music with all modern conveniences.'

Advancing through the past was common enough in the arts at the time, and The Rite has obvious connections with the 'Scythian' movement among Russian artists, who looked to the country's pre-Christian traditions for clues to its future: Gorodetzky's poetry may have given Stravinsky a hint,[8] and Roerich was a man whose interests as a cultural historian and as an artist already went in this direction. But the most essential groundwork for the piece had been laid by Stravinsky himself, in Petrushka. As in that work, musical ideas are treated as objects, to be repeated, dismembered and overlaid without excuse. As in that work, too, the great steering is provided not by harmonic modulation but by pulse. But of course there are vital differences too. As has already been mentioned, there is almost no pantomime: the whole work dances, or, in the introductions to each part, waits to dance. More centrally, the clear diatonic planes of Petrushka are exchanged for denser harmonies, the melodic motifs are almost never more than a few beats long, or else they are very obviously chains of such motifs, as if the melodies are analysing themselves as they go along, and the orchestral world is quite different. These are, of course, linked features: the thicker harmony of The Rite almost necessitates the elimination of the tuned percussion instruments that had brightened Petrushka, and indeed The Firebird, both these earlier scores being for virtually the same resources. The Rite is scored for a distinctive orchestra overwhelmingly of wind instruments and drums, the wind sections being enlarged (and this time Stravinsky did not mitigate the force of the first eruption in a later rescoring, nor did he ever conduct a cut version – though he did, astonishingly, sanction one for Ansermet), the drums reinforced by the emphatic chords that make up so much of the strings' music.

The jump from Petrushka to The Rite, and the 'twenty-year' leap from The Firebird, can be seen by comparing Ex. 3 with Ex. 4, from the 'Dances of the Young Girls'. Not only is the music harmonically and texturally denser – it has just outgrown its only key signature, of three flats, introduced at the start of this section, though even there the

---

[7]Debussy Letters, ed. François Lesure and Roger Nichols, trans. Nichols (London, 1987), p. 270.
[8]See Lawrence Morton: 'Footnotes to Stravinsky Studies: Le sacre du printemps', Tempo, 128 (1979), pp. 9–16.

Ex. 4

The Rite of Spring: The Augurs of Spring

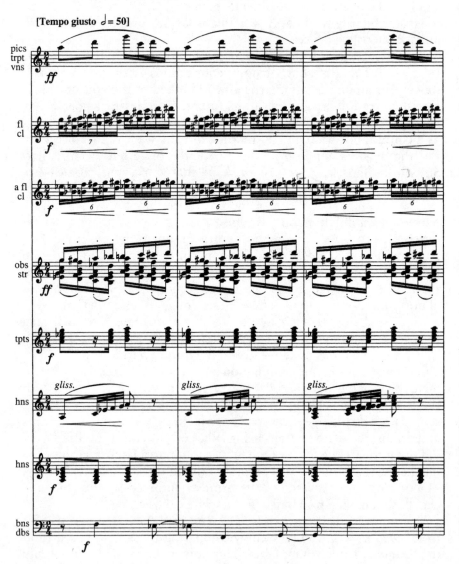

combination of E flat and F flat harmony, which may well have been the key to *The Rite*,[9] left the signature with little relevance – but now everything is ostinato. The dance is a machine, and the work's

[9]See, on this and so much else, Pieter C. van den Toorn: *Stravinsky and The Rite of Spring* (Oxford, 1987).

principal methods of proceeding are the mechanical ones of repetition, accumulation and flat contrast. The musical mill turns, as in this section, and as it turns it converts any new ideas into rotating ostinatos, building up to a point of overload which determines a switch to something else. There is a mechanical increase too, of speed, in the large-scale form. For example, the tempo is doubled from the Introduction to the 'Dances of the Young Girls', and then doubled again in the succeeding 'Ritual of Abduction', the joins being assured in each case by an elementary version of what Elliott Carter would later call 'metric modulation', the establishing of a new rhythmic unit within a senescent metre, as when the quaver ostinato of the 'Dances of the Young Girls' begins as a semiquaver pattern before the Introduction is over. On the largest scale the gearing is again mechanical. Each part of the work is rigged to a double wave of increasing dynamism, and the final dances of each part, the 'Dance of the Earth' and the 'Sacrificial Dance', are related in speed by a ratio of 2:3.

The dominance of pulse, which is of course the most conspicuously revolutionary feature of *The Rite*, is equally obviously the main source of its primitivism: this is music restored to its condition before European civilization. The wind–drumming instrumentation is important here too, and the reduction of melody to basic elements in what is, continuing in the direction of *Petrushka*, a play of signals and tattoos. Some of these melodic elements have been identified as folksongs,[10] but nearly all of them could have come from the same stores of folk memory. Such things as the omnipresent ostinato of the 'Dances of the Young Girls' – down a minor third, up a fourth, down a fourth (see Ex. 4) – are the rudiments of Russian folksong released into separate being, things more primitive than what is already a primitive stock. *The Rite of Spring* is well made for its subject matter.

But at the same time, again as with *Petrushka*, the music is executing a drama on its own terms, and the dancing of the ritual is only a paraphrase of another ritual being played out by instrumental soloists and choruses. The great machines of accumulation and destruction do not need any excuse from the stage: they are working with purely musical energies of pulsation, repetition and obliteration. Messiaen's term 'rhythmic characters',[11] introduced to explain what is going on in the 'Sacrificial Dance', is just: the few ideas here are not only

[10]See Richard Taruskin: 'Russian Folk Melodies in *The Rite of Spring*', *Journal of the American Musicological Society*, xxxii (1980), pp. 501–43, and Morton, op. cit.

[11]See Claude Samuel: *Entretiens avec Olivier Messiaen* (Paris, 1967), p. 71.

accompaniment to the dance but themselves actors in a drama of sacrifice. On one level, the sacrifice being played out throughout the work (whose original title was 'The Great Sacrifice') is that of everything Western music had nurtured: individuality and fluidity of melody, subjugation of clock rhythm to continuity, seemlessness and complexity of form, harmonic motivation. But the rhythmic characters in the 'Sacrificial Dance' are dancing a sacrifice of their own. Within an overall *ABACA* pattern of refrains and verses, one slicing character is introduced at the end of the second *A* section to catastrophic effect in the final *A* section, where in its repetitions it seems to be dispatching everything else (see Ex. 5). *The Rite* is, simply in its musical operation, a dance of self-extinction, a dance prompted not only by the ostensible

Ex. 5

The Rite of Spring: Sacrificial Dance

subject but by a dynamic rage, for Robert Craft has testified that Stravinsky 'repeatedly said that he wrote *Le Sacre du printemps* in order "to send everyone" in his Russian past, Tsar, family, instructors, "to hell".'[12]

It may also, while it was happening, have extinguished the self of its composer, as he suggested in saying he was 'the vessel through which *The Rite* passed'.[13] This seems to be more than just the later composer's distancing of himself from youthful savagery, partly because it gains support from his continuing difficulties in setting down what the music should be,[14] and partly because the work is so different from anything else in his output. Not only did he keep clear of it when ranging over his earlier output in search of numbers to arrange for violin and piano (though to be sure, such a polite abstraction from this score is hard to contemplate), but the particular sound world of *The Rite* is curiously rarely evoked in other works. This is not just a matter of the orchestra's being so much larger than any Stravinsky would use again: the Violin Concerto shows that cross-references are entirely possible with lesser resources. That they are so rare may be because the vessel cannot refill itself, or because Stravinsky realized that *The Rite*, though in so many ways essential to the future of music, was inimitable.

This separateness of *The Rite* is shown most remarkably in the works Stravinsky was writing at the same time: the Balmont songs, *Zvezdoliki* and the Japanese Lyrics. *Zvezdoliki*, using an orchestra on almost the same scale, sometimes evokes the Introduction to the second part of *The Rite* in its glowing smoky harmonies, but nothing could be more different from its great contemporary than this static icon. An apocalyptic vision of Christ, the work is far removed from anything else in Stravinsky's output at the time, and indeed from anything later, in its creation of a religious image with something other than scriptural or liturgical words. However, the feeling here for harmony as resonance, as the afterlight of chant and bell, is entirely Stravinskian, and quite particularly sacred-Stravinskian. What is most un-Stravinskian about it, adding to the mystery, is the fact that it was not prompted by some occasion or commission. The only thread of a purpose it discloses is the wish to honour Debussy, in the dedication and in some allusions to Debussian style, as when horns echo as if from a distance. Possibly Stravinsky was spurred by Debussy's admiration for the 'sonorous magic' of the 'Tour de passe-passe' in *Petrushka*, and

---

[12]*Glimpses*, p. 14.　　　[13]*Expositions*, p. 148.
[14]See Louis Cyr: 'Writing *The Rite* Right', in *Confronting Stravinsky*, ed. Jann Pasler (Berkeley and Los Angeles, 1986), pp. 157–73.

for that work's 'orchestral *certainties* such as I have encountered only in *Parsifal*.'[15] In any event, the debts to Debussy, though slim, weigh more than any to Skryabin, even though the work seems to belong in a very Russian tradition of devotional utterance.

The tiny Balmont songs are different again. The revolving modal ostinatos and larger-scale repetitions, though cued by repetitions of word, rhythm and rhyme in the texts, belong close to *The Rite of Spring*, and far away from Stravinsky's previous song diptychs. But these are delicate chimes and whispers where *The Rite* was a roar.

[15]*Debussy Letters*, pp. 256–8.

6

Three Japanese Lyrics and a Chinese opera

Two days after the unleashing of *The Rite* Stravinsky was admitted to a sanatorium at Neuilly-sur-Seine, having contracted typhus. He therefore missed the opening of *Khovanshchina* on 5 June, again in the Théâtre des Champs-Elysées. In July he left for what would be his last summer in Ustilug, where he resumed work on *The Nightingale* after four years that had seen *The Firebird*, *Petrushka* and *The Rite of Spring*. Though none of those ballets had been staged yet in Russia, news of them had of course reached home, and there had been concert performances of the *Firebird* suite and *Petrushka*. Serge Koussevitzky, at the St Petersburg première of the *Firebird* music on 5 November 1910, was so impressed that he had determined to add Stravinsky to the stable of his publishing company, Edition Russe de Musique, and a rapidly growing reputation was also responsible for the commission from the Free Theatre of Moscow that led Stravinsky to take up *The Nightingale* again.

In September he returned from Ustilug to Clarens, and continued at the opera, except for making a revision in October–November of three little folksong settings, published with the subtitle 'Recollections of My Childhood'. On 14 January 1914 the Three Japanese Lyrics had their first performance in Paris, and the next day the Stravinskys' fourth and last child, Maria Milena, was born in a sanatorium at Leysin. The composer and his older children, with Berthe, moved into the Grand Hotel there, where they were visited in January by Dyagilev (the Free Theatre had folded, and so *The Nightingale* could now be secured for the next Ballets Russes season) and in March by Cocteau, hoping to catch Stravinsky's interest in a ballet on the subject of King David. On 27 March, at Leysin, *The Nightingale* was completed.

Six days later, in Montreux, Ernest Ansermet conducted a performance of the early Symphony, initiating a long professional and personal relationship (for a period more professional than personal) with the composer. This was the start, too, of Stravinsky's career on the podium, for he had conducted part of a rehearsal on 30 March before leaving for Paris and the first concert performance of *The Rite*, at the Salle du Casino again under Monteux, after which he was fêted. He went back to Leysin and wrote the first of the Three Pieces for string quartet (completed on 26 April). Then it was back to Paris for the first performance of *The Nightingale*, at the Opéra on 26 May, with Monteux conducting and the stage sumptuously bedecked by Benois.

Several histories converge on the tiny space of the Japanese songs. The work was, most celebratedly, the occasion of Stravinsky's single close encounter with Schoenberg before the latter's death in 1951: hearing *Pierrot lunaire* while he was engaged on the composition (and on *The Rite of Spring*, much of which had been written exactly while Schoenberg was at work on *Pierrot*), he scored the piece for a similar, though expanded, ensemble; he also had the cue, perhaps, for the widened harmonic range and independence of line displayed in the instrumental colloquy of the second song, and for the motivic echoings of the third, suggestive of the passacaglia of *Pierrot*. The first song, written before the experience of *Pierrot*, stands somewhat apart, but thereby links the set to other pasts: to the preceding Balmont songs (much later brought still nearer by being scored for the same ensemble), and more distantly to *The Rite*, in that this song is an ostinato of twelve and a half cycles, bent in shape and instrumentation under the impress of other ideas. The apartness of the first song is also justified thematically, in that it is a winter poem coming before the rush and flowering of spring, the whole little cycle being linked by images of whiteness (flowers, snowflakes, ice floes, clouds) that concur with the harmonic stasis, brilliance and delicacy of the music. And those qualities also set the work in a distinctly French history of Japanese-imitating refinement. These Japanese lyrics (though he was still setting texts in Russian), not the Verlaine songs, were Stravinsky's first essay in the French style. They were dedicated to French colleagues, and devised alongside similarly scored works by two of these friends: Delage's *Quatre poèmes hindous* and Ravel's *Trois poèmes de Stéphane Mallarmé*.

Stravinsky's other collaboration with Ravel, on *Khovanshchina*, produced a final chorus which is essentially his composition,[1] and lost him his friends in the family of his teacher Rimsky-Korsakov, whose own performing version of the work was thus implicitly criticized. So more links with Russia were being loosened, as they were in the

---

[1]See Richard Taruskin's essay published with the 1989 Deutsche Grammophon recording of the opera.

composition of *The Nightingale*. Stravinsky had gone back to this old work – exceedingly old on the time scale of his present development, since the first act had been completed before *The Firebird* – on behalf of a new Moscow enterprise, but it became yet another Dyagilev exhibit for Paris.[2] At the same time, as Stravinsky was the first to point out,[3] there is a sharp movement away from the Russian tradition within the substance of the piece. The first act, though he revised it, still has moments of languorous exoticism reminiscent of *Sheherazade*, while the later two are not only suddenly more alert but explosive with announcements of coming theatrical works. The 'entr'acte' at the start of the post-*Rite* material has almost no dramatic function in its context, but as an exhilarated ostinato-driven ceremonial for soloists, chorus and orchestra it strikingly anticipates *Les noces*. There are also intimations of *Histoire du soldat* in the episode for bassoons, trumpet, viola and cello in the 'Chinese March', and of *Renard* in the piano's repeated arpeggio-summons.

In those three works, all to be conceived during the next four years, Stravinsky would find new ways of creating theatre by musical means; *The Nightingale*, on the other hand, seems almost to have been designed to show opera's desuetude. And this is even true of the 1908–9 first act. Before any action takes place there is a double frame: first an orchestral prelude strongly suggestive of Debussy's *Nuages* (and also therefore of Musorgsky's song cycle *Sunless*), an image of 'Once upon a time . . .', and then the song of the Fisherman, waiting in his boat for the Nightingale to sing. Since he is not connected with the rest of the drama, and since his song returns at the end of the act (as also at the ends of the second and third acts), the central action presents itself as an opera within the opera, and is further distanced by its very brevity: the whole three-act piece is over within three-quarters of an hour. Opera, it seems, is an old story, as Stravinsky almost said in an interview early in 1913: 'I dislike opera. Music can be married to gesture or to words – not to both without bigamy. That is why the artistic basis of opera is wrong.'[4]

To be sure, there is not very much conventional opera here, even allowing for the straitened confines of the work. The first act, inside its frame, is essentially a comic scene for palace servants searching for the Nightingale, which they take to the Emperor. The second act is taken up mainly with tableaux – the introductory entr'acte, the Chinese March to which the Emperor and his court arrive – and then stationary numbers (the Nightingale's song, for high soprano; the

[2] See *SSC II*, pp. 197–218.   [3] See *An Autobiography*, p. 51.   [4] *SPD*, p. 95.

bicinium of the Japanese envoys, tenor and bass, bringing in the gift of a mechanical nightingale and recalling another two-part vocal invasion from an alien world, that of the Catholic monks in the forest scene of *Boris Godunov*; the song of the mechanical nightingale, for oboe with a harp—celesta ostinato, using a musical machine to create the image of a machine, as Stravinsky was to do again in *The Rake's Progress*). Only in the third act is there sustained dialogue, as the Emperor is claimed by Death for having preferred the mechanical nightingale to the real one, to be rescued by the latter, whose returning song charms Death away. But this act also includes the most curious dismissal of an obvious operatic possibility, when the Emperor's showing of himself to a surprised court is underplayed. It is as if the music has already gone off with the Nightingale, back to the natural world represented by the Fisherman.

However, the opposition of nature (bird) and artifice (automaton) is not as central to the opera as it was to Andersen's tale. Stravinsky shifts the emphasis from the narrative, from the story once told, to its recurrence, to its metaphorical enactment of dawn (the Nightingale sings as dawn approaches; the Emperor's revival from the hands of Death is the awakening of day from night), an enactment valid for every day of eternity. The framed, ritual, anti-natural aspects of the work are thus not at all faults, as they might be in a traditional opera (the sort of opera, surely, to which Stravinsky was objecting in that 1913 interview), but on the contrary are manifestations of this concern with story as wheel rather than line.

The other principal theme of the opera is that of music's magic power, and in particular its power over natural forces. In the final act the Nightingale's song gains successive victories over time (in the shape of an alto chorus coming to gather the sick Emperor into his past), and then over Death itself, an alto soloist (though the remarkable female soloist in Stravinsky's recording sounds like a high tenor, and the role could well be assigned that way). The Nightingale's interview with Death is bewitchingly scored for small groupings, and it is surely here, much more than in the ostensibly Japanese episode, that Stravinsky profited from what he had just achieved in the lyrics, in their small-scale repetitiveness as well as their economy (see Ex. 6). Where *The Rite of Spring* ended with a dance of death to assure the continuation of time, *The Nightingale* ends with a song of resurrection to stop the advance of time (or at least the first of its endings ends so: there is still the desultory conclusion of the plot to come, and the final appearance of the Fisherman's song). It would be possible to read the opera as a Christian fable, especially in the light of the Fisherman's

Ex. 6
The Nightingale: Act III

[I like to hear your songs, why did you stop?

I want to hear more. Sing again!]

references to the 'spirit'. However, the regeneration is more general and perhaps also more intrinsic: a creative regeneration that this work, covering the six years from *Fireworks* to the Three Pieces for string quartet, is uniquely placed to observe within itself.

The problems of the piece – which are problems of scale and programming, given that this is effectively a one-act opera for large resources, as well as problems of genre – were resolved when, three years later, Stravinsky created from it an orchestral digest, *Chant du rossignol*, which he described as a 'symphonic poem' (according to his own report,[5] it was, following the pattern of *Petrushka*, conceived as an orchestral work before the inevitable suggestion came from Dyagilev that it should be danced). The use of instruments here to sing (solo flute or violin for the Nightingale, trumpet for the Fisherman) or, even more conspicuously, to declaim (trombones for the Chamberlain's announcement of the Emperor's approach) brings the music near *The Rite* and *Petrushka* as an instance of orchestral theatre, and the dialogue scenes are either omitted – the servants' comedy goes along with the entire first act – or considerably reworked, the central part of the last act becoming an exchange between musical characters, an exchange which is not resolved but simply cut off for the funeral procession. The new version is also more practical, Stravinsky's slimming of his orchestra presaging what would happen to *Petrushka*; the enhancement of verse-refrain forms, as in the last act, suits the ideas; and there is now, with the removal of all the pre-*Firebird* material except the Fisherman's song, no stylistic disparity. But the problems of the operatic *Nightingale*, and the lavishness, belong to its fascination.

[5]SPD, p. 80.

7

Around *Les noces*

On 18 June 1914, three weeks after the Paris opening, Stravinsky was in London for the first night of *The Nightingale*. During this visit he was impressed by the bells of St Paul's (though the composer of *The Firebird*'s magic carillon perhaps already knew enough about such sounds) and by a performance by the clown Little Tich, who became the subject of his next composition, the second quartet piece: this was finished on 2 July in Salvan, in the canton of Valais, where Stravinsky and his family had recently settled. On the day after, he set off for a quick visit to Ustilug and Kiev, returning after ten days with published collections of Russian folk verse that he needed for his next stage work, *Les noces*, already being planned. The outbreak of war in the following month made any further travelling across Europe impossible, and he was not to go back to Russia again until 1962. Soon after returning to Salvan he wrote the third and final quartet piece (25–6 July), and then in August made settings of three traditional Russian poems, the first three *Pribautki*. After adding a fourth to this set at the end of September (the Stravinskys had now moved into Ansermet's villa La Pervenche in Clarens), Stravinsky wrote an unpretentious *Valse des fleurs* for piano duet. And this was the essential pattern of his output throughout the war: folk rhymes (seemingly offshoots from growing stage works: *Les noces* and *Renard*) and duets (the stimulus for these presumably coming from the composer's children).

Dyagilev had been planning to open a Ballets Russes season in Berlin in October 1914, but that was now impossible, and there were no more performances until December 1915. However, Stravinsky and Dyagilev continued to meet: for instance, in the autumn of 1914 in Florence, and in February 1915 in Rome, on which occasion the composer played what he had written of *Les noces*. After the Florence meeting Stravinsky returned to Clarens and composed a piano duet Polka dedicated to Dyagilev (dated 15 November), beginning a set that was completed with a March for Alfredo Casella (19 December) and a Waltz for Erik Satie (6 March). During this winter of 1914–15 he also began a new series of folk verse settings with the third and fourth, as they would become, of the Four Russian Peasant Songs for female chorus. There was also another crucial encounter when, dining with Ansermet at the Geneva Maxim's on 28 January, Stravinsky was captivated by the cimbalom played in the restaurant by Aladár Rácz.

In June 1915 Stravinsky and his family moved from La Pervenche into the Villa Rogivue in Morges; he had started yet another folk verse cycle, the *Cat's Cradle Songs*, composed between May and November. His only other composition of this period was a piano miniature, *Souvenir d'un marche boche* (1 September), though of course there was the unseen progress on *Les noces*. At the end of the year he made his public début as a conductor, performing the *Firebird* suite in Geneva (20 December) and the complete ballet in Paris (29 December), on both occasions at benefit evenings for the Ballets Russes.

Much of the next year was taken up with the composition of *Renard*, commissioned by the Princesse Edmond de Polignac on 4 January 1916 and completed in piano score on 1 August (though there was no performance until 1922). Otherwise there was only another female chorus, the start of a new song group, *Three Tales for Children*, and perhaps the piano *Valse pour les enfants*, written in December 1916 or January 1917. By the summer the family had moved into another villa in Morges, Les Sapins; in May Stravinsky had made his first visit to Spain, where the Ballets Russes were performing after a visit to New York which he had not joined.

1917 was more evidently busier. By early April he had written the last of the female choruses and a new set of piano duets, the Five Easy Pieces, besides creating the *Chant du rossignol* out of his opera. Then he went to join the Ballets Russes in Italy, and conducted *The Firebird* and *Fireworks* at the Teatro Costanzi in Rome (12 April), the latter work given as a dancer-less light show, with a stage full of geometrical objects designed by Giacomo Balla. Before the performance, since the tsar's abdication had rendered the Imperial hymn obsolete, Stravinsky conducted an arrangement of the 'Song of the Volga Boatmen' he had made four days earlier for wind and percussion. During this Italian trip, which continued to Naples, he also had his first meeting with Picasso, who drew his portrait. Back in Morges he completed the *Three Tales* in May–June, before going for the summer to Les Fougères in Diablerets (Vaud), where he met Gide in order to talk about a projected musical production of *Antony and Cleopatra*. In October the Stravinskys moved into a new place in Morges, the Maison Bornand at 2 place St-Louis, where they remained until 1920. *Les noces* was completed there in sketch score on 11 October, and the first sketches for *Rag-time* may date from the same month. In November, the month of the Boleshevik Revolution, Stravinsky wrote an Etude for pianola, and in December came a *Berceuse* for voice and piano.

After *The Nightingale* – or maybe just before its completion, when Stravinsky and Cocteau attended a Jewish wedding in Leysin in March 1914 – began the longest gestation in the composer's life: a period of nine years leading up to the first performance of *Les noces*, in striking contrast with the rapidity with which the earlier works, including even *The Nightingale* once it had been restarted, had moved from conception to fulfilment. Of course there were practical reasons. The Ballets Russes were appearing only intermittently, and in 1914–15 Dyagilev seems to have been more concerned with his projected balletic mass *Liturgie* than with *Les noces*:[1] without the prospect of a performance, Stravinsky would be encouraged to delay completion, as with *The Rite of Spring*. Meanwhile he needed money: hence the importance of the Polignac commission, causing further delay.

But this was also a work that created problems of its own, and of two kinds. In the first place, following the experience of *The Nightingale*, which had been given by what was of course a ballet company, with the title role and the Fisherman's song delivered from the pit, Stravinsky was moving towards a form of spectacle in which music, words and movement would be linked not as in conventional opera (the impossible alliance of his 1913 newspaper interview) but as in ritual observances, a direction prepared by *The Rite of Spring* as well as *The Nightingale*. That meant reconsidering the resources, to arrive at an ensemble in which singers, dancers and instrumentalists are ideally all part of the action. Secondly, the choice of subject matter, that of a Russian peasant wedding, involved Stravinsky in closer, deeper contact with folk music and folk verse, bringing about a change to a pithier, earthier style – unless, of course, it was the change of style, already beginning in the last act of *The Nightingale*, that encouraged him to look towards peasant art.

A new direction can, as so often, be ascribed to quite different causes. There was also the outbreak of war, disrupting not only the Ballets Russes but cultural life generally: the Flonzaley Quartet played Stravinsky's Three Pieces in Chicago in 1915, and there was a performance of the female choruses in Geneva in 1917, but these were the only Stravinsky premières between that of *The Nightingale* just

[1]See *SSC II*, pp. 15–19.

before the war and that of *Histoire du soldat* at its close. Those conditions themselves may have encouraged a move to smaller forces, while Stravinsky's comparative isolation (though he travelled to Spain and Italy) could have brought out a kind of home-made music, a music rooted in peasant rhymes and children's tales when not explicitly domestic. And everything he wrote between the quartet pieces (spring–summer 1914) and *Rag-time* (winter 1917–18) is of this sort: an enacted village wedding, a dramatic farmyard fable, sets of invented folksongs, an episode for the homely pianola, piano duets with easy parts for beginners. His social life too was becoming more local and circumscribed, with the grand Paris friends of the pre-war years – fellow composers (Ravel, Delage, Schmitt, Casella), socialites, acolytes of the Ballets Russes – replaced by a Swiss entourage that included Ansermet, Ramuz and Cingria.

However, the jump in musical style was not so abrupt as it now appears, for *Les noces* as originally planned seems to have been both more 'operatic'[2] and more magniloquent: André Schaeffner's report[3] makes it sound like a super-*Rite*, with an orchestra of a hundred and fifty in categories of wind (including voices) and percussion (including strings). The three-act project appears to have been condensed and formalized at an early stage, but only gradually did the two categories of the ensemble find their definitive realization in groupings of voices only and of pianos plus percussion. By the autumn of 1917 Stravinsky had almost finished an instrumentation for orchestral wind with a rich percussion ensemble (including piano, harpsichord, cimbalom and two harps) and just eight strings, a formation not unlike that he had planned in 1914 for a stage work based on the comic verses of *Koz'ma Prutkov*, rapidly aborted in response to Benois's dismissiveness.[4] Then in 1919 came a new scoring, up to the end of the second scene, for an amended version of just the keyboard–percussion group, comprising timpani, percussion, harmonium, two cimbaloms and a newcomer, a pianola. Stravinsky apparently abandoned this solution because of the scarcity of cimbalom players and the difficulty there would be in synchronizing the pianola with the more biological music makers; the piece was then set aside until 1922.

Meanwhile Stravinsky gave the cimbalom – the nearest concert instrument to the peasant Russian *gusli*, or portable psaltery, he had mentioned early in the *Les noces* story[5] – a leading role in *Renard* (1916) and wrote a pianola study the next year, a piece that seems to

[2] *SPD*, pp. 145–6. [3] See White, p. 254.
[4] See *SPD*, p. 133. [5] Ibid., p. 151.

have been one of the first written for, and spectacularly exploiting, the multitudinous fingers of this instrument's spectral performer. In such ways, and surely in others less tangible, the story of *Les noces* intertwines with those of the other works of 1914–17. For instance, the clangorous pianos of the final *Les noces*, ensemble are presaged in the duets and song accompaniments, though this is an ancestry that, as has already been intimated, goes back as far as the 1908 studies. Conversely, the orchestral version of *Les noces*, cross-cutting among different ensembles associated with different phrases, may have left a permanent mark on the mixed groupings of *Pribautki* and *Renard*.

The first new work of 1914, as a little triptych for string quartet, stands rather apart. This is an oddity in Stravinsky's output, one of his very rare contributions to chamber music, and it seems to have been started without a commission, the Flonzaley Quartet entering the picture only after the first piece had been written.[6] Just possibly the work became a repository for ideas sparked off by fruitless dramatic projects: the third of the quartet pieces is an evocation of slow antiphonal chant that may relate to *Liturgie* (Stravinsky gave it the title 'Cantique' when he orchestrated it), while the other two movements – rustic and urban, but both sighted on low culture – suggest the fascination with circus and music-hall to be found in the contemporary endeavours of Debussy, of Picasso, and of Cocteau.

Rather more than the biblical king's dance around the ark, however, the first piece suggests a peasant fiddler. The first violin keeps repeating a line against a grid of 3 + 2 + 2 beats supported by a pizzicato ostinato from viola and cello, while the viola also holds a D drone and the second violin sporadically interjects a brusque descending scale fragment in Dorian C sharp (F sharp–E–D sharp–C sharp), a fragment having no notes in common with the curtailed Mixolydian G of the tune. Because the number of beats in the latter is not a multiple of seven, at each repetition it finds itself at a different place in the metrical grid, while the second violin's intrusions come ever earlier (regularly so in the case of the double entry, not so regularly for the single one: the entries are marked here with arrows, and the lines below the tune show its rebarrings in its three and a bit recurrences – see Ex. 7).

This is an extreme point in Stravinsky's automatism, and may reflect the machine aesthetic of the time: quite apart from the interest in the pianola that was soon to be manifested creatively, he was aware of the futurists through his visits to Italy. But perhaps he needed no outside

[6]Ibid., p. 126.

Ex. 7
Three Quartet Pieces: I

stimulus, having been an artificer of musical machines at least since the second op. 7 study. Besides, the drone, the ostinato and the four-note exercises (Mixolydian, Dorian, and chromatic for the lower strings) all suggest a rural ambience, miles and aeons away from the urban–industrial noises of the Italian (and later Russian) futurists. What Stravinsky offers is a futurist photograph of something ancient. As in a Balla painting, the edges of the object are blurred by shifted repetition, with the shifts made not in space but in time, against the grid and against the memory of how the tune went last time. And of course the effect is emphasized by the presence of so much repetition at a finer level, which gives tiny motifs a quick metrical reinterpretation and breaks up symmetry, rather as the symmetries of his first Russian folk-rhyme group, the Three Little Songs of 1913, were to be broken up by pauses and reiterations in the orchestral version of 1929–30. In this first quartet piece the thing disrupted, the object in the photograph, is perhaps the melody as far as the first cadence, a melody which can easily be heard as in four 2/4 bars with a half-bar upbeat. What follows is echo and ripple: a repeat of the cadence, then a reversal (A–G–A–B–C–B–A in bars 5–7 of Ex. 7 exactly mirroring A–B–C–B–A–G–A in bars 1–3) leading to a repeat of the double cadence, then a repetition of this whole last phrase, with an upbeat (though the identity here is of course compromised by the rebarrings in its later appearances). The self-analysis that the tune acts out – breaking into fragments, reversing some – is a legacy from *The Rite of Spring*, but uncommonly acute here because of the simplicity of the basic material. It also shows how close Stravinsky was to serial thinking, at the very time when Schoenberg was just beginning to formulate his method, and forty years before he himself would explicitly take the same path – close, but also widely distant, for where Webern saw serialism as a way of continuing to compose naturally ('Otherwise, one composes as before'),[7] Stravinsky's efforts were directed at showing even the most rudimentary melody as unnatural.

The third of these quartet pieces, otherwise so different, is similar in its reworkings of elementary melodic ideas, except that the reworkings are essentially harmonic, a matter of small displacements within the homophonic repetitions, and only subsidiarily rhythmic. The middle movement has its distorted repetitions too, but within a much more diverse context of clownish jumping from one bizarre posture to another. Altogether the oddity of the music (the second violin and viola in this piece are instructed to 'quickly turn the instrument upside-down' in order to execute an arpeggiando) is that of an outsider behaving as if unaware that the string quartet had a distinguished history. The tone is not so much irreverent or insolent as simply ignorant, a signal that Stravinsky still had hold of his naivety, and in that respect at least, these quartet pieces – which he kept with him, revising and orchestrating them during the war – belong with the peasant songs and dances that quickly followed.

But there are other connections too. For instance, the first of the *Pribautki* (the title indicates a kind of near-nonsense rhyme) starts out attached to a three-bar grid like that of the first quartet piece, and drones and ostinatos are common accompanimental features of all these works. Equally common are techniques of alteration whereby, as most plainly in the first and last quartet pieces, simple motifs give rise to longer melodic utterances. The evident deliberateness of these processes suggests links not only with serialism but also with the constructivism of Malevich and other contemporaries among Russian painters. There are tempting parallels, too, with developments in cubism around the same time. In *The Rite of Spring*, as in analytical cubism, objects (folksongs) had been splintered into their most elementary components; now the effort, as in the synthetic phase of cubism, was to build those components into new unities, but without appeal to an old system of organization, whether tonal harmony or the rules of perspective. The alternative, for Stravinsky, seems to have been a sequence of improvised solutions.

[7]*The Path to the New Music* (Bryn Mawr, Pennsylvania, 1963), p. 53.

Ex. 8 illustrates this in four settings of what is essentially the same melodic motif, from four different works of 1914–17 (see Ex. 8 below and opposite). These show the motif in different modes: Mixolydian in *Les noces* and the choral piece, Aeolian or Dorian in the rhyme and the duet. There are also obvious rhythmic differences. Stravinsky's nimble restressing is shown from one to another of the three Russian vocal pieces, and within the fragment from the *Pribautki*: this was something the folk rhymes themselves made play with, and 'the recognition of the musical possibilities inherent in this fact was one of the most rejoicing discoveries of my life'.[8] In the duet piece, of course, the rhythmic transformation goes much further, bending the motif to the skip of a tarantella; but the essential point here is that there is no discontinuity between Stravinsky's Russian pieces and his postcards from other places. And what the four extracts also together show is the variety of

Ex. 8

(a) *Les noces*: Scene 2

(b) Four Russian Peasant Songs: III

---

[8]*Expositions*, p. 121.

his accompaniments to the same idea: a kind of dissonant negative image in *Les noces*, a counterpoint in an opposed mode in the choral song, an ostinato in the *Pribautki*, a guyed banal pattern in 'Napolitana'. Just about the only general principle to be observed here is the complete avoidance of the fifth, the tonal dominant, as part of a caustic mismatching of tune to setting, an avoidance of conventional harmonic coherence. Clearly, no amount of abrasion and contradiction can stop the basic motif from sounding cadential, but in these anti-tonal settings it becomes a cadence that enforces itself on the music, rather than coming from within. It becomes the portrait of a cadence, with the frame provided by the accompaniment.

By withholding harmonic affirmation of his melodic cadence, Stravinsky also cuts himself off from the forward drive of tonal harmony. These are static moments – snapshots of a musical idea – which may be linked to others by repetition or continuation of some element (ostinato, drone, instrumentation), but never by smooth flow.

Ex. 8 cont.

(c) *Pribautki*: IV

(d) Five Easy Pieces: Napolitana

At the same time, they are snapshots of something in action. Because there is such a decisive gap between melody and accompaniment, the association of the two must always seem provisional: there is no single best solution, as there might be in a chorale harmonization, but an infinity of options, as Ex. 8 begins to suggest, showing too how there is a wide range of possible rhythmic interpretations of the idea, and another universe of timbral settings. Nothing is settled here, nothing fixed. It could all be different; it could all immediately become different, as in the example from the *Pribautki*. Alongside the rigidities – the frames, the ostinatos, the mechanical rhythms – there is, then, a sense of the haphazard. That is what gives this music its versatility, extending from a Russian wedding song to an Italian dance without moving from the spot. That is also what contributes to its humour.

These are some of the music's contradictions: its severity and its comedy, its fixity and its accidental character, its melody and its accompaniment. Perhaps this was one of the attractions of folk culture, that it found no problems in embracing contradictions – that, for example, a wedding could be at once ritualized and humorous, as the wedding of *Les noces* is (and of course Stravinsky's wheeling of different instrumentations through that score is of a piece with his constant recompositions of rhythm and accompaniment within works and among them: *Les noces* is the matrix composition of this period not only in its size and its long duration in progress but also in its mutability). One may remember too that the essentially comic character of severely precise, short, cross-cut forms was being realized at this time in the cinema, and that Stravinsky's contemporaries included – besides Picasso, Malevich and Balla – Chaplin and Keaton.

Instead of the silent cinema he offers, in the songs and instrumental pieces, the dark theatre, where gesture is created purely in sound. A striking instance comes at the end of the first *Pribautki* song, where the cadenza for oboe and clarinet sounds, as White observed, 'like the gurgle of an emptying bottle'[9] (this is of course a drinking song). But gesture can be just as graphic, and just as comic, without being onomatopoeic: it may be a matter of oddity, as in the central quartet piece or the string ostinato in Ex. 8c, or it may work through allusion to other music, as in the dislocated bass line of Ex. 8d. What is always crucial, though, is that the vividness of the gesture is heightened by its separation from its context, by the lack of an explanation for it, a before and an after, just as photographs of athletes or of running animals will provide more distinct, more powerful images of motion

[9]p. 237.

50

than will a film. Where Stravinsky's music connects with film, rather, it is in the jump-cuts that help to wrest events from environments.

The two works in which the dark theatre becomes light, *Renard* and *Les noces*, are still full of vital gestures existing on an exclusively aural plane, as they can be when Stravinsky's refusal of explanation operates not only sequentially but simultaneously, in a jamming together of text, music and action contrarily to fusion, so that musical events are not necessarily linked to words or to stage happenings (though they may be to either or both). The dislocation of music from action, in particular, seems to have been facilitated by the Ballets Russes productions of *The Nightingale* and of Rimsky-Korsakov's *Golden Cockerel*, the latter also given in 1914, with the singers standing at either side of the stage while the action was danced. In *Renard* and *Les noces* this double casting is taken into the fabric, and extended, with decisive results. The characters, represented by dancers and so not needing singers to embody them, are dissolved in the musical setting, which can obey different rules from those of sung dialogue. In *Renard* the four characters of the farmyard fable – Cock and Fox, Cat and Ram – are often sung by the two tenors and two basses respectively, but it is also possible for all four singers to be delivering the Cock's words, and *Les noces* goes much further in this direction. The solo soprano and solo bass are fleetingly identified with the bride and groom, but they can also sing the words of other characters – the bride's mother and the best man, for instance – though most usually they are caught up anonymously with the chorus.

There is, simply, no illusion that the soloists are singing for themselves, in character. They may seem to be delivering instead strings of quotations, as in a sense they are, since Stravinsky adapted the text from 'a complete script of a ritual'[10] in the Kireyevsky collection he had bought in Kiev. They are not enacting the wedding but rather reporting on it, reporting across a gulf of time and space that the music actualizes. Its materials are geographically and temporally strange, for unlike Bartók, who was creating the basis of a national tradition in his use of folk music, Stravinsky was engaged in showing his culture abroad. Right from *The Firebird* his works had been written primarily for a non-Russian audience, had been projections from one place into another, and also, since their subject was old Russia, from one time into another. But with *Les noces*, the first stage work he shaped entirely himself (*Apollo* was perhaps its only

[10]Simon Karlinsky: 'Igor Stravinsky and the Russian Preliterate Theater', *Confronting Stravinsky*, ed. Jann Pasler (Berkeley and Los Angeles, 1986), p. 9.

51

companion in this respect), the estrangement becomes part of the substance of the piece. The singers relate an action they cannot join, in a language which the intended audience cannot understand, and in a form made remote by formalization.

For though the liturgical moment of marriage is the very event Stravinsky's libretto excludes (and did exclude right from the first draft),[11] the effect of the work is to create a liturgy out of the extra-ecclesiastical necessities: the braiding of the bride's hair, the preparation of the groom, the departure of the bride, the wedding breakfast. Nor is it that old rituals here are being evoked in any anthropological manner, even if the script is an old one, for the ritual form comes from the music rather than the words. It is a matter of constant chanting (the work is more than half advanced before the instruments play a single bar alone, and they come fully to the fore only for the coda). It is a matter of verse–refrain and other closed repetitive forms projected, of course, over a much greater span than in the songs. It is a matter of modality. And it is a matter of unyielding pulsation, which keeps the music stitched into the objective time of the clock. Nearly all the music is geared to one of three pulse rates in the ratio 1:2:3, and there are no smooth transitions of tempo: this is a time machine more rigorous than *The Rite*, a world in which the uncertainties, hesitations and accelerations of psychological time are as impossible as is the individuation of character.

The final instrumentation, which makes this so much a work of voices and bell-like resonances, is another ritual aspect (Russian churches have bells, of course, but Orthodox practice forbids other instruments). At the same time, the omnipresence of piano tone conveys something of the atmosphere of a rehearsal, so that any performance of *Les noces* seems an appeal to an ideal that has still to be achieved. There is, therefore, another respect in which the work bodies forth one world into another: not just old Russia into the present-day West, but a noumenon into the universe of the senses. *Les noces* is a marriage in many dimensions: female and male (the first scene is begun and largely carried by women's voices; the second brings the men into prominence, and after that the shares are equal), ancient and modern, ritual and machine, voice and instrument, narrative and action, song and dance. But perhaps its deepest, and most deeply Russian, binding is of holiness and humour, the holiness of a ceremony going on beyond the senses and the humour of drunken guests at a wedding party. It is both comedy and icon.

[11]See *SPD*, pp. 145–6.

8

Histoire du soldat and other rags

On 25 March 1918, the day Debussy died, Stravinsky completed the piano version of the main work (apart from the set-aside *Les noces*) hanging over from the previous year: *Rag-time*. Also during this spring he made sketches that would find homes in the *Piano-Rag-Music*, in a new set of Russian songs, and in the Symphonies of Wind Instruments, to be dedicated to Debussy's memory. However, his main task of 1918 was the musical play *Histoire du soldat*, a local piece created in collaboration with Swiss friends (C. F. Ramuz as writer, Ansermet as conductor, René Auberjonois as designer, Georges and Ludmilla Pitoëff as dancers and choreographers), and put together swiftly, between April and the first performance in the Théâtre Municipal of Lausanne on 28 September.

After that, in October–November, came the set of Three Clarinet Pieces as a thank-offering to Werner Reinhart, the patron (and amateur clarinettist) who had financed the production of *Histoire du soldat*; there was also the instrumentation of *Rag-time*, finished on another significant day, 11 November, that of the armistice. During the ensuing winter Stravinsky completed the set of Four Russian Songs, revised the Three Quartet Pieces (December), celebrated New Year's Day with an arrangement of the *Marseillaise* for solo violin, and made a new *Firebird* suite (February 1919). It was perhaps during the following spring, when there is a gap in the record of Stravinsky's datings, that he worked at the version of *Les noces* with pianola and cimbaloms. Otherwise the only work between February and September, when *Pulcinella* was begun, was the *Piano-Rag-Music*, completed on 28 June.

Earlier that month, on the 6th, the two sets of folk rhymes with ensemble accompaniment, the *Pribautki* and *Cat's Cradle Songs*, had their first performances under the auspices of Schoenberg's concert society in Vienna (though the former set had been sung with piano accompaniment in Paris the previous month). Stravinsky was not present; but Webern was, and wrote enthusiastically of the event to Berg: 'These songs are wonderful. This music moves me completely beyond belief . . . How those three clarinets sound!'[1] Maybe their sound remained in his mind when he came to write his Latin canons for soprano and clarinets a few years later, though the links here are thicker and deeper. Webern and Schoenberg were already using small, mixed ensembles: Schoenberg, of course, had been doing so since *Pierrot lunaire*, surely as much the paradigm in Vienna as it was in Morges. Just at that moment – and it was a brief moment – Stravinsky could be accepted as a corresponding member of the Viennese School.

So the quite unusual chaos of Stravinsky's composing while he was drafting *Les noces*, between 1914 and 1917, continued for the next couple of years. Where before and after this period he generally concentrated on one major work at a time, now there were nearly always several in train at once. Single works (*Les noces*) or collections (the female choruses) remained in progress for years; sketches were left awaiting definitive form and instrumentation, including some that would enter the Symphonies of Wind Instruments and, most conspicuously, one for a bassoon duet that would have to wait more than thirty years for realization. Some of this can be blamed on the lack of opportunities for performance, for when such a goal seemed in sight, with *Renard* and *Histoire du soldat*, Stravinsky could work straightforwardly towards it (though *Histoire du soldat* was based on earlier sketches, including some meant for *Antony and Cleopatra*). But the incompletions and the changes, including especially the incompletions and the changes in *Les noces*, might suggest a need for validation that could no longer be answered. Stravinsky was cut off from the main cause of what he was doing, and though he had for several years been engaged in presenting Russia to the West, his Russia had now doubly disappeared, made unreachable in space by war and revolution, and irretrievable in time by the new direction the country was taking. To go on making pictures of old Russia would have been to risk the most un-Stravinskian emotion: nostalgia. There would have to be another way of examining history, and soon there was. Meanwhile the repertory of Russian songs came to an abrupt end with the set of the first postwar winter; Stravinsky suddenly switched to looking West, to ragtime, rather than East; and he gave a Russian tale a more generalized aspect in *Histoire du soldat*.

According to his own account, he based his rags of 1917–19 on material brought back from the United States by Ansermet.[2] How-

---

[1]Hans Moldenhauer: *Anton von Webern* (London, 1978), p. 229.
[2]See *Dialogues*, p. 54.

ever, Debussy's 'Golliwog's Cake-walk' is evidence that ragtime had been known in Paris at least a decade earlier, and Ansermet's American tour, with the Dyagilev company, had been in 1916, well over a year before Stravinsky began *Rag-time*. Perhaps the more immediate stimulus was Satie's use of the style in *Parade*, first produced by the Ballets Russes in Paris in May 1917. Stravinsky was not at the première, but he knew the music before he saw the piece for the first time in 1921,[3] and his use of low musical forms in the duets of 1914–17 certainly has its parallels in Satie – though the original debased valse is that of *Petrushka*, which has anterior claims to the Polka Stravinsky favoured as the prototype of neo-classicism.[4]

This word has been debased itself by the variety of cases it has been grabbed to cover: just within Stravinsky's own output it may refer to the use of past forms with a consciousness of their pastness (not only the polka and waltz but also the fugue, or the sonata allegro, or the pastoral–lyrical slow movement), to the adaptation of existing music (as in *Pulcinella* or the Bach Variations – themselves quite different in tone), to the use of a classical orchestral ensemble, to the appeal to classical models of harmony or phrase structure, to the imitation of particular composers, or to the pervasive self-conscious reference to some work or repertory (as in *The Rake's Progress*). But yet there is some meaning here, which has to do with Stravinsky's externality, with his concern for mechanism rather than motive, with his view of history not as a developing stream in which he had a place, but rather as a welter of efforts making no larger sense and all equally separate from, or close to, himself (the more temporally distant – Bach, Monteverdi – might well be much closer than Wagner and Brahms). This dispossessed condition may have been exacerbated by his exile – or to put it another way, he may have needed to be exiled in order to achieve it (in either case the *Petrushka* example is pertinent, since this was his first major work written in the West) – but the musical and biographical evidence is that his dislocation had already begun long before, at 66 Krukov Canal.

The pervasiveness of cross-reference in Stravinsky's music means that the mapping of influences is, as usual, dependent on guess and assumption (though clearly it mattered to Stravinsky, who persistently condescended to composers he felt himself to have outgrown: Musorgsky, Skryabin, Ravel, Satie). More important in these rags and polkas is his participation in an enthusiasm for popular art that characterized the period, and at the same time the utter distinctiveness

[3]See *An Autobiography*, p. 93.   [4]See *Dialogues*, p. 41.

of his contributions. *Histoire du soldat*, for instance, is full of forms that Satie cultivated – marches, chorales, café dances – but fashioned with a complexity that is completely different.

The style is remarkably different, too, from that of the immediately preceding works. *Renard*, for instance, is similarly a piece of rough theatre for reduced resources, even if it is perhaps a portrait of a peasant performance rather than something actually to be done in a village square: it has a march to bring the players on and take them off again, whereas the march at the start of *Histoire du soldat* is already part of the piece. But the biggest jump is in the nature of the music. The orchestra of *Renard* is kaleidoscopic, and beautifully composed around the jangling tones of the cimbalom, whereas *Histoire du soldat* has a severity and sameness of sound, and its ensemble seems to have been chosen for the greatest possible disparity and abrasion: clarinet and bassoon, cornet and trombone, violin and double bass, and percussion. The score appears to exist in exile from the juicy Russianness of the works of 1914–17, and when Stravinsky's own past is evoked it is from a perspective of distance, as in the music for clarinet and bassoon at the end of the 'Pastorale', suggesting *The Rite* (this was, after all, his first purely instrumental composition for mixed ensemble since that work).

Of course, the essential difference from *Renard* and *Les noces*, as this comparison with *The Rite* brings out, is the absence of voices in *Histoire du soldat*. The exuberant variety of the instrumental writing in *Renard* is given an occasion, as in the chamber orchestral version of *Les noces*, by the chops and changes in the vocal scoring, the fact that the instruments are following and enhancing a concatenation of rhymes. Without that framework, the instruments in *Histoire du soldat* look partly to borrowed forms and styles, partly to the mechanical ostinatos of the Three Quartet Pieces. The 'Little Concert', the one movement not to use a stock pattern, is full of examples, as here, where the double bass ostinato supports – or, rather, exists in friction with – violin and woodwind lines that give the coarse timbral mix harmonic and metrical substance as well (see Ex. 9). But the clashing of instrumental colours, modes and metres here is also a clashing of tenses, since the woodwind are recalling the prominent cornet theme from the start of this movement while the double bass has gone back to its figure from an earlier section, the 'Airs by a Stream'.

The score is full of such cross-references, and inevitably the opportunity for them becomes greater as it proceeds, and generates more material out of its tugging polyphonic machinery. The music

Ex. 9
Histoire du soldat: Petit concert

thus has a capacity for holding on to the past that is denied the hero, for the Soldier meets his doom when he tries to go back home to his former life while keeping the Princess he has acquired during his travels (it is hard not to see Stravinsky's own misapprehensions about home reflected here, no matter how non-autobiographical an artist he was). This final gesture – the Soldier, about to cross the frontier into his home country, looks back at his Princess, and is recaptured by the Devil – makes *Histoire du soldat* his first treatment of the Orpheus myth, and the connection is reinforced by the fact that the Soldier's soul is represented by a musical instrument, his violin (an instrument which is duly prominent in the score). But the piece is also a Faust story, in which the Soldier is duped into selling his soul to the Devil in exchange for earthly riches.

The nature of Stravinsky's collaboration with Ramuz is unclear, though the composer would seem to have been the senior partner, given that he had earlier been using Ramuz as the translator of his Russian texts, that Ramuz's few letters from this period contain suggestions that were not in fact carried through,[5] that the final version abbreviated the spoken material,[6] and that the roots of the work were Russian rather than Franco-Swiss.[7] Besides, there are resemblances of theme with *Renard* (both are parables of good and evil), and the intertwining of narration and action, of past and present, is carried over from both *Renard* and *Les noces* (Ramuz deserves credit at least for the juggling of tenses and viewpoints in his lines for the narrator, who remains outside the play except at its crucial juncture). But in any event, it is the music that takes control as the work unfolds, for where the first half includes only an introduction and interludes, the second half is full of music, and important episodes are given entirely in music and dance, with no verbal accompaniment or explanation. The piece thus drifts from play into ballet, without coming near opera, which would have required Stravinsky to match his music to what was still the alien medium of French words. That was something he would, remarkably, evade until *Perséphone* fifteen years later, remaining in exile.

Most of the movements of *Histoire du soldat* show, along with cross-referencing, the kind of persistent repetition and reconsideration demonstrated in the case of the first quartet piece (Ex. 9 has a little of this again). But the most substantial instance of this cubist technique – and, with a duration approaching five minutes, Stravinsky's longest instrumental movement between *The Rite of Spring* and the Symphonies of Wind Instruments – is *Rag-time*. The presence of the cimbalom, in what is effectively a small-scale concerto for the instrument, inevitably recalls *Renard*, but there are close links with *Histoire du soldat* in terms of instrumentation (six of the Soldier's seven are among these eleven, including the important violin and the cornet inherited from the orchestra of *Petrushka*), of motif, and of course of musical subject. But Stravinsky's three rags are as much different as they are alike. The one in *Histoire du soldat* is developed to

[5]See *SSC III*, pp. 33 and 35–6.
[6]Ibid., pp. 469–74.   [7]See Karlinsky, op. cit., pp. 12–13.

make a substantial finale for the Princess's set of three dances, following a tango and a waltz: the 4/8 metre is persistently being jolted by added or subtracted beats and by small-scale repetitions as well as by syncopation, but the violin assures continuity. *Rag-time*, on the other hand, keeps to its 4/4 but is comically unsteady in its cut-and-paste construction from clichés and frustrated cadences: again one might recall the cinematic parallels. Then in the *Piano-Rag-Music* Stravinsky sometimes takes advantage of the solo medium to abandon barring that would inevitably mask the cross-metres (as it does in Ex. 9 and in much of *Histoire du soldat*). What remains is the absolute consistency of pulse, suggesting at least two reasons why Stravinsky might have found ragtime appealing: because it accorded with the principle of restressing he had already drawn from, and applied to, Russian folk verse, and because it sounded as if made for the pianola.

Of course, ragtime was also exotic – like the Spanish music he heard on his visits[8] and brought exuberant into the pianola study and into the 'Royal March' of *Histoire du soldat* as well as into the duet 'Española', though his view of Spain was partly slantwise in the mirror of Glinka and Rimsky-Korsakov. More direct, but now ending, was his inspection of Russian folk music. The Four Russian Songs of the winter after *Histoire du soldat* are a disparate quartet, the first belonging with the children's tales, the second a tiny counting song with postlude that makes a pendant to the *Pribautki*, the third a divination song close to the female choruses, and the last a spiritual lament quite unlike any of the other sets in its narrow chromatic melismas. There are also signs that the songs, though composed contiguously, were not planned as a set for voice and piano. The counting song is accompanied entirely by cimbalom-like rapid iterations and glissandos, and the final piece was composed for voice, flute and cimbalom: some of the flute part remains, unexplained, printed above the piano part in the published version, and it was perhaps in order to do justice to this number, in particular, that Stravinsky in 1954 prepared the Four Songs for voice, flute, harp and guitar, where it is joined with three nursery rhymes of this period. In this later version the harp and the guitar together provide a last imitation of the *gusli* from long-post-cimbalom days, though the flute part is considerably changed from the original.

The Three Pieces for clarinet are connected historically to *Histoire du soldat*, both in that they were written straight afterwards, and in

[8]See *An Autobiography*, p. 69.

that they were intended to thank Reinhart. But their musical aura is that of the Russian folksongs, again with modal images presented and immediately avoided, cut or distorted in the manner of the first quartet piece. These are wordless songs, as the chants of the Symphonies of Wind Instruments, already starting, were wordless. Before it could learn French, Stravinsky's music would have to forget Russian. And of course it never would.

9

Pergolesi and after

Prompted by Dyagilev, who had reconstituted his company for performances in London throughout the last third of 1918 and most of 1919, Stravinsky set to work on a new ballet, *Pulcinella*, and left *Les noces* for the more distant future. But his residence, and his musical liaisons, remained Swiss. On 8 November he took part in a concert in Lausanne including the first performances of his recent small-scale instrumental pieces: *Piano-Rag-Music* and the piano *Rag-time*, played by José Iturbi, the Eight Easy Pieces, played by Iturbi and the composer, the clarinet pieces and the suite from *Histoire du soldat* in the arrangement for violin, clarinet and piano. The programme was repeated in Zurich on 20 November and Geneva on 17 December; also in Geneva, eleven days before, Ansermet and his Suisse Romande Orchestra had given the first performance of *Chant du rossignol*. Two months later, on 2 February 1920, that work had its first stage production by the Ballets Russes at the Paris Opéra, again with Ansermet conducting. The choreography was by Leonid Massine, with designs by Matisse and a cast including Karsavina as the Nightingale and Lydia Sokolova as Death.

Pulcinella was finished on 20 April 1920, a week before the first performance of the ensemble version of *Rag-time*, given under Arthur Bliss in London. Stravinsky was not there: presumably he was involved in rehearsals for *Pulcinella*, which was introduced on 15 May, again by the Ballets Russes at the Paris Opéra with Ansermet on the podium. Again, too, the choreographer was Massine, who also danced the title role, with Karsavina as his Pimpinella. The designs were by Picasso.

The next month Stravinsky and his family moved from Morges to Paris, though they were not there long before leaving for the Hôtel Charles in the Breton resort of Carantec, where Stravinsky resumed work on the Symphonies of Wind Instruments, completed a short score of the work (on 2 July), and went on to the Concertino. That piece, for string quartet in its original version, was finished in the villa Bel Respiro in Garches, Seine-et-Oise, on 24 September; Stravinsky had moved into the house, owned by Coco Chanel, earlier in the month. Like the set of Three Pieces, the Concertino was first performed by the Flonzaley Quartet in New York (on 23 November) in Stravinsky's absence: another four years were to pass before his first visit to the United States.

A week after this distant première he completed the instrumentation of the Symphonies. The only other achievement of the next four and a half months was a set of tiny piano pieces, *Les cinq doigts*, finished on 18 February. But exactly two months after that Stravinsky sent a telegram to Ansermet informing him that *Les noces* would be scored for four pianos and percussion. Also in April he moved from Garches (the affair with Chanel – one of several during the period since 1914 when his wife became a permanent convalescent – was over) into an apartment provided for him at the Maison Pleyel in Paris, the idea being that he would work on pianola transcriptions of his works, as indeed he did, and with enthusiasm. Increasingly he was living a life apart from his family (he had spent Easter in Spain again with the Ballets Russes), and in May Catherine and the children moved to Anglet, near Biarritz, where Stravinsky would come for visits and holidays. In June he was in London, attending a performance of *The Rite* under Eugene Goossens in the Queen's Hall (7 June) and, three days later, the first performance in the same place of the Symphonies of Wind Instruments, under Koussevitzky.

The story of Dyagilev's jealousy of his protégé's Swiss achievements seems to have its origins in the latter's *Autobiography*.[1] But none of the new works Stravinsky had completed in Switzerland was suitable for the Ballets Russes. *Renard* and *Histoire du soldat* were both chamber pieces (though Dyagilev came to the rescue of the un-performed former work in 1922); *Les noces* was still unfinished; and the only orchestral scores of the war were *Chant du rossignol* – which Dyagilev did take on, which he may even have prompted,[2] and for which in 1916–17 he had planned a futurist production with designs by Fortunato Depero – and versions of the quartet pieces and some of the duets. (Neither of these last projects was unveiled until much later. The quartet transcriptions gained titles: 'Danse', realizing the fife-and-drum image behind the first; 'Excentrique', putting the lopsided antics of the second into Petrushka's cell, with prominent piano; and 'Cantique', laying out the chants as symphonies of both wind and string instruments. They also gained a more upbeat finale, 'Madrid',

[1] p. 79.   [2] See *SSC II*, pp. 28–9.

made out of the pianola study, but that was not until a decade later. The arrangement of the eight duets, to make two four-piece suites for small orchestra, also went on into the 1920s.) One need not imagine a peevish impresario, only a man anxious to get something new from his leading composer into his repertory now that the war was over and his company could resume its seasons in Paris.

His solution turned out to be almost as much a masterstroke as his original commissioning of Stravinsky a decade before. Maybe that was instinct, maybe luck. He could just have been trying to follow up two successes he and Massine, whom he had advanced to principal choreographer after his break with Nijinsky in 1916, had had with scores that were pots-pourris of earlier music: *Les femmes de bonne humeur*, by Vincenzo Tommasini out of Domenico Scarlatti (introduced in Rome in April 1917: this was Massine's choreographic début; Stravinsky was there), and *La boutique fantasque*, by Respighi out of Rossini (London, 1919). But his choice of Pergolesi as Stravinsky's collaborator – or rather of 'Pergolesi', since much of this music is now known to have been falsely attributed during the mid-eighteenth-century Pergolesi craze – was peculiarly apt. Stravinsky's main excursions from Switzerland during the war had been to Spain and Italy to be with the Ballets Russes, and his musical excursions had, besides the rags, been in the same directions. Naples (in this case the postcard, 'Napolitana', had come before the visit) was a particular attraction, possibly because it mixed the two national temperaments: Stravinsky remarked on its 'half Spanish' character,[3] on the pleasure he and Picasso in 1917 had found in the aquarium and in the Neapolitan water colours, and on their attending a *commedia dell'arte* performance there[4] (strikingly premonitory of *Pulcinella*, these images of the two artists watching: watching fish, watching clowns). Pergolesi, or 'Pergolesi', offered him Naples in music. At the same time, this was music that was neither too good to destroy nor too bad to be worth destroying, neither so familiar that Stravinsky's contribution would be spotted at once as external, nor so unfamiliar that dislocations would not be recognized. In a sense, one cannot imagine *Pulcinella* having been made with anything but this music. In another sense, it enables one to imagine almost anything from the mid-seventeenth century to the late eighteenth *Pulcinella*-ized, since what it presents is not so much a work as a way of hearing.

That way of hearing is curious in both senses: enquiring and intensely watchful, but also askew. The general way with

---

[3] *An Autobiography*, p. 67.   [4] See *Conversations*, pp. 104–5.

eighteenth-century music, as practised for example by Tchaikovsky in *Mozartiana*, was to make the borrowed pieces as much as possible like one's own. But Stravinsky had no concept of 'own': lack of ownership was one of the conditions of exile – or, more likely, had come about through his rapid, repeated outgrowings of himself in his twenties–or, perhaps more likely still, was the lot of an autodidact and outsider. Ex. 8 was enough to show how what might have been a basic symptom of style – a melodic shape – could be approached in very different ways. Certainly by this point Stravinsky no longer had a style so much as an attitude, a pair of ears listening to anything – ragtime, paso doble, folksong, Orthodox chant – from somewhere in the wilds of pre-Westernized, pre-diatonic Russia. He could not recompose Pergolesi, so bright with the discoveries of major-minor harmony that were thoroughly alien to him, as his own possession; what he could compose was the act of possessing. This is possibly what he meant when he spoke of approaching his model not with respect but with love.[5] *Pulcinella* is not the record of a satisfactory affair: it is the act.

As such it makes one alert to two participants. There is no dissolving of Pergolesi into Stravinsky, as there is of Mozart into Tchaikovsky. What happens is more a brightening achieved not only by the orchestration but also by the illumination from a new harmonic angle, so that the original pieces, when one hears them, seem more like the shadows of originals that are here in *Pulcinella*. The effect of the scoring is all the more remarkable given that Stravinsky, lacking a place of his own even in terms of orchestral resources (each of his orchestral scores – the recent quartet arrangements show this – has a sound world that is its alone, not an aspect of something more generally his), meets Pergolesi on the latter's ground, or nearly: the work is for a small string orchestra with concertino quintet, and with pairs of flutes, oboes, bassoons and horns, besides solo trumpet and trombone as less regular visitors. What results from the new harmonic light is not only addition, though there are indeed new voices, richer chords and repetitions to create ostinatos, but may equally be exclusion or displacement, besides the partitioning brought about by the instrumentation. Stravinsky had already shown, in much of his Swiss music, how meaning might inhere not in the substance of passages but in how they are placed and arranged (the crude meanings of the cadences and jog-trots in *Rag-time*, for instance, are always being subverted, so that subversion becomes the real subject, the meaning, of the piece). Now *Pulcinella*, the last work completed in

[5]See *An Autobiography*, p. 81.

Morges, presents the two levels of meaning at once, the Stravinskian all the way along the length of the Pergolesian.

A little of how this is achieved may appear from a look at one short section, here given in its versions before and after Stravinsky, the former from a trio sonata in B flat, transposed into Stravinsky's key for ease of comparison (see Ex. 10). Here there are virtually no additions (the only exceptions are brought about by the inversions and, for the bassoon, octave shift to give repeating life to the octave bounce figure at the end of the first phrase): on the contrary, the Stravinsky has fewer notes – not only, trivially, because it is an abbreviation, cutting the passages between square brackets in Ex. 10a, but also because there is no realization of the figuring until the tailpiece. As Stravinsky himself noted, 'the remarkable thing about *Pulcinella* is not how much but how little was added or changed'.[6] It was enough to excise some chromatic passages that might have introduced an unwonted *affettuoso*, to collapse the upbeat into the first downbeat, to break up a bit the regular phrasing, and, especially, to parcel the music out to wind ensembles, effectively constraining the rhythmic give that the original would seem to imply.

Nearly half of *Pulcinella* is worked up from trio sonatas; the rest comes from keyboard pieces, orchestral movements and arias. These last retain their words, though the parts may be differently distributed (for instance, a minuet aria for bass becomes a trio with soprano and tenor). And though the placing of the songs seems to have been determined at least in part by the action (there is a serenade early on, for example), there is no more matching of singer to character than there was in *Renard* and *Les noces*, and the singers are surely meant to stay in the pit. Meanwhile the action, of which an outline is printed in the score, is an adaptation of a *commedia dell'arte* piece, with Pulcinella, the carnal trickster, outwitting his companions and getting the girl of his fancy. Not only the subject but also the brilliant diatonic machinery has points of contact with *Petrushka*, and on Picasso's side too the *commedia* seed fell on ready soil. But the nature of the masquerade needs to be carefully stated. This is not a work in which Stravinsky adopts bygone manners, except in his choice of orchestral ensemble, which he then makes sound not at all eighteenth-century. The bygone manners are there because bygone music is there, and in that sense the piece is not neo-classical. There is a mask, a shockingly colourful one, but there is also a very evident gap between mask and face – or perhaps better, between puppet and puppeteer.

[6]*Expositions*, p. 113.

Ex. 10
(a) 'Pergolesi': Trio sonata: I

Ex. 10 cont.
(b) *Pulcinella*: Scherzino

If one were to try to disentangle the two, to see Ex. 10b as the product of Ex. 10a and something else, then that something else might look not unlike the Symphonies of Wind Instruments, which similarly features compartmented groupings answering one another. That is not to say that this other great work of 1919–20 represents the 'real' Stravinsky, only that it is a considerably less complex

67

occasion, with of course no Neapolitan line-drawing to be over-painted, but also with no allusions to concerto grosso texture or lingering Hispanic echoes (like the shudderings of fandango rhythm at the very end of the Pergolesi ballet, though inevitably the principal steps here are Italianate and eighteenth-century – tarantella, minuet, siciliana, gavotte – with the overture a march, if an altogether more courtly, balletic one than in *Renard* and *Histoire du soldat*).

Like *Les noces* but now completely, the Symphonies is a pulse machine, geared in the ratios $1 : 2 : 3 : 4$, with the slowest pulse reserved for the concluding chorale, as if the music had come to its rhythmic fundamental. The resonance model, of fundamentals and overtones, also seems to guide the harmony: the very last chord, for instance, could be interpreted as composed of the second, third, fifth, seventh, twelfth, fifteenth, sixteenth and higher harmonics (C–G–E–B–G–B–C–G–B–D) of an extremely low C that is not sounded. But the effect is of inharmonic vibrations, of bell chimes ringing from these wind instruments quite as much as they were to ring from pianos in the final version of *Les noces*. The melodic patterns resounding on these wind bells, and played by smaller ensembles of reeds and pipes in the quicker sections, are all modal, as in the Russian–Swiss works for which this score provides a culmination and an epitaph – an epitaph because, though written as a tribute to Debussy (as Stravinsky's earlier wind orchestra piece had been for Rimsky-Korsakov), this is also a memorial to a phase in his own music. As so often, his own verbal description is the best: 'an austere ritual which is unfolded in terms of short litanies between different groups of homogeneous instruments'.[7]

The fact that the work fits its particular medium of homogeneous instruments (but not totally homogeneous instruments) so well makes it surprising to discover that early sketches were for harmonium and for strings, and that the piece drew itself apart from a body of material that also gave rise to compositions so dissimilar from it as the *Piano-Rag-Music*, the Concertino and the Octet.[8] Of these, the Concertino is a brisk survey of recent territory. Commissioned by the Swiss Flonzaley Quartet, who had given the Three Pieces their first performance, its main substance tugs at a simple up–down scale motif rather in the manner of the first piece from that set, its ending brings the same motif into the calm of the third piece, and there are also windows into the worlds of *Histoire du soldat* (a 2/4 march with the leader as soloist) and *Pulcinella* (bright, bouncing, wide-spaced

[handwritten margin note:] just possible but Griffiths ignores much more straight-forward overtone-series derived harmony in The Rite and Les Noces: the source would be discussed – is this the 'Promethean' Skryabin (Griffiths consistently – ironically – underestimates the latter's importance as an influence on Stravinsky's early music)

---

[7]*An Autobiography*, p. 95.   [8]See *SPD*, pp. 225–6.

chords). The 1952 rescoring for violin and cello with wind decet brings out other vistas of the Symphonies, though they are brief – and surprisingly so, given that sketches for the latter work include some for just such a combination.

It is in its hint of *Pulcinella*, but now without the borrowed façade, that the Concertino is most forward-looking, and the arrow continues through Stravinsky's next work, a set of simple piano pieces given the title *Les cinq doigts* because the right-hand parts (and in the first of the eight the left-hand too) are five-finger exercises, often keeping to the same bare compass of a fifth throughout a movement. Since, too, only the last piece includes chords of more than two notes in either hand, the materials are exceedingly reduced. But the simplicity does not seem to be in the interests of child performers (the single concession to the picturesque is the final tango, a dance form perhaps not likely to feature prominently in most children's experience) so much as of the composer, re-making himself after *Pulcinella* rather as he had had to re-make himself after *The Rite of Spring* in the songs and duets of 1914. Except that in this case the return to basics is much more severe and the re-making much more in evidence. In *Les cinq doigts* Stravinsky plays his hand openly, in his patent shuffling of elementary ideas, in his unexplained interruptions, in his rhythmic shifts, and maybe most of all in the disparity he keeps between treble and bass, the harmonic unease. That unease now exists, more than in any original Stravinsky piece since *Petrushka*, against a background of major or minor tonality. There are some direct recollections of *Pulcinella*, notably in the siciliana rhythm of the fourth piece, but now Stravinsky is learning how to write this music himself. The mask is beginning to twitch into life.

10

A Russian opera and an octet

On 14 July 1921 (the date was remembered as an anniversary) Stravinsky began an affair with Vera Sudeikina, eventually his second wife, and from this point his regular companion in Paris and abroad. There was no subterfuge. Stravinsky habitually acted, as Robert Craft has neatly put it,[1] logically rather than psychologically, and logically told his wife that he could not live without Vera. Catherine had always been solicitous only of her husband's well-being, and now she seems simply to have extended her concern to Vera. But, as with so much in Stravinsky's biography and indeed in his music, the action is far more conspicuous than the motive. The published letters from Catherine to her husband suggest a woman pious and unworldly,[2] but more recently Craft has suggested that 'the primary motive of her letters, conscious or otherwise, may have been to punish her husband with feelings of guilt'.[3]

One feels bound to return to the role of dispassionate observer, and to see Stravinsky, during the rest of this summer of 1921, spending his time with Catherine and the children at Anglet, arranging the Three Movements from *Petrushka* for Artur Rubinstein and beginning the one-act comic opera *Mavra*. In the autumn the family moved from Anglet to the villa Les Rochers in Biarritz, and the Ballets Russes production of Tchaikovsky's *Sleeping Beauty* opened at the Alhambra Theatre in London (2 November), with two movements orchestrated by Stravinsky; Sudeikina was the Queen.

Mavra was completed on 9 March 1922 in Biarritz, and put on the stage on 3 June by Dyagilev's company at the Paris Opéra, with Gregor Fitelberg conducting. Bronislava Nijinska, sister of the great dancer, was the director, with designs by Léopold Survage and a cast including Oda Slobodskaya as Parasha. Nijinksa had also choreographed, and danced the Fox in, the first production of *Renard* on 18 May, also at the Paris Opéra under Dyagilev's auspices; this time

[1] *Stravinsky: Glimpses*, p. 13.
[2] *SSC* I, pp. 3–19.   [3] *Stravinsky: Glimpses*, p. x.

Ansermet was the conductor and Mikhail Larionov the designer. Between August and November Stravinsky was in Berlin, awaiting the arrival of his mother from Petrograd. He was back in Paris to conduct *Fireworks* and extracts from *The Firebird* and *The Nightingale* at a concert in Paris on 25 November, his taking the baton still being a rare event.

On 6 April 1923 he at last finished *Les noces* in Monaco (the Ballets Russes were appearing in Monte Carlo), and the work had its first performance by the Dyagilev company at the Théâtre de la Gaiété-Lyrique in Paris on 13 June, once again with Ansermet conducting and Nijinska as choreographer. The designer was Natalya Goncharova; Georges Auric was among the pianists. In between the completion and the première Stravinsky had finished his Octet in Paris (on 20 May). He conducted the first performance at one of Koussevitzky's concerts at the Paris Opéra on 18 October, and the next month made a partial recording, his gramophone début, but unpublished. Other events of the year included a performance of *Histoire du soldat* in Weimar, which Stravinsky attended, and where he met Busoni and Hermann Scherchen. In December he returned to one of his oldest pieces, the Pastorale, to make an arrangement for violin and wind.

The achievement of *Pulcinella* could have been as much an encumbrance to Stravinsky as the non-achievement of *Les noces*, in that the way forward from it was not obvious: one could not just go on rehashing minor eighteenth-century masters. Certainly, apart from finishing off the Symphonies and the Concertino, he wrote unusually little in the year after the Pergolesi piece: just *Les cinq doigts*. And this was an artist who liked to say that he composed 'every day, regularly, like a man with banking hours.'[4] But then the path cleared in these two blocked directions, and from the middle of 1921 Stravinsky was able to move both back to *Les noces* and forward to his first major work since *Pulcinella*, the one-act comic opera *Mavra*. Maybe the affair with Vera Sudeikina was a release, though Stravinsky, always sharply resistant to interpretations of music as autobiography, preferred to regard the new opera as coming out of an affair with Tchaikovsky that started at very much the same time.

There are a lot of subtexts here. Stravinsky's lauding of Tchaikovsky, so unexpected at the time of the *Sleeping Beauty* production that apparently it was not believed,[5] was an identification with a Russian composer who had turned his gaze towards the West, in contrast with

---

[4]*Dialogues*, p. 107.   [5]See *SPD*, p. 231.

the avowed Russianism of Rimsky-Korsakov, Musorgsky, Borodin, Cui and Balakirev. It was a setting aside of his own earlier works, or at least of earlier views of his earlier works, an affirmation that he was now Tchaikovsky–Stravinsky, the clear articulator of musical form, not Musorgsky–Stravinsky, the diviner of the Russian soul (this was a setting aside that, of course, he would actualize musically in his numerous revisions of the 1940s). It was a statement of separation from Russia, which he seems to have regarded, because of his own history, as dominated by Shteynberg and others of the Rimsky school. It was also the claiming of a new parent. What Tchaikovsky had grasped in *The Sleeping Beauty*, according to Stravinsky, was the possibility of an invented past:

> This cultured man, with his knowledge of folksong and of old French music, had no need to engage in archaeological research in order to present the age of Louis XIV; he recreated the character of the period by his musical language, preferring involuntary but living anachronisms to conscious and laboured *pasticcio*: a virtue that appertains only to great creative minds.[6]

There can be little doubt but that Stravinsky included himself in this last category, and though what he was writing was ostensibly a defence of Tchaikovsky to be published in *The Times* on behalf of Dyagilev's *Sleeping Beauty* production (a defence required because here was the company of *The Rite of Spring*, revived in 1920–21 with new choreography by Massine, going back to spun sugar), his words, with a few changes, apply to the work he was engaged on himself, *Mavra*, and to its predecessor, *Pulcinella*. This cultured man (another category in which Stravinsky surely included himself), with his knowledge of folksong and of old Russian and Italian music, had no need to go to scraps of Pergolesi in order to present another age; he could recreate the character of any period by his musical language. This was the essence of his neo-classicism. It was not a 'return to the past'; it certainly had nothing to do with nostalgia. It was, rather, the invention of pasts, the creation, as it were, of imaginary Pergolesis as collaborators, models or screens through which music might issue, probably with some degree of force.

It was, of course, a deeply ironic exercise. Again to risk an autobiographical gloss, Stravinsky, now definitively cut off from the Russia that had fed and validated his music, had to invent a new homeland, and then, for each new work, another and another. First, in *Mavra* (or perhaps better, behind *Mavra*), came a new 'old Russia'. Old Russia is there before the music begins, in the triple dedication 'to the memory of Pushkin, Glinka and Tchaikovsky'. Then all three ghosts are called up again by the piece, which is based on one of Pushkin's verse tales, and which places itself musically – Stravinsky's repeated pronouncements made sure the point would not be missed[7] – in a zigzag line out of bel canto through *Ruslan and Lyudmila*.[8] But the newness is equally unmistakable, in the overlapping at times of two or three irreconcilable harmonic–metrical streams (irreconcilable, that is, in terms of conventional homogeneity), in the evident artifice of ideas built up, as in *Les cinq doigts*, from within a narrow pitch range, in the dislocation of regular metres and harmonic progressions, and in the dislocating effect, too, of the wind-band scoring. This can be comically heavy, notably in the writing for a quartet of horns, or it can be dry and abrupt, so much of the accompaniment being staccato; but in either event there is the suggestion of the 'wrong' colour being used, as in *Pulcinella*, except that in this case the projected string original is not some real past music but a virtuality.

Mavra is a work which makes no secret of its lack of depth, a work whose realism is its own consciousness of itself as a fabrication. For all Stravinsky's appeals, implicit and explicit, to the 'good tradition' of Glinka and Tchaikovsky, his practice is wilfully unsound, in the ways just mentioned. There is no attempt to make something which could be mistaken for a lost piece by either of the forebears claimed, nor to create a smooth continuation from them: on the contrary, the essence is disharmony, the simultaneous presence, as much as in *Pulcinella*, of model and contradiction. Something of how this works, and of the contrapuntal spirit that breaks into Stravinsky's music through the cracks in this divided opus, may be clear from a brief example from the elaborate love-duet near the end of the work (see Ex. 11). This is a stock nineteenth-century Italian opera cadence, but teased by added parts, by extension, by the landing somewhere other than in the expected C, and by the swivel from utterly traditional styles of accompaniment (the juicy cellos) to untoward byplay. Here, no doubt, the intention is mocking. But though that is by no means always the case, divergence is heard right through the opera much more than meeting, divorce more than marriage.

The work's breezy discrepancy is not only musical. The story depends on a trick of disguise: Parasha, a young girl, finds her mother

---

[7]See for example *An Autobiography*, p. 98.   [8]See *SPD*, p. 233.

Ex. 11
Mavra: Duet

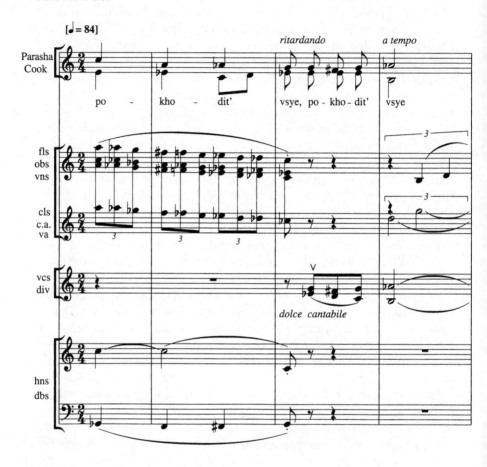

a new cook, who is her hussar lover in drag, but the deception comes to a quick end when mother discovers the cook shaving. However, this surface element of masquerade is rather incidental to the opera, as distinct from the story – and the opera is indeed very distinct from the story. One sign of that is, quite precisely, the treatment of the ending, which comes not with an *opera buffa* wallop but with a trailing away, as if the opera could not maintain interest in the story once the denouement had been set up. The scale and nature of other musical numbers, too, is often out of proportion to their function in the story, as when the Mother and her Neighbour unfold an elaborate duet on the most banal chit-chat, or when all four characters begin a solemn

Ex. 11 cont.

[We'll live in our new dream.]

elegy for the recently departed cook. What matters, then, is not the dressing-up *in* the story so much as the dressing-up *of* the story, the treatment of it in ways that may be manifestly exaggerated, inadequate or misleading. Just as *Pulcinella* proposes a method to be applied to past music, so *Mavra* is an opera kit. Its techniques were indeed applied by later opera composers, including Weill, Shostakovich, Hindemith and, not least, Stravinsky himself; one could even argue that no single Stravinsky work, not even *The Rite*, had a more widespread immediate influence, with its wind-based scoring affecting the musical colour of the decade as much as its unhooking of music and drama was decisive for the future of opera. But as an original it was unrepeatable.

The importance of *Mavra* has probably been (but unbenignly) disguised by the infrequent performance inevitable in the case of a piece that demands large orchestral resources and a stage production (this is definitely not an 'opera–oratorio') yet lasts under half an hour. Its musical importance is that of the neo-classical prototype, inventing a new way in which the bifurcation that had been characteristic of Stravinsky since *Petrushka* could operate. Previously the bifurcations had come from dialogues with something outside himself, whether Russian folksong or light music or Pergolesi, but now the dialogue is internal, so that it becomes impossible to give credence to one of the rivalling intentions more than to another. One can accept that *Mavra* is, on one level, what Stravinsky said it was: a little comedy in Italian–Russian style. One can also easily see that it is more than that, a parody of that. But the greater challenge it provokes is to hold it in view as both at once, as with those optical illusions where a cube is seen either recessed or advancing from the page.

One common response has been to see the doubleness as duplicity – as frivolousness or the striking of poses. But the seriousness of *Mavra* is in creating a world in which pose and authenticity are irrevocably intertwined and undistinguishable. Even where they seem to be peeling apart, as in Ex. 11, the work demands the simultaneous presence of both, and throughout most of its length it twins them much more tightly than here. There is no stable ground (the absence of a definitive bass in the harmony may be significant here); this is not a work one can trust. Nor are these characters one can trust. Once again, they have taken into themselves conflicts that Stravinsky earlier expressed through double casts of singers and dancers (in *Renard* and *Les noces*), or of narrator and actors (in *Histoire du soldat*). Some gap between the what and the how of expression is of course common in opera, is maybe what makes comic opera worth having, but the form it takes in *Mavra* is new. Insincerity in *Don Giovanni* is the insincerity of Don Giovanni, of Don Ottavio, of Donna Anna (however different, illuminatingly different, those insincerities may be). Insincerity in *Mavra* is the insincerity of Stravinsky.

To call this 'insincerity', though, is to appeal to a musical morality that Stravinsky and Schoenberg both at this point recognized as defunct. After atonality, which Stravinsky had at least confronted in his attendance at that Berlin performance of *Pierrot lunaire*, there were no more guarantors. Schoenberg's reaction was painstakingly to make the resulting desert, the fully chromatic desert, become its own justification through an implied generation from some ordering of the chromatic scale; and at the time of *Mavra* he was just producing his first twelve-note serial pieces. Stravinsky's response was to erect imaginary palaces in the desert, but without pretending that they were anything else but that. His 'insincerity', then, is the sign of a deeper sincerity, and his diametric opposition to Schoenberg (whose music he rarely encountered during the four decades between *Pierrot* and Schoenberg's death)[9] the sign of a deeper confluence.

One important mark of the failure of the old sincerity is the increased objectivity of Stravinsky's music from this point: the clean lines, the precision of sound, the lack of rubato – things that had always been characteristic of Stravinsky but were now intensified, coming perhaps from inside the musical conception rather than being applied to something potentially more amorphous. His essay on his next piece, the Octet for wind, begins boldly with the full-paragraph statement: 'My Octuor is a musical object'.[10] And during the next few hundred words it advances the tenets that would be developed in *An Autobiography* and the *Poetics of Music*, including the central axiom that this 'is not an "emotive" work but a musical composition based on objective elements which are sufficient in themselves'. The direct correspondence now with Schoenberg, rather than mirroring anti-nomy, is remarkable, in the search for 'objective elements' – elements which, one may understand, could provide the fixity and support no longer to be expected from the simple rules of major-minor harmony – and in the avoidance of string instruments in favour of winds (Stravinsky based *Mavra*, the Octet and the following Piano Concerto all on wind formations; Schoenberg's Wind Quintet comes from the same period) or pianos and percussion (Stravinsky's final scoring of *Les noces* was done alongside *Mavra* and the Octet; Schoenberg at the same time was writing his Five Piano Pieces and Piano Suite).

The Octet has many of the features of the instrumental writing of *Mavra*: the relative scarcity of expressive and even dynamic markings, the light, clear-cut planes of sound – indeed the objectivity. In the formal domain that objectivity provides the necessary disjointing. For the first time since his student symphony Stravinsky was writing against background of traditional form, but it was now very much against, in contrast to, that background, and not within it. The three movements are, in some respects, a sonata allegro with slow introduction, a set of variations and a rondo (with ragtime tendencies, as there are occasionally too in *Mavra*), but traditionally these were forms created by subjects, not by Stravinsky's exactly delineated, self-contained objects, which seem rather like bright kites carried on the winds of orthodox musical movement and shaping.

---

[9]See *Dialogues*, p. 106.   [10]In White, pp. 574–7.

The stories of the Octet's genesis are as varied as its contents. According to Stravinsky's *Autobiography* he 'began to write this music without knowing what its sound medium would be . . . I only decided that point after finishing the first part'.[11] Later he gave a vivid description of having encountered the ensemble in a dream, then starting the composition the next day[12] (this was not his first musical dream: a motif for *Histoire du soldat* had come from the same source).[13] There is also apparently evidence of Octet sketches being entangled with others that would be used in the Symphonies.[14] But perhaps these stories should be considered as forming an acerbic counterpoint like that of the music they concern: there was the intention to create a pure structure in sound; there was the aesthetic preference, the experience and even some unused bits of material all pointing towards a combination of wind instruments. A dream could have clinched the matter.

One further deciding factor might well have been the wish to avoid anybody else's 'interpretation' – another central item in Stravinsky's credo to which the essay on the Octet devotes half its space. Of the three conductors outside Russia who had so far been most closely associated with him, Monteux was in Boston, Ansermet seems to have had some doubts about *Mavra*,[15] and Koussevitzky had been blamed for the failure of the Symphonies of Wind Instruments to make much impression at its first performance.[16] But as yet Stravinsky himself had little practice in conducting; a small ensemble, therefore, might give him a suitable launching pad as composer–performer – and quite apart from his artistic objections, he now needed, with no income from Russia, performing fees to supplement the subsidies he had been receiving during the last few years from the Princesse de Polignac, Werner Reinhart, Eugenia Errazuriz and Coco Chanel. The Octet was just the beginning. Henceforth, until Movements thirty-six years later, Stravinsky would be responsible for nearly all his first performances, whether as conductor or as pianist.

[11]*An Autobiography*, p. 103.
[12]See *Dialogues*, p. 39.
[13]See *Conversations*, p. 7.
[14]See *SPD*, p. 225.
[15]Ibid., p. 232.
[16]Ibid., p. 222.

11

Piano and pianola

In the early months of 1924 Stravinsky's career as a conductor began to take off. There was a concert in Brussels on 14 January, when his programme comprised the Octet, *Pribautki*, *Mavra* and the *Firebird* suite. He then spent most of March in Spain, where he was to return regularly, this time conducting concerts in Barcelona and Madrid that included many of his smaller works and suites from *The Faun* to *Pulcinella*. From Spain he went to be with his family in Biarritz, where he completed the Piano Concerto, apparently intended for himself,[1] on 21 April; the work had its first performance a month and a day later, at the Paris Opéra, with Koussevitzky conducting. In July he made a trip to Copenhagen with Vera, and then returned to Biarritz, where on 21 August he completed the first movement of another work for himself as pianist, the Sonata. The two later movements were completed in October, by which time the family had moved from Biarritz to the Villa des Roses, 167 boulevard Carnot, Nice.

At the end of October he left on a concert tour that included performances of the Concerto in Amsterdam under Mengelberg (23 November) and in Leipzig under Furtwängler (4 December), as well as appearances in Winterthur, Warsaw, Prague and Berlin. After only a couple of weeks back in France, he left on 27 December by ship for New York and his first American tour. This lasted until the middle of March 1925, when he made his first, again unpublished recording as a pianist in New York, playing six pieces from *Les cinq doigts*. He then continued into a new piano work for himself, the third in succession: the Serenade in A, of which the last movement, the first to be composed, was completed on 9 May. On 17 June he was at the Paris opening of a new Ballets Russes production of *Chant du rossignol*, choreographed by Balanchine, and on 16 July the Sonata had its first performance, given not by him but by Felix Petyrek in Donaueschingen.[2] The following month he finished the first move-

---

[1] Whether this was so from the start is uncertain, but some time before the end of November 1923 he had been trying to arrange American performances with himself as soloist: see *SSC I*, p. 432.
[2] I am grateful to Stephen Walsh for this information.

ment of the Serenade, and then a suite after *Pulcinella* for the violinist Paul Kochanski.

On 8 September 1925 he played the Sonata at the festival of the International Society for Contemporary Music in Venice. During this trip he bought a life of St Francis in Genoa, and was struck by the idea of a special language (French for the saint) being reserved for prayer.[3] He completed the Serenade, with its second movement, on 9 October, and two days later wrote to Cocteau proposing 'an opera in Latin on the subject of a tragedy of the ancient world.'[4] On 25 November, in Frankfurt, he gave the first performance of the Serenade and also, with Alma Moodie, that of the Suite after *Pulcinella* for violin and piano. This was during a tour that also included concerts in Basle, Berlin and Copenhagen. Then on the last day of the year he finished orchestrating the Suite no. 1 from wartime duets, its companion piece having been completed in 1921.

The piano was central to Stravinsky's composing. Though briefly ousted by the cimbalom during the war (that interruption was an affair, like the affairs with Pergolesi and ragtime), the piano had featured in many of his larger scores since *The Firebird*, and prominently of course in *Petrushka* and 'Excentrique'. It had recently, quadrupled, provided a long-awaited destination for *Les noces*, and there had been a good deal of music featuring it alone: the wartime duets, and ambitious solo pieces from the early sonata to the *Petrushka* concert transcriptions. There were also piano versions of nearly all the orchestral and chamber works – not only the ballets, of which keyboard reductions were required for rehearsal purposes, but also the quartet pieces, *Rag-time* and even the concluding chorale from the Symphonies of Wind Instruments. These one could regard as returning the music to its original medium, given that Stravinsky always composed at the piano, and that keyboard sounds and gestures are so often discernible in his music, alongside, and without paradox, his characteristically precise adjustment of material to medium (an example is the Octet, of whose instrumental acuity he much later expressed approval even while noting his reference point in the last movement was Bach's two-part inventions).[5] And yet, until the mid-1920s, his private pianism was not publicly expressed. Ony at the Swiss recitals of 1919, it appears, had he played before an audience (and then, presumably, it was in the easy parts of the duets). Perhaps

[3]See *An Autobiography*, p. 125.
[4]*SSC* I, p. 94.   [5]See *Dialogues*, pp. 39–40.

Les cinq doigts was intended as not only a creative rediscovery but also a stepping stone towards a concert repertory for himself, a repertory that he began in earnest with the Concerto for piano and wind (1923–4), and continued with his next two works, the Sonata and the Serenade. These, together with his second concerto, the Capriccio of 1928–9, he played in numerous European and American cities during the 1920s. But he seems to have been a solo performer only out of necessity. In the 1930s he preferred to appear in partnerships, with the violinist Samuel Dushkin and with his pianist son Soulima. Then in America his performing career turned wholly in the direction of conducting.

This little history bears out the evidence of his recordings,[6] and indeed of the music he wrote for himself, that he was not a born virtuoso, in contrast with such contemporaries as Bartók, Prokofiev and Rakhmaninov. Illusion had to be at work: the illusion of music that appears flamboyant without being excessively difficult (it becomes hard to say how much the preference for lean two-part counterpoint and staccato, even rhythm is conditioned by practical rather than aesthetic considerations as Stravinsky's music passes, perhaps with permanent consequences, through the filter of his pianism in this exclusively keyboard-directed period of 1923–5); the illusion of another Stravinsky as a lifetime pianist–composer, out of whose repertory a chunk suddenly inserts itself into the real Stravinsky's output (and just a single chunk, for his only significant later piece for or with piano solo was Movements, belonging to quite a different world); the illusion of debts to traditional form, texture and harmony which the music does not honour, but dishonours with genius.

The Concerto and the Sonata are both, like the Octet, in three movements, and both in a traditional pattern of fast–slow–fast. There are even inducements, again as in the Octet, to hear the formal process within each movement as traditional – to hear the first movements, for example, as sonata allegros, with a slow introduction in the case of the Concerto, where it returns, not so traditionally, as slow coda. But the essential harmonic motivation of sonata form is missing, for Stravinsky avoids the root-position triads necessary to give tonal harmony a grounding. There may be the signposts – of thematic recollection, or of development-like complexity and chromaticism – but they are signposts in the air.

This makes it difficult to keep track of quite where one is: the form is not an enveloping entity, a logical unfolding. Stravinsky's own failures

---

[6]The most accessible are 1930s accounts of the Serenade, *Piano-Rag-Music* and Concerto for two pianos, with a 1945 *Duo concertant*, on Sony SM2K 46297.

of memory in performing the Concerto, therefore, seem of more than anecdotal interest, and certainly as more than further proof of his lack of expertise. At the first performance, just before beginning the slow movement, 'I suddenly realized that I had entirely forgotten how it started.'[7] 'Another time . . . I suffered a lapse of memory because I was suddenly obsessed by the idea that the audience was a collection of dolls in a huge panopticon. Still another time, my memory froze because I suddenly noticed the reflection of my fingers in the glossy wood at the edge of the keyboard.'[8] These are marvellous accidents. The composer, playing music that is mask-like and mechanical, sees himself being heard, or rather unheard, by a public with the same qualities. And then music which has sprung from the play of fingers on keys is interrupted by a sideways confirmation that that is what it is. Beneath the mask there is nothing (we are well along the line from *Les cinq doigts*, of masks that have snapped into life, absorbed all life): beyond the machinery, the hardware, there is nothing.

The principal features on the mask, of course, are those of Bach; once again the Octet provided the example, and it is astonishing how quickly, after the operatic cavortings of *Mavra*, Stravinsky fastened on Bach, even while maintaining the wind scoring (and, more incidentally, the ragtime echoes) of that score. Of course, what he fastened on was not the historical cantor of Leipzig, and certainly not the Bach of present-day performance practice, but the Bach of the 1920s, the Bach, perhaps quite particularly, of Wanda Landowska, who was living in Paris at this time. It is the resolve, the unyielding tempo and the level dynamics of 1920s Bach performance – and, of course, on a less practical plane the contemporary view of Bach's abstractness – to which Stravinsky makes his appeal, and the contrapuntal mastery of the two-part inventions that is his model as much in the Sonata as in the finale of the Octet. If he did not now choose to recognize this (in *An Autobiography* he barely mentions Bach, and certainly not in connection with the Concerto or the Sonata, preferring to see the latter as descendant from Beethoven), that may be because it is hard to see one's own mask, or because the connection was too banal to be interesting, or because the clarion call of 'back to Bach' had already become a cliché (Hindemith, so much more prolific, had grasped the implications of *Pulcinella* and *Mavra* even before Stravinsky).

But Schoenberg could see what was happening. In his chorus 'Vielseitigkeit' – written in November–December 1925, by which time the Octet, Concerto and Sonata were all in print, even if, as Stravinsky

---

[7] *An Autobiography*, p. 114.   [8] *Expositions*, p. 47.

states,[9] Schoenberg had missed hearing him play his last work in Venice in September – he made clear reference to his contemporary:

> So who's that coming along?
> Why, it's little Modernsky!
> Just had his hair cut in a bob;
> Looks quite good!
> Like real false hair!
> Like a wig!
> Quite (according to how little Modernsky sees himself),
> Quite the Papa Bach![10]

Desperately unfunny though this may be, it at least shows a recognition (if hardly a comprehension) of Stravinsky's enterprise. It is also interesting as a document of the rift between the two leading composers of their generation, a rift that had far more than professional rivalry to explain it, and that continued through Schoenberg's weary criticism of *Oedipus rex*,[11] through the years of mutual silence in Los Angeles – a rift so fundamental that one has to speak of two contradictory histories of music from this point onwards, with only rare, spindly bridges between them in, for example, Weill and Hindemith.

Indeed, it is the fraying of history that Stravinsky's music of this period is most deeply about. There is the faltering of the continuously progressive line from Bach through Mozart, Beethoven and the rest, after the disintegration of the old harmonic system which had supported that progression: time was now going forward without music's onward development being inseparably fixed to it, so that the threads of music could twist back immediately to touch on Bach, or anything else. There is the faltering of progress, too, within the substance of each piece. And it was not only during performance that even the composer could lose track, for there is another pregnant story, relating to the period of composition: 'Some pages of the manuscript disappeared mysteriously one day, and when I tried to rewrite them I found I could remember almost nothing of what I had written. I do not know to what extent the published movement differs from the lost one, but I am sure the two are very unlike.'[12]

With the possibility, perhaps at at any point, of going forward in radically different directions (the latent possibility which the composer at least may recall when he is seated at the keyboard), the music has an improvisatory lightness, despite the severe fixity of speed, so that it feels

[9]See *Dialogues*, p. 106.
[11]See *Style and Idea* (London, 1975), pp. 482–3.
[10]Three Satires op. 27: no. 2.
[12]*Expositions*, p. 46.

rather like running on the spot. At the furthest extreme, though this is not so very far from the case in the Octet or the Concerto, each movement of the Sonata and the Serenade proceeds to its end without a change of tempo, and there are also very few dynamic indications, most of those being the basic *p* or *f* (the last movement of the Serenade reaches the perfection of complete absence of dynamic marks). This was an item of policy;[13] it also made the music not only sound but look like Bach (or perhaps one should again be more cautious and suggest that it made the music look like Bach editions of the 1920s). But despite its look, despite its sound, the music's airiness is being played, as in the Octet, not through the image of Bach but against it. It is not, as Schoenberg supposed, that Stravinsky is pretending to be Bach and failing; the failing is the point.

The unrooted feel of the music, its gliding through conventional forms rather than propelling them, its freedom – these are all most easily seen and heard in the Serenade, partly because its movements are shorter (the story goes that Stravinsky, writing the work soon after making his first gramophone recordings, planned the movements so that each could fit on to one side of a ten-inch 78 r.p.m. disc),[14] partly because the music is more relaxed, and partly because, even so, there seems to have been some didactic intention to show that 'in A' need not mean what it meant in κ.488. Properly one should recognize that fact by always using the full title: this is not a Serenade that happens to be in A; this is a Serenade in A, as afterwards there would be a Symphony in C.

The four movements are not only studies in different kinds of keyboard texture and velocity but also four different ways of being in A, as they show emblematically in their four different final cadences (perhaps the title of the last, 'Cadenza finala', is to be understood as this, as final cadence, and not final cadenza; it is not very cadenza-like), none of them anything like perfect. What is distinctive too, and accordant with the music that prepares the cadence, is the way the ending comes not so much with a step as with a dissolve, leaving the titular keynote in open octaves: alive to the resonance possibilities of the instrument, Stravinsky in three cases uses Schoenberg's technique of depressing keys silently so that the corresponding strings can vibrate in sympathy. The A – and it is the note A that is at issue, not the tonality of A major or A minor – is not a goal but a line which has always been there, and around which the music has been playing its

[13]See his note on the Octet in White, p. 575.
[14]See White, p. 323.

improvisatory gambits, with a teasing avoidance, precisely, of commit-
ment to A as a goal, as a key.

A few bars can provide an example:

Ex. 12
Serenade in A: I Hymne

This is from the first movement, 'Hymne', which is a succession of
flights and allusions coming from a bell-fanfare of five chords at the
start. Its pattern is everywhere in the background here, but so too is the
image of Bach (in the first two bars, before it slips aside to reveal the
image of boogie-woogie) and the ideal of A major. This is the expected
destination of the first bar, but instead Stravinsky supplies a rest, and
then a shift up for a restart. Once again there is the promise of A major,
for the sixth quaver of this second bar, but when the chord arrives it has
sagged a semitone. Perhaps an even truer title for the piece would be
'Serenade not in A'.

However unmistakable the Bachian references of the counterpoint in
this passage, the rigidity and weight of the keyboard style are enough to
suggest that what we are hearing through Stravinsky is not Bach
absolutely but the Bach of a particular period. Stravinsky preserves
ways of playing and hearing Bach, rather as other ways are preserved,
and sometimes quite as self-consciously, in Brahms or in Mozart; of
course this becomes, and will become, ever clearer with increasing
distance in time. Simultaneously, the advance of time brings the arrival
of new works which touch back to Stravinsky as much as he touched

back to Bach – or perhaps which touch back to Stravinsky as played and heard in the time of their composition. For example, the Serenade's playfulness with tonality now seems to have much less to do with Bach than with the Ligeti of the Etudes for piano. And this is perhaps the ultimate lesson of neo-classicism, not that there are irrefragable canons of art holding through the generations, but rather the resemblances between works of different periods will constantly change as those works move through time, like planets, towards new conjunctions.

One other encounter inscribed into these piano works of 1923–5, as with so many of their predecessors, is with the pianola. The Pleyel company had provided the composer with a Paris base since 1921 so that he could work on pianola transcriptions of his works, and during the next few years he produced versions of a great many, from *The Firebird* (a luxury edition, with what may be the composer's own account of music and action printed on the roll so that it can be read by the pianolist, rather in the words-alongside-music manner of Satie's *Sports et divertissements*) up to the first movement of the Sonata. He also made some rolls for the American Duo-Art company, and on his first arrival in New York, in 1925, gave an interview in which he said his aim was: 'Not a "photograph of my playing" . . . but rather a "lithograph", a full and permanent record of tone combinations that are beyond my ten poor fingers to perform.'[15] Quite apart from any futurist glamour of the machine, which anyway seems to have faded in Stravinsky's mind since the Etude for pianola and the pianola-toned project for *Les noces*, the instrument would provide the composer with a direct route to his public; it would also present the music with that supposedly Bachian objectivity. Perhaps the appeal to Bach was, after all, an appeal to a composer who had, as it seemed, prefigured the pianola. Perhaps the regular, dry staccato of the Sonata and the Concerto should be heard as more pianolistic than Bachian, as if this music's real place were the pianola, and the piano only a makeshift.

[15] *SPD*, p. 165.

12

A Latin opera

Stravinsky began work on *Oedipus rex* on 2 January 1926, though also this month he was engaged on a new round of revisions of *The Rite of Spring*. In February he worked on the opera–oratorio with Cocteau in Villefranche, before leaving for Amsterdam, where for the first time he conducted *The Rite* on the 28th, beginning a concert tour that lasted over a month and took in Brussels, Budapest, Vienna and Zagreb as well as the Netherlands. In March, en route from Zagreb to Nice, he took his first flight, from Trieste to Venice, and then joined a pilgrimage to Padua. A spiritual epiphany at the shrine of St Anthony was followed by a setting of the Lord's Prayer in Slavonic.

Oedipus was resumed in Nice in April, then set aside for a long summer break, during which Stravinsky conducted *Petrushka* and *The Nightingale* at La Scala, Milan, in May, and returned to Milan the next month for concerts including the Piano Concerto. In August he went back to *Oedipus* in Nice, and now worked at the piece with comparatively little interruption. He did, though, go to London to conduct a new Ballets Russes production of *The Firebird* on 25 November, with designs by Goncharova and with Lifar and Balanchine in the cast. He finished the sketch score of *Oedipus* in Nice on 14 March 1927, then worked on the orchestration before leaving for Paris on 3 May. On 30 May the work had its first performance, in concert form, under Ballets Russes auspices at the Théâtre Sarah-Bernhardt in Paris, Stravinsky conducting. The cast included Stephan Balina-Skupievsky as Oedipus, Hélène Sadoven as Jocasta and Pierre Brasseur as the Speaker.

There was another sense in which the piano–pianola period of 1923–5 was an insertion: it interrupted Stravinsky's work for the theatre. From 1908, when *The Nightingale* was begun, to 1923, when *Les noces* was at last finished, there had always been at least one theatrical work in progress. Then nothing. One reason may have been a dissolving of his ties with Dyagilev, who seems to have become more interested in nineteenth-century French opera and in commissioning ballets from the younger French composers, such as Poulenc, Auric, Milhaud and Sauguet. The four-year gap in the published correspondence, from 1922 to 1926, may be a mark of that, as may the way in which the correspondence was resumed, with a letter from Stravinsky, dated 6 April 1926, telling Dyagilev that he intends to take communion for the first time in twenty years, and asking therefore for forgiveness.[1] But by this time, of course, *Oedipus rex* was already under way, though Dyagilev was kept in the dark about it until a late stage, in order to surprise him with a gift to mark the twentieth anniversary of his theatrical enterprises.

If in the event Dyagilev found it 'un cadeau très macabre',[2] he may have had good reason. Oedipus by the 1920s had ceased to be a myth and become a complex: if Dyagilev was Stravinsky's substitute father, the choice of subject was not very happy. However, Stravinsky's treatment of the subject is in the least possible degree psychological, the result at once of the musical–dramatic manner, the preferred style of stage presentation (alone among Stravinsky's scores, this one comes with a detailed production note, including a sketch by the composer's son Theodore) and not least the choice of language for the libretto, which, it is clear from the correspondence with Cocteau,[3] came before the choice of subject. Latin would be for the new work what Russian had been for *Mavra*: a bar to the acceptance of the characters as natural people who just happen to sing. They would be essentially different; they would be estranged; they would be in their own self-enclosed world, operating according to its own rules.

Perhaps too, even though Cocteau's libretto was translated into classical and not church Latin by Jean Daniélou, and even though Stravinsky's use of 'k' is an insistence on schoolroom rather than ecclesiastical pronunciation, there is an aura about the piece not only of an alien language but of a sacred one. It is, after all, in church, and in church music, that Latin is usually encountered in the twentieth century. There is also the derivation of the idea from St Francis, according to one of the most vivid and familiar Stravinsky anecdotes, and the coincidence of this work with the composer's return to formal Christianity. Again, there is the flavour of the Bach Passion about the rehearsal of a myth through a succession of arias and choruses presented by a narrator – though there are certainly no chorales in which the audience ideally could join: on the contrary, the speaking narrator in evening dress, like a museum guide giving his spiel (and occasionally getting things wrong), emphatically underlines the

[1]See *SSC II*, p. 40.   [2]*Dialogues*, pp. 24–5.   [3]See *SSC I*, p. 94.

distance between the audience and the objects on view. And finally there are the sporadic Christian resonances in the piece, such as the description of the Shepherd as 'omniskius' (omniscient), or, in one of the few phrases not traceable to the original Sophocles, Oedipus's offering of himself alone, without Creon's aid, to set the world to rights.

However, *Oedipus rex* is no more a Christianization of the story than it is a psychological interpretation in the way of Hofmannsthal (or of the later Cocteau of *La machine infernale*). Indeed, it is quite decisively non-Christian in allowing no dialogue whatsoever between man and heaven, in presenting characters whose fates unwind like clockwork. Or seen in another way, it makes no statement about the nature of human beings, because its characters are not easily read stand-ins for real people. Not only do they discourse in Latin, but they behave like 'living statues', as the score's preface has it, with only their masked heads and arms visible as the singers stand behind cut-out representations of their characters. This is not an opera in which we encounter Oedipus and Jocasta, but rather one in which monuments of Oedipus and Jocasta are caused to sing.

The petrification has gone so far that the interventions of the Speaker are not really necessary to draw attention to it, and Stravinsky himself later professed his weariness with the device, while acknowledging that the whole piece is structured and paced by it.[4] Even at the time he kicked against it, by presenting vital events that the Speaker fails to prepare or even remark upon (notably the arrival of the Shepherd), and conversely by contradicting what the Speaker has just said ('And now you will hear the celebrated monologue "Jocasta's divine head lies dead"' declares the Speaker, and what in fact we hear from Stravinsky's Messenger is, as he was to put it, 'only a four-word singing telegram').[5] The tension between Cocteau and Stravinsky, between showing-off and showing, is petrified into the piece as much as the myth.

Another, deeper tension is that between Sophocles and Stravinsky, revealed straight away in what Stravinsky chose to leave out. These omitted passages are registered in italic in the following synopsis:

SPEAKER: Introduction to the piece, and to the ensuing number.
CHORUS AND OEDIPUS: The chorus (*in the Sophocles a priest*) implores Oedipus to save the city from plague. He says he will do so, and that he has sent Creon to ask the oracle what he must do. The chorus welcomes Creon.
SPEAKER: Introduction to the following events.

[4]See *Dialogues*, pp. 29–30.   [5]Ibid., p. 30.

CREON: In an aria (*not in dialogue with Oedipus*) he relates the oracle's pronouncement, that the murderer of the old king Laius is hiding in the city and must be found and expelled.

OEDIPUS AND CHORUS: Oedipus, with more choral encouragement, says he will find the criminal, he alone.

SPEAKER: Oedipus will question Tiresias; Tiresias will avoid replying. Oedipus will accuse him of wanting to help Creon to the throne; then he will speak, and say that the king's murderer is himself a king.

CHORUS: The gods are called to the city's assistance. (*Oedipus asks for information; none is forthcoming, only the rumour that Laius was killed on the road. Oedipus then curses the criminal, and anyone who has helped or shielded him.*) The chorus (*not Oedipus*) hails Tiresias and asks him to speak.

TIRESIAS: It is impossible, it is not right to speak. But Oedipus accuses him of being the murderer, and he then duly issues the Speaker's formula (*though in the Sophocles his words are direct*).

OEDIPUS: Envy, he says, has made Tiresias and Creon plot against him. (*Tiresias, to Oedipus's fury, prophesies his doom. He goes, and the chorus contemplates his words. Creon enters, indignant at the accusation made against him. He and Oedipus dispute the matter*).

CHORUS: Jocasta is welcomed. This ends the first act. The chorus is repeated to start the second.

SPEAKER: Introduction to the following events.

JOCASTA: In an elaborate aria she chides the princes with causing disturbance in a stricken city (*there are no interventions from them and the chorus*) and says that oracles cannot be trusted: Laius was told that he would be killed by his son, whereas he was killed by thieves at a crossroads and their son was put out on the mountainside to die. The chorus repeats the fatal word 'crossroads' (*not in Sophocles*).

JOCASTA AND OEDIPUS: He joins her to voice his fear: he killed an old man at a crossroads. (*He goes on to tell of the other oracular prophecy, that he will kill his father and marry his mother, which is why he cannot return to Corinth.*) He asks to speak to the Shepherd who witnessed the old king's murder; Jocasta says he must not; he insists (*this dispute is jumped back from a later point*). (*The chorus calls for the gods to be honoured. Jocasta, saying that Oedipus is unwell, prays to Apollo.*)

SPEAKER: A messenger will announce the death of Polybus of Corinth, and say that Oedipus was only his adoptive son. Jocasta will understand, try to hold Oedipus back, and go, making Oedipus think she is ashamed to be the wife of a parvenu. Then will come his fall.

CHORUS AND MESSENGER: The chorus hails the arrival of the Shepherd and the Messenger. The latter says that Polybus is dead, and that he, the Messenger, found the boy Oedipus in the mountains and took him to Polybus from the Shepherd. (*Jocasta tries to draw Oedipus back; failing, she goes. The chorus asks why. Oedipus says she must be ashamed. But he will know the truth: this is the great declaration that comes earlier in the Stravinsky, at the end of the Jocasta–Oedipus duet.*)

CHORUS: Oedipus must surely be the son of a god.

SHEPHERD: It would, he says, have been better to keep silent about Oedipus's origins. (*in the Sophocles he is being drawn out by Oedipus*).

OEDIPUS: He notes Jocasta's exit, as he thinks ashamed, and looks forward to hearing of his ancestry (*the reference to Jocasta came earlier, and the expectation not at all*).

SHEPHERD, MESSENGER AND CHORUS: Together they state and amplify the waiting message: Oedipus is the son of Laius and Jocasta (*in the Sophocles this comes out in dialogue between the Shepherd and Oedipus*).

OEDIPUS: Now he sees it all: the wrong of his birth, his marriage and his killing. This is the one point where the Stravinsky and the Sophocles coincide almost word for word.

SPEAKER: He announces the Messenger's 'celebrated monologue' telling how Jocasta has hanged herself and Oedipus blinded himself with her gold clasp. Then the epilogue. Oedipus is compelled to display himself. He will be made, but with care and love, to leave.

(*The chorus ponders on what has happened.*)

MESSENGER AND CHORUS: They sing of the death of Jocasta and the blinding of Oedipus (*they, and not the attendant whose monologue this is.*)

CHORUS: As the music of the opening momentously swings back, they hail Oedipus and bid him farewell. (*And here is the largest omission: a full two hundred lines in which Oedipus reappears in lament and self-loathing.*)

As may appear from this, the collapsing of the Sophocles accelerates as the piece unfolds, as if it were rushing towards its destination. That apart, the main changes are to bunch together Jocasta's appearances –

the only woman in this male-voice world – and, most significantly, to eradicate dialogue almost entirely. This is done partly by a fierce abbreviation of Creon's part. The telescoping of the catharsis swallows up his lines there, and his altercation with Oedipus also goes, though there are references to it in the spoken narration and in Jocasta's aria (another, even more crucial loss from the sung drama is that of the oracle binding Oedipus to kill his father and marry his mother: if such an essential element can be left out, we are perhaps hearing broken fragments from an ancient text, glued together, not quite adequately, by the Speaker). The other way in which Stravinsky avoids dialogue is more pervasive. The myth of Oedipus is a story of converging stories, and in the play those stories are elicited through dialogue – principally through dialogue with Oedipus, questioning in turn Creon, Tiresias, the Messenger and the Shepherd. But in the opera –oratorio (Stravinsky's term for a work which carries an oratorio style of objective narration into the theatre) all four speak in pronouncements, and their unwillingness to speak is expressed not by the need for Oedipus to drag the truth out of them, but instead, again, by pronouncement. Only in Tiresias's aria is there any vestige of dialogue (the sole vestige in the whole work), and this is just one short interjection from Oedipus necessary to tilt the seer from silence into speaking. The duet for Jocasta and Oedipus is a duet for two people who happen to be singing at the same time, but not to each other. Or rather, what they listen to in each other is the musical line and not the text.

There is, throughout the work, the sense of people delivering prepared statements rather than singing of, for and from themselves. No doubt that has to be the way living statues behave, and it is conveyed by the choice of language (classical Latin was nobody's natural means of expression by 1926–7, of course, and it was the wrong language too for the characters of the Sophocles), but still more by the way language is musically straitjacketed. Stravinsky is as free here in his changes of accentuation as he is in the Russian works, even shifting the stress in the way Jocasta pronounces the protagonist's name. That may suggest we are hearing something cramped by the exigencies of translation: for instance, the chorus's awkward 'Gloria' as they hail Jocasta (dotted minim, quaver, quaver) could easily be a refitting of music composed to the Russian equivalent 'Slava' (dotted minim, crotchet). But much more generally the lumpy word-setting implies that the lines are compelled by musical rather than verbal considerations, that the words are being shuffled and jostled along by music with its own purposes and processes.

The sway of the music over the voices is what makes it inevitable that Jocasta and Oedipus in their duet should be heeding it rather than each other:

Ex. 13
Oedipus rex: duet

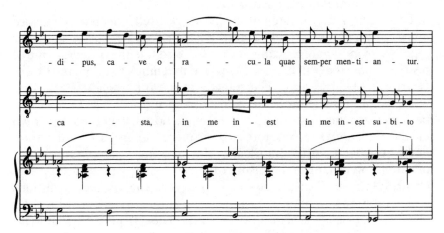

[Jocasta: Be wary of oracles, Oedipus: they always lie
Oedipus: Suddenly, Jocasta, I am filled with fear]

Like monsters of vocal egotism, they remain on separate rhythmic–harmonic tracks (it is of course the unrootedness of Stravinsky's tonality that makes this possible), taking their own cues from the orchestra, as in their separate, disjunct imitations of the woodwind line. Oedipus's fear does not touch Jocasta, nor does her assurance touch him. Indeed, they are not really touched by these feelings themselves: Jocasta is wound up by the orchestra: Oedipus is a counterweight somewhere else in the clockwork. And when Jocasta imitates Oedipus's line, it is not verbal communication but vocal rivalry, a parody of nineteenth-century Italian operatic style.

The tumbling of parodies into this music parallels, without in any way expressing, the tumbling of stories into the story. The Bach connection has been mentioned; equally obvious is the brush with Verdi, most especially in Jocasta's aria form of cantabile followed by cabaletta, and the atmosphere of Gluck in the sequence of declamations and choral tableaux. Of course, Stravinsky's own past is also part of the parade. This was his first full-orchestral score since the war, and its dynamic tuttis occasionally echo *The Rite of Spring*, which he had been revising during the early stages of the composition. However, what is chiefly remarkable is not its similarity to earlier orchestral scores but rather its difference, especially when one considers that the instrumental formation is very close to that of *Petrushka*: it is rather *Mavra*, with its breezy wind homophony and its ostinatos, that is evoked. Then, in the central role, there is the proudly virtuoso but unsubstantiated sound of the Stravinsky tenor carried over through *Mavra* from *Renard*.

This is the voice of fate within the work itself, this barely masked intervention of the past, of so many pasts. It was, Stravinsky said, 'put together from whatever came to hand',[6] and it is the heartless rule of history that is the trap here, the 'infernal machine', to quote the title of Cocteau's Oedipus play. The tragedy inside the tragedy is that of a work being blown through by gusts from musical history, and the peripeteia is when it suddenly, in the final chorus, brings back its own past. But if *Oedipus rex* is, too, a comic piece – openly so, for instance, in the nonchalant horn remark after the Messenger has announced the death of Polybus, or in the rushes of musical energy that sweep voices absurdly along, or in the disparities between the Speaker's captions and what in fact happens, or in the vocal competitiveness of Ex. 13 – that is because it is also able to stand aside from all its models. Obedience is carried to the point of caricature; Stravinsky makes public oblations to the past but privately goes his own way – without, it would seem, very much feeling of Oedipal guilt.

[6]Ibid., p. 27.

13

The muses' summer

In June 1927, the month after the first performance of *Oedipus rex*, Stravinsky visited London to play his Piano Concerto for the BBC. He then turned to a new ballet, *Apollon musagète*, begun in Nice on 16 July and finished there on 9 January, at the end of an otherwise uneventful period. On 10 February he conducted his first full concert in Paris, with a programme of *Chant du rossignol*, *The Rite* and *Petrushka*. On 25 February he was at the Kroll Theatre in Berlin for the second stage production of *Oedipus rex* (the first had taken place a couple of days earlier in Vienna), produced and conducted by Otto Klemperer on a programme with *Mavra* and *Petrushka*. In March he gave concerts in Barcelona.

The first performance of *Apollon musagète* (later renamed *Apollo*) took place at the Library of Congress in Washington, DC (the work had been commissioned by the Coolidge Foundation), with choreography by Adolph Bolm, who also danced the title role. Stravinsky was not there, being involved as conductor in performances of *Oedipus rex* in Amsterdam (24 April) and London (12 May). But he was present, and conducting, at the European première, given by the Ballets Russes at the Théâtre Sarah-Bernhardt on 12 June, with choreography by Balanchine, designs by André Bauchant, and Lifar as Apollo. He also went with the production to London, where he recorded *Petrushka* (27–8 June).

Another ballet, *Le baiser de la fée*, was begun in July and finished on 30 October (earlier that month the Four Studies for orchestra had been completed). This had its first performance on 27 November by Ida Rubinstein's company at the Paris Opéra, with Stravinsky conducting, Nijinska directing, designs by Benois and Rubinstein as the Fairy. Then on 24 December Stravinsky took up the Capriccio, beginning with its third movement. Work on this continued, with short interruptions for concerts in Dresden, Paris, London and Berlin, and in May for a recording in Paris of *The Rite* (the gramophone now ousted the pianola as his chosen means of fixing his music for the future). On 19 August Dyagilev died: Stravinsky and his family were spending the summer at the Châlet des Echarvines, Talloires, on the Lac d'Annecy, as they had in 1927 and 1928. The Capriccio was finished in full score on 9 November, and first performed on 6 December at the Salle Pleyel, with Stravinsky as soloist and Ansermet conducting. Back in Nice, Stravinsky orchestrated his Three Little Songs during the Christmas period.

A chronological progress through Stravinsky's output inevitably gropes for patterns. It finds a consecutive sequence of three works sharing unusually relaxed, euphonious features – *Apollo* (to use the title Stravinsky came to prefer), *Le baiser de la fée* and the Capriccio – and interprets them as representing a stylistic development. But the calm may be deceptive, as deceptive as the harsh solemnity of *Oedipus rex*; it may be just that the composer has moved to another set of masks, or puppets. It is with the whole oeuvre as it is with each work, that jump-cuts are more typical than developments, and that surface elements of style may be self-contradictory. Even the large-scale division into three periods – Russian, neo-classical and serial – comes to seem unhelpful as increasing distance in time shows up how little classicism there is in neo-classicism, or how the manipulation of given idioms is omnipresent, or how Stravinsky never lost his thick Russian accent (in word setting, in closeness to folksong and Orthodox chant, in apartness from the Western symphonic tradition).

The distinction of *Apollo* may be most essentially that here suddenly Stravinsky's chosen musical language is through and through – not intermittently as way back in the Japanese lyrics and the iconic Balmont chorus – French. And perhaps that came about because he was, for the first time since *The Rite of Spring*, planning a ballet without a sung scenario (as in *Les noces* and *Renard*) and without existing music (as in *Chant du rossignol* and *Pulcinella*). It had been seventeen years since the first vision of *The Rite*; he could not go back to taking his patterns from Russian folksong. One of his remarks on *Apollo* is quite explicit on the need to find an alternative 'melodism',[1] but the search was for an alternative model to bounce off, too, and the most resilient available, because it was the strictest, was the *ballet de cour* of Lully and Louis XIV. (Of course, *Apollo* need not have been a ballet at all, since Elizabeth Sprague Coolidge had merely commissioned a half-hour instrumental score; but composing a ballet enabled Stravinsky to fulfil that commission and provide something for Dyagilev at the same time. There was also what it is hard to avoid

[1] *Dialogues*, p. 32.

seeing as a resistance to, or a discomfort with, abstract music that would lack the projecting energy of a soloist – a resistance or discomfort not overcome until the 'Dumbarton Oaks' Concerto another decade later.)

Following French Baroque style meant beginning with a French overture, in slow–fast–slow form, with the slow music imposing and dotted, and continuing with a set of formal dances. It also meant writing for string orchestra; and among much in *An Autobiography* that begins to sound edgily defensive of 'classical' perfection, Stravinsky's reference to 'the pleasure of immersing oneself again in the multisonorous euphony of strings'[2] has its mark in the music. Ever since *Petrushka* the strings had been distinctly secondary in his orchestra, even when they were not omitted altogether. *Apollo* has a sense of relishing new treats, and of doing so to the full, with a norm of six-part texture (the cellos being divided), sometimes with the further teasing out of one, two, three then four members of a solo quartet, and with writing, most conspicuously for the solo violin, that is remarkably unlike that of *Histoire du soldat*: the new melodism, a new diatonic serenity, had indeed been found.

The French Baroque model also demanded a classical subject, and *Apollon musagète* (Apollo as leader of the muses) fits in well with such Lullian titles as *La naissance de Vénus* or *Les muses*. At the same time it offered a nice historical pun – a ballet of the sun god in the manner of the court of *le roi soleil*[3] – besides labelling the work as one of Apollonian grace, constraint and rule (the Apollonian–Dionysiac antithesis, so much a favourite of Stravinsky criticism, seems to have been sanctioned by the composer). Finally, the French Renaissance and Baroque concern with classical poetic metre, and with its musical application, receives a belated contribution here.

The idea of *musique mésurée à l'antique*, which had been an item of faith for Claude Le Jeune and others in the second half of the sixteenth century, is pursued in a work whose 'real subject . . . is versification'. 'The basic rhythmic patterns', Stravinsky goes on, 'are iambic, and the individual dances may be thought of as variations of the reversible dotted-rhythm iamb idea.'[4] This is made explicit in the score in the case of Calliope's variation (economy, perhaps Dyagilevian economy, leaves this Apollo with only three muses to lead), but oddly, because Stravinsky subtitles this dance 'the alexandrine' and quotes two anapaestic lines from Boileau, whereas the model for the music is a line of six iambs. Elsewhere too, in keeping with the composer's later

---

[2]p. 136. [3]See *Dialogues*, p. 34. [4]Ibid., p. 33.

*but that's what an alexandrine **is**, for heaven's sake: a line consisting of six iambs* 97

remark, the music's rhythmic step is iambic, and one may wonder whether he was aware of Maurice Emmanuel's efforts to put Greek verse rhythms into music, efforts that would be carried further by the latter's pupil Messiaen.

However that may be, there are certainly other ways in which the French Baroque template of *Apollo* is adjusted by later history. For example, the suite of dances, begun with something like an allemande in Apollo's variation, and receiving its gigue in Calliope's alexandrine, has shades of the waltz in the intervening 'Pas d'action', passing hints of more recent dance measures in the syncopations (though with the string instrumentation now suggesting a *thé dansant* more than ragtime), and a big 'Pas de deux' in the Adagio–Allegro form of nineteenth-century ballet. Then again, the diatonic style evokes more a twentieth-century than a seventeenth-century Hellenism, an ancestry in Satie, Debussy and Ravel. The Gallic spirit of *Apollo* is a complex superimposition of Lully and Delibes, *Daphnis* and the Ritz.

It is, though, a harmonious superimposition, far from the abrasions of *Histoire du soldat* or the jarring of levels in *Oedipus rex*, and its musical expression can similarly attain a calm overlapping of different time scales, especially towards the end of the 'Pas d'action', where the same melodic idea unfolds at four different rates (see Ex. 14). Also notable here is the scarcity of accidentals, matched though by a scarcity of root-position triads. This is timeless polphony, where a quaver can stretch to a breve, and goalless harmony, where the music glides in a region above and beyond such considerations as B flat major, G minor or Phrygian D.

Quite apart from the fact that the historical references of *Apollo* are quite different from those of *Oedipus*, its euphony, to repeat Stravinsky's term, breathes a quite different sort of irony, less astringent and compelled. The costumes, whether Louis XIV, Second Empire or up-to-date, are ones in which the composer is comfortable. But the clothes he fitted best were still Tchaikovsky's, and after *Apollo* came one of his most extraordinary enterprises: *Le baiser de la fée*. What is extraordinary about the piece is its creative humility, for where the use of Neapolitan arias and sonatas in *Pulcinella* had resulted in a piece of almost aggressive self-assertion, the collection and scoring of Tchaikovsky pieces here produces a corporate personality. Gestures that sound like Tchaikovsky – and there are many of them, like the breasting rise of the strings in the trio to the scherzo in the third scene – have the aura not of parody but of self-parody. Things that closely recall Stravinsky – like the *Petrushka*-like cross-cutting of folk dances in the second scene, or the final wide-spanning figures across suspended

Ex. 14
Apollo: Pas d'action

harmony in a characteristic apotheosis of static repetition – still suggest an extension out of Tchaikovsky rather than a modification, still less a contradiction. The identification is now complete.

The case becomes perhaps most unsettling in the grand 'Pas de deux', with an Adagio section that makes rapturous use of Tchaikovsky's song 'None but the lonely heart', complete with cello solo. One wants the music to declare itself, to say whether it is a send-up or a homage. But it remains proudly silent. Tchaikovsky was the only other composer whose music Stravinsky regularly conducted, his repertory in the 1940s and 1950s including the occasional symphony or the Serenade. Tchaikovsky was the only composer whose music he continued to honour in straight arrangements, for Dyagilev in 1921 and for Balanchine twenty years later. And Tchaikovsky was the only composer who remained in his pantheon all the way from his student days, the days of the Sonata in F sharp minor and *The Faun and the Shepherdess*, to his old age, when he chose Sibelius's Canzonetta to arrange for Finland because of its Tchaikovskian associations. There may be a touch of contrariness in this, the man who insisted that 'art is arbitrary and must be artificial'[5] identifying with the man whose music is taken as the paradigm of frank emotional self-expression. But Stravinsky's long love affair may suggest too that there is no real paradox here, that construction expresses and expression constructs.

'I dedicate this ballet to the memory of Peter Tchaikovsky,' Stravinsky's prefatory note to the score reads, 'relating his muse to this fairy, in which respect the work becomes an allegory. His muse similarly marked him with a fatal kiss, whose mysterious imprint manifests itself in every work of this great artist.' But if Stravinsky saw himself so clear and whole in the mirror of Tchaikovsky, the allegory may be also a self-portrait. There is no indication that the scenario, also printed in the score, was the work of anyone but himself, and it seems to have been addressed as a surprise even to Benois,[6] who was responsible for the idea of using Tchaikovsky's music[7] as well as for the designs. The Swiss setting of the second scene, with its rustic dances, may also be significant in view of Stravinsky's long stay in Switzerland. But this is a fairytale and not a travelogue. The kiss of the muse-fairy isolates the unnamed hero from his mother, when he is a baby, and then from his fiancée, when he is a young man; her second kiss comes at the end, when she has carried him off to 'a land beyond time and place', a land perhaps where France and Russia are one, and where Lully and Stravinsky – and Tchaikovsky – are contemporaries.

[5]Ibid., p. 33.   [6]See *SPD*, pp. 284–5.   [7]See *An Autobiography*, p. 146.

It is in this never-nowhere land – where distinctions dissolve between model and creation, between mask and face, between past and present (as in *Le baiser de la fée*, whose elements of the 1860s and of the 1920s may be so tightly fused as to make the music's date undecidable), between comedy and tragedy (see *Oedipus rex*), between triviality and idealism (see *Apollo*) – that the Capriccio happily sits. Stravinsky's explanation of the title is particularly unconvincing (one has to remember that all his published books were, quite as much as *Le baiser de la fée*, joint creations, with a series of assistants including Walter Nouvel for *An Autobiography*,[8] Roland-Manuel for the *Poetics of Music*[9] and Robert Craft for the late essays and dialogues): 'I had in mind', he avers, 'the definition of a *capriccio* given by Praetorius, the celebrated musical authority of the eighteenth century. He regarded it as a synonym of the *fantasia*, which was a free form made up of *fugato* instrumental passages.'[10] Leaving aside the fact that Praetorius died in 1621, and the suspicion that his name has just been grabbed to lend a spurious classical authority, the only word here that applies well to the music is 'free', each movement being a chain of events, with repetitions pasted on in order to give a semblance of formal propriety (the slow movement thereby becomes a ternary structure, and the opening Presto gains a sonata-style recapitulation besides, as in the Concerto for piano and wind, a return of the introduction as coda). The title seems to have less to do with ancient precedent than with a taste for piquantly unassuming descriptions (Serenade, Divertimento), and also with a wish to avoid the form 'Piano Concerto no. 2'. Stravinsky's titling of his symphonies, chamber concertos and string quartets similarly avoided any implication of a series, and therefore of development. All his works carry an implicit 'no. 1' tag.

Besides, the Capriccio is different in kind from the Concerto of only five years before. Not only is it scored for full orchestra (with concertino strings inherited more from *Pulcinella* than *Apollo*), but it is far less chromatic and far more playful, profiting in these respects from its two ballet predecessors. From this point Stravinsky could have become Poulenc.

[8]See *SSC II*, p. 492.   [9]Ibid., pp. 503–17.   [10]*An Autobiography*, p. 159.

14

Symphony of Psalms

The chronicle of 1930 is largely the chronicle of the Symphony of Psalms. The work was begun, with its third movement, on 6 January. Stravinsky left twelve days later on a concert tour through Berlin, Leipzig, Düsseldorf, Bucharest and Prague, returning to Paris at the end of February; he also conducted a pair of concerts in Barcelona in late March. On 27 April he completed the third movement of the symphony, and went on to the second, finished on 17 July, and then the first, completed at the Châlet des Echarvines on 15 August. The only important interruption had been a recording of the Capriccio with Ansermet, made in Paris (8–10 May).

From the start of October until early December there followed a concert tour through Switzerland, Germany and Vienna. The German part of the tour began in Mainz, the home of Schott, with whom Stravinsky had recently begun to deal for the publication of his music. Willy Strecker of Schott suggested he write a violin concerto, and he jotted down a first idea on 27 October, though did not begin the composition in earnest until March, after a busy winter of performing. Also during this German tour Ansermet conducted the first performance of the Four Studies in Berlin (7 November). It was Ansermet, too, who conducted the Symphony of Psalms for the first time, in Brussels on 13 December, with Stravinsky playing the Capriccio on the same programme. He was not, therefore, at the first American performance of the Symphony six days later, when it was conducted by Koussevitzky, who had commissioned it for the fiftieth anniversary of the Boston Symphony Orchestra.

One further distinction remaining to be dissolved was that between the divine and the human, and this Stravinsky achieved in the Symphony of Psalms, right from its disarming double dedication: 'This symphony composed to the glory of God is dedicated to the Boston Symphony Orchestra on the occasion of its fiftieth anniversary.'

The Boston commission was, one has to recall, the first invitation to write an orchestral concert work without soloists that Stravinsky had received, or at any rate accepted, since before *The Firebird*: all his many orchestral scores of the last two decades had been theatre works, or concertos, or adaptations of music conceived for other means. For an artist increasingly inclined to appeal to classical authority, and abhorring any notion of music as illustrative, it would have been unthinkable to offer Boston a symphonic poem. The new work would have to be a symphony, just as Stravinsky's subsequent orchestral concert pieces created *ab nihilo* were symphonies. 'Symphonic form as bequeathed to us by the nineteenth century', however, 'held little attraction for me', and yet clearly something abstract and entire was demanded: hence the idea 'that my symphony should be a work with great contrapuntal development', which would make it 'necessary to increase the media at my disposal'. 'I finally decided on a choral and instrumental ensemble in which the two elements should be on an equal footing.' If there would therefore have to be words, it would be best to seek them 'among those which had been written for singing. And quite naturally my first idea was to have recourse to the Psalms.'[1]

This account of the work's genesis matches cogency with implausibility, and must say more about the cool, logical attitude Stravinsky wished to present (to present through his music, too, of course) than about his creative process. There is nothing here about signs and miracles, nor about going to confession and communion (matters of keen importance in the letters of 1926–7),[2] nor about the setting of the Lord's Prayer that had been written before the Symphony of Psalms or those of the Creed and Hail Mary that soon followed. Nor is there any mention of the Russian émigré composer Arthur Lourié, who had been part of Stravinsky's inner circle since the mid-1920s, and whose *Sonata liturgica* (1928) and *Concerto spirituale* (1929) would seem too close to Stravinsky's symphony in date and scoring for coincidence. Nor finally is there any reference to Jacques Maritain, whom Stravinsky came to know through Lourié, and whose ideas about rule, order and authority, divinely sanctioned, clearly had much more bearing on Stravinsky's neo-classical theorizing than did any study of Mozart.[3]

What is interesting here is not the influence that Lourié and Maritain may have had on Stravinsky's music, as opposed to the words about music that he wrote or condoned, for it needed rather weightier figures – Schoenberg, Webern, and indeed Mozart (not to mention Modoc the elephant) – to have any musical influence on him

[1]*An Autobiography*, pp. 161–2.
[2]See for example *SSC I*, pp. 111–12, and *SSC II*, pp. 40–42.
[3]See Louis Andriessen and Elmer Schönberger: *The Apollonian Clockwork*, pp. 86–96.

from this period onwards. What is interesting, rather, is the implied self-doubt that made him vulnerable to ideologues. Some part of that may have been his long-standing feeling, going back to the afternoons in Rimsky's studio, that he was under-educated. He had also lost his sheet-anchor with the death of Dyagilev, however frayed their relationship may have become since the first giddy years of the Ballets Russes. So far from being a confident assertion of symphonic and divine order, therefore, the Symphony of Psalms might be more a record of doubt, searching and prayer.

This would be its difference from *Oedipus rex*: not dead men hearing the dictates of dead gods, but living people in search – the living people whom the singers represent, as those in the opera–oratorio represent the citizens of Thebes. As Ansermet put it, the work 'expresses the religiosity of others – of the imaginary choir of which the actual singing choir is an *analogon*'.[4] And yet this is not quite complete, because there is also a posited hearer of the imaginary choir's psalmody. The search is on two levels. There is the icon-like image of a choir processing through prayer (the march-like imploration 'Exaudi orationem meam'), promise (the double fugue 'Expectans expectavi') and praise (the final 'Laudate Dominum', the 'new song' to which the preceding movement looked forward). There is also the search to bring that choir into focus, perhaps to join it, to make the work a real and not an imaginary liturgy, to call the God of the Psalms out of retirement.

This double perspective – of a choir moving forward through time, and of a view of that choir from a time outside their time – may be implicit in the nice distinction Stravinsky made just as he was finishing the composition: 'It is not a symphony in which I have included Psalms to be sung. On the contrary, it is the singing of the *Psalms* that I am symphonizing.'[5] That meant choosing resources not entirely for their acoustic balance but also for their traditions of sacredness. The score asks for children's voices in the upper parts if possible, though Stravinsky was rarely able to achieve that in performance,[6] and none of his four recordings is with a children's choir.[7] Then the exclusion of clarinets, violins and violas from the orchestra not only widens the split between voices and instruments but also leaves a reedy, brassy ensemble that may suggest a super-organ, while bells (at first cracked bells) are evoked by pianos and harp.

The largely homophonic choral chanting, even in the fugal movement, and the atmosphere of Orthodox modality are taken up

---

[4]*Fondements de la musique*, as quoted in White, p. 366.
[5]*SPD*, p. 297. [6]See *Dialogues*, pp. 46–7.
[7]See Alan Blyth, ed.: *Choral Music on Record* (Cambridge, 1991), pp. 254–7.

from the recent unaccompanied Lord's Prayer, but the instrumental sounds look back further, to the Symphonies of Wind Instruments and *Les noces*, which, as Stravinsky pointed out,[8] the symphony closely

[8]See *Dialogues*, p. 46.

Ex. 15

(a) Symphony of Psalms: I

(b) Symphony of Psalms: III

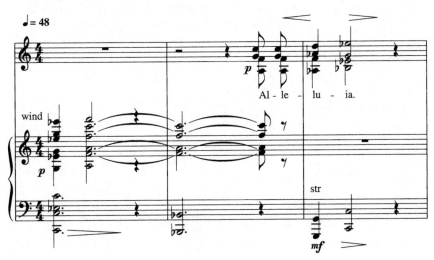

approaches as it ends, with the winds and strings holding a haze of reverberations over the choir while pianos, harp and timpani ring in octaves. Just as characteristic of the 'Russian period' is the working with small motifs, especially the rise through a minor third that gives the first movement its goal and the finale its starting point (see Ex. 15). We also know that Stravinsky began the Symphony as a Russian piece, setting Slavonic words, and that though he rather scorned suggestions of Byzantinism he by no means denied them.[9] There is, too, the greatest possible difference between the steady, fixed purposefulness of the opening movement, setting out again and again to trudge away from a grim E minor, and the elated improvisatory careering of the Capriccio.

However, the patience, the severity and the Russianness are perhaps all qualities of the imaginary choir. Stravinsky's hearing of that choir comes with the strain and the artificiality of his more recent music, though without the smart allusiveness. The central fugue, for instance, is remarkably free from echoes of Bach, given how much Stravinsky had delighted in such echoes in the contrapuntal piano displays of 1923–5. What it does convey, though, is stretching and hazard, a cautiousness as if dealing with material that might break at any moment: the instrumental fugue is exposed in a frail treble register exclusively by oboes and flutes, and though it sets out from the minor-third rise that gives the whole work its motto, the impression is of pitches and intervals being assembled one by one, with care. Another example is the hurrying of piano and wind in the last movement, which Stravinsky said 'was inspired by a vision of Elijah's chariot climbing the Heavens',[10] but which is curiously rickety and unsafe, not so much a vision as a fragile hope that a vision might be possible.

[9] Ibid., pp. 45–6.   [10] Ibid., p. 46.

15

Stravinsky's violin

The almost immediate recording of Stravinsky's new works, begun with the Capriccio in 1930, continued with the Symphony of Psalms in Paris on 17 February 1931, at rehearsals for a concert to take place a week later. There were also concerts in London around the beginning of February and in early March. Then on 27 March Stravinsky completed the first movement of his next work, the Violin Concerto. Late in April he made a brief visit to Venice before returning to Nice, where there were consultations with Samuel Dushkin for whom the Concerto was being written. The two central movements were finished on 20 May and 6 June, the latter ten days before Stravinsky went with his family to Voreppe, just north of Grenoble, where they found a new home in the Château de la Vironnière. There he finished the fourth movement of the Concerto on 4 September, and the full score three weeks later.

From October to December 1931 there was another long concert tour, beginning in Oslo. The first performance of the Violin Concerto, with Dushkin playing and Stravinsky conducting, was in Berlin on 23 October, followed by performances in Frankfurt, London, Cologne, Hanover and Paris. After the tour, on 27 December, Stravinsky went straight into another violin work, the *Duo concertant* designed for Dushkin and himself to play in recitals. At the end of March 1932 they gave further performances of the Concerto in Florence and Milan, on the latter occasion playing the violin–piano reduction. The next month Dushkin visited Stravinsky in Voreppe, and a transcription of the 'Russian Dance' from *Petrushka* was made for violin and piano, the first of several such miniaturized excerpts. In Paris, during the period 6–9 May, Stravinsky recorded the suite from *Histoire du soldat* and the Octet. He completed the *Duo concertant* in Voreppe on 15 July, and three days later a new version of the violin–piano suite from *Pulcinella*, retitled *Suite italienne*. Both these works were played for the first time by Dushkin and Stravinsky in Berlin on 28 October, after which the two musicians gave recitals in Danzig and Paris, where on 14 November Stravinsky began the first movement of another big recital piece, the Concerto for two pianos.

Another interlude, this violin-centred period of 1931–2. Or perhaps the interludes have now become so frequent that Stravinsky's creative life has to be seen as a sequence of interludes, a capriccio, a succession of responses to opportunities, of which the latest was another, different round of concert engagements, and therefore another, different repertory, with Dushkin. His praise of artisanship seems significant here, his approving quotation of Tchaikovsky's aim to compose 'exactly as a shoemaker makes shoes.'[1] And yet that degree of unselfconsciousness is far removed from the music he was writing, and surely embodies a utopian dream shared by many artists in the twentieth century. At the same time, his appeals to authority appear increasingly disconnected from the music. 'Lyricism', he affirms (and again he is even using an authority to appeal to authority, here quoting his friend Cingria), 'cannot exist without rules, and it is essential that they should be strict.' But this is said in connection with the *Duo concertant*, which sublimely makes up its rules as it goes along.

So much seems arbitrary here: the great length of the gigue, the way the second movement introduces, repeats and then abandons a raw bagpipe tune, the cadences (the final chord of the first movement is held long enough that it can appear to resolve, can become appropriate), the absence of barring for substantial sections of the second and last movements, even the titles of the work and of its movements. This is not a display piece in the sense of Weber's *Grand duo concertant*: indeed, part of the appeal of the relationship with Dushkin, quite apart from the violinist's amiability,[2] was perhaps the possibility of conversation more than bravura. As for the movement titles, 'Eglogue' and 'Dithyrambe' (for what is a slow finale, far more Bachian than Bacchanalian) would seem to have been chosen to give the work a Hellenic aspect, just as Stravinsky's description of it as 'a work of musical versification'[3] says more about his wish to align it on the side of *Apollo* than about the nature of the piece. The arbitrariness here is not the same as the arbitrariness of the potentially mutable and forgettable Piano Concerto or the elated Capriccio; it is more like unconcern, a shoemaker's dispassion.

The concerto for Dushkin is strikingly different. This and the set of clarinet pieces were the only two original works in which Stravinsky could let virtuoso flamboyance have its way without being limited (if also of course stimulated) by what his own fingers were telling him – and the qualifying 'original' is necessary only because the *Petrushka* transcriptions for Rubinstein have to be counted in this narrow

[1]*An Autobiography*, p. 171.   [2]See *SSC II*, pp. 295–6.
[3]*An Autobiography*, p. 170.

Stravinskian category too. There is often a sense of the music cutting across the grain of the instrument, as Stravinsky appears to recognize, and indeed be gratified by, in citing Hindemith's advice that not being a violinist 'would make me avoid a routine technique, and would give rise to ideas which would not be suggested by the familiar movement of the fingers'[4] (though this was an assurance the composer of *Histoire du soldat* hardly needed). A prominent example – placed right at the start of each of the four movements, a 'passport' to the work as Stravinsky described it[5] – is the wide-spanning D–E–A chord, where something utterly in the nature of the instrument (the sound of the three upper open strings) is estranged by having the middle note shot up two octaves. But so much of the music comes from a twisting or exaggeration of clichés and obviousnesses.

One instance is the turn figure, out of which grows the first theme of the opening movement and the whole of the third movement (and, indeed, the finale of the *Duo concertant*). In its sympathy with traditional ornament, and in its passages of strict counterpoint and its zest for chamber combinations, the work bears out Stravinsky's own suggestion of a correspondence with Bach rather than with subsequent violin concertos.[6] However, his discounting of its virtuoso pedigree, almost in the same breath, is less easy to swallow. Dushkin may not have been on a par with such contemporaries as Heifetz and Szigeti (the version of the *Pulcinella* suite written for him is less demanding than the one prepared for Kochanski a few years earlier), but the Concerto is written around exhibiting the soloist, who plays almost continuously. It is not that Stravinsky goes in for empty display, but rather that empty display is the subject matter. Hence the feeling sometimes of a circus band accompanying the high-wire act of the first movement, for instance.

This first movement has a more convincing outward show of sonata form than anything hitherto in Stravinsky's output, in that there is a wholesale recapitulation. But the reprise is merely repetition, without tonal change, and the whole form is essentially sectional, motivated by the soloist's alighting from one idea on to another in the manner of a trapeze artist, perhaps, more than a tightrope-walker. Stravinsky's heading, 'Toccata', allows that its principal impetus is that of pulsation rather than harmony, with, characteristically, no change of tempo from beginning to end. The finale, another 'Capriccio', has a husk of rondo form, but again the energy is pulsed and the soloist

[4] Ibid., p. 168.
[5] See Dushkin's reminiscences in *Stravinsky*, ed. Edwin Corle (New York, 1949).
[6] See *Dialogues*, p. 47.

swings from one caper to another. The following examples from this movement show how a semitone signature (with a strong rhythmic correspondence between the first two, consecutive ideas) can give rise to passages quite different in nature, the last of these three suggesting the Soldier's violin playing at the 'Sacrificial Dance':

Ex. 16
Violin Concerto: IV

Stravinsky's musical relationship with Dushkin lasted until 1937, covered his next two American tours, and produced an extraordinary number of little arrangements quite apart from the two original works and the two major transcriptions (the *Suite italienne* and the Divertimento, the latter a suite from *Le baiser de la fée* which appears to have preceded the orchestral version with the same title). There might have seemed the threat in the 1930s that Stravinsky, having given up the pianola idea, would be turning out all his music in arrangements for violin and piano. But his willingness to extract gems from *Petrushka* or *The Nightingale* would only be puzzling in a composer of less severely sectional music, and his readiness to provide domestic alternatives has its rationale in the shoemaker's wish to be useful.

16

A French melodrama

In February and March 1933 Stravinsky gave more recitals with Dushkin in Munich, London and Winterthur, and then in Paris, on 6–7 April, made recordings with him of the *Duo concertant* and smaller pieces, including a new version of the Pastorale for violin and wind. In May he began his first stage work since *Le baiser de la fée* of five years before, the commission again coming from Ida Rubinstein, and the subject to be the myth of Persephone, treated as cantata and melodrama with verse by André Gide. During the autumn he took time off from this to make another version of the Pastorale, for violin and piano, and also a suite from the last Rubinstein ballet for Dushkin and himself to play, the 'Divertimento'. He also moved his Paris pied-à-terre in October from the Maison Pleyel to an apartment at 21 rue Viète.

The next month, in Barcelona, he conducted the Capriccio with his son Soulima as soloist, making his public début. Henceforth he appears not to have played his concertante works in concert, preferring to conduct, or to play in duo recitals with Dushkin and with Soulima. He made a tour with Dushkin to England in February 1934 (*Perséphone* had been completed in full score on 24 January), performing the Violin Concerto in Manchester on the 22nd, and giving recitals in Liverpool on the 23rd, Cambridge on the 26th, London on the 27th and Oxford on the 28th. More recitals with Dushkin followed in Turin and Kaunas the next month, and then a second sacred chorus, the *Ave Maria*, dated 4 April. On 30 April *Perséphone* had its first performance by Ida Rubinstein's company at the Paris Opéra, with Stravinsky conducting. The choreographer was Kurt Jooss, the director Jacques Copeau and the designer André Barsacq. Rubinstein spoke the title role and René Maison sang that of Eumolpus.

Stravinsky's second work for Ida Rubinstein is, with *Oedipus rex*, one of his biggest pieces between *The Nightingale* and *The Rake's Progress*, but it is also one of his least often performed, and its defenders have understandably felt themselves engaged in a Persephonic effort of rescue. Stephen Walsh, in particular, presents a wide range of evidence in support of the piece: the fact that here we have a Christianized spring ritual that is supremely Russian and supremely Stravinskian; the marriage of genres (cantata, ballet and recitation) that is also highly characteristic; the spontaneity revealed by superficial awkwardness; the individuality of a score which poses so much pure diatonic harmony and melody in a world calmed by the exclusion of cadences; the bell sounds and the other beauties of the scoring.[1]

Even Walsh, though, is bound to recognize that these are frail virtues – that the limpidity, for instance, can seem more bland than pure, or that the spoken recitation is a problem in its style and in its failure to integrate with the music. As far as the latter is concerned, Stravinsky himself, always eager in the later dialogues to point out faults in his own earlier works as well as in those of others, admitted the weakness of Gide's lines and of the melodrama device,[2] but there is a certain aptness in having Persephone sounding as if from another world, in having her the subject of a pageant which she can only observe, and especially so when the other soloist, the priest Eumolpus, is also outside the action which he invokes (increasingly the part draws towards monotone chant on E, towards the high pitch of a tenor Russian deacon).

The greater problem is the simplicity of so much of the harmony, or at least of the chording, and of the rhythm, or at least of the metre. To a large degree these features are carried over from *Apollo*, for *Perséphone* is a further step taken by Stravinsky as *musicien français* (his citizenship came through just five weeks after the première), following the French tradition of white-note Hellenism and also looking back to the Baroque tradition of cantatas on classical subjects. But where in *Apollo* the levels of French–Greek form, Russian irregularity and café charm live in a teasing harmonious disparity, in *Perséphone* the dislocation is over. It can even be made to be over retrospectively, if Stravinsky was right in saying that one segment of the music came from a 1917 sketchbook[3] (other material came from the recent and abandoned Petrarchan *Dialogue de la Joye et de la Raison*), so that here Eumolpus would be singing to music written sixteen years before (see Ex. 17). But in a manner inconceivable for 1917, the lines glide by in static pandiatonic harmony, glide over the harp ostinatos, and the barline is extraordinarily enfeebled, with only

[1]See *Dialogues*, pp. 154–8.   [2]Ibid., p. 37.   [3]Ibid., p. 38.

Ex. 17

Perséphone: II Perséphone aux enfers

[He gives it (a pomegranate) to Persephone, who is amazed.]

the first flute seeming to remember its former power (it is certainly powerful elsewhere, for instance at the start of the third section, but there the banality of the gesture and the odd clattery quality of the scoring suggest in a different way that the machine is running down).

Stravinsky's willingness to take up old ideas and even older clichés

113

(Ex. 17 repeats the quintessential combination for its French tradition, one found for example in Debussy's music for the Bilitis poems of Louÿs), so curiously without the irony recently rampant in the Violin Concerto – may simply have been caused by the speed with which he had to work: at no other time did he complete nearly an hour of music in eight months. It may just have been, too, that he was here working like a film composer, writing to a plan of the stage action, and willing to sacrifice a purely musical coherence: there is a strange affinity of self-effacement with his other score for Ida Rubinstein, except that here the invited partner is not Tchaikovsky but rather a tradition of Grecian grace going back to Botticelli. Stravinsky being so dilute, it is hard to tell quite why this Primavera is smiling.

17

Cards and concertos

In July 1934 Stravinsky made more recordings, of the Serenade and *Piano-Rag-Music* in Paris and of *Les noces* in London. On 11 September he met Berg at a concert in Venice, and on 28 November conducted *Perséphone* in London. The next month he and Dushkin made a concert tour from Liège down to the south of France, and embarked from Villefranche for New York. Stravinsky's second American tour, including his first visit to California, then lasted until April 1935; in May he gave concerts in Copenhagen, Bologna and Rome (where he met Mussolini). In the summer, at Voreppe, he returned to the long-suspended Concerto for two pianos (remarkably, there had been no new major work since the completion of *Perséphone* in January 1934), finishing the second movement on 13 July and the fourth (originally third) on 1 September. There was then more work with Dushkin: a tour of Scandinavia, and a recording of the Violin Concerto in Paris on 28–9 October. On 9 November he completed the two-piano Concerto, and twelve days later gave the first performance with Soulima at the Salle Gaveau in Paris; they gave repeat performances in Paris and Lausanne before the end of the year.

His next work, the ballet *Jeu de cartes*, followed between 1 December 1935 and 6 December 1936, during which time there were more concert tours. In February and March he and Soulima appeared in Milan, Rome, Barcelona and Bournemouth, performing the Concerto for two pianos and the Capriccio. In April he played the Concerto with Soulima in Baden-Baden, his last public appearance in Germany until after the war, though he returned in 1938 to record *Jeu de cartes* in Berlin. His attitude towards the Third Reich remained ambiguous until the start of hostilities between Germany and Russia: snobbish contempt for the Nazis, and a genial taste for the Latin dictators, were typical of his age, nationality and class.[1] Then between April and June he was in South America.

Between January and May the next year, 1937, he made his third

---

[1]See *SPD*, pp. 547–58.

visit to North America, again with Dushkin. In January they gave concerts and recitals in Toronto, Montreal and New York; in February Stravinsky conducted the General Motors Symphony in Detroit and the Cleveland Orchestra; in March he spent most of the month on the west coast, giving recitals with Dushkin and conducting the San Francisco and Los Angeles orchestras. He also found time, on this long tour, to compose. The Praeludium for jazz ensemble was finished on 6 February, and on 3 March, in Evanston, Illinois, he made his first notation for the Symphony in C. On 27 April *Jeu de cartes* had its first performance, as *The Card Party*, at the Metropolitan Opera House, New York, with Stravinsky conducting a triple bill that also included *Apollo* and *Le baiser de la fée*. The company was American Ballet, the choreographer Balanchine, and the designer for the new ballet Irene Sharaff. Also this month Stravinsky made his last transcription for Dushkin, the 'Chanson russe' from *Mavra*.

During the summer Stravinsky stayed at the Château de Monthoux, Annemasse, to be near his wife and daughters, who were in a sanatorium in Sancellemoz. In September he paid a visit to Venice (where he conducted the European and concert première of *Jeu de cartes*), Rome, Positano and Paestum, and in October he conducted his latest ballet again in London. He also set a *Petit Ramusianum harmonique* for his old collaborator's sixtieth birthday the following year (the piece is dated 11 October 1937). His larger work after *Jeu de cartes* was the Concerto in E flat, completed in Paris on 29 March 1938, the month after recordings of *Jeu de cartes* in Berlin and the two-piano Concerto with Soulima in Paris. On 8 May the new Concerto had its first performance at Dumbarton Oaks, Washington, DC, conducted by Nadia Boulanger. Stravinsky was not there, but he did attend a twenty-fifth anniversary performance of *The Rite* under Manuel Rosenthal in Paris on 30 May, and on 4 June, also in Paris, he himself conducted the European première of the Concerto.

Schoenberg's complaint of *Oedipus rex* was that it said what it was not, rather than what it was,[2] but the criticism is even truer of *Perséphone* (which it is hard to imagine Schoenberg sitting through), not because this lyrical melodrama counters and frustrates the obvious path – it would have been a central Stravinsky work if it had done so – but rather because it goes blithely along with what is expected of it. There is rather the same outward correctness, though with a return of

---

[2]See *Style and Idea* (London, 1975), pp. 482–3.

humour, in Stravinsky's next works: two concertos, of which the first had been begun before *Perséphone*, and a ballet.

The Concerto for two pianos bears the same relationship to the Capriccio as the *Duo concertant* does to the Violin Concerto, in being a piece which the composer–conductor and his soloist could play in cities where there was no orchestra, or no time to prepare one. But it is a much more excited musical occasion, with a nice sense of self-observation as it goes about the business of behaving like a proper symphonic piece. The rapid even staccato in the first movement suggests the impatience of fingers keen at the keyboard and also that of a musical mind in invention. The form, as in the Violin Concerto, makes deep bows in the direction of sonata conventionality (the opening theme recalls the energy of the start of the last part of *Perséphone*), but the structure is no less sectional, and wittily admits as much with its abrupt hesitations. Then comes a slow Nocturne of which one could imagine – much more than of *Threni*, of which this was true – that it was written on a night-club piano after hours. The last two movements were to have been a prelude and fugue followed by a set of variations, but after completing the work Stravinsky decided to place the variations first, so that their theme comes after them, as a point of arrival rather than departure. This is particularly appropriate when the last of the four variations has shown that Stravinsky, thirty years after the event and in a work with very different stylistic assumptions, could still come near the 'Dance of the Earth' from *The Rite of Spring*, so that the theme comes as the clearing after a storm. It also fits that the fugue should refer to the *Perséphone*-like material of the first movement, and come back to its E tonality, now major rather than minor.

The applicability of key names is one of the symptoms of the difference of Stravinsky's current music from that of the 1920s. The Violin Concerto is 'in D' in an altogether more conventional sense from that in which the Serenade is 'in A': it was now possible to keep a key signature throughout a movement (except for the middle section of the first Aria), staking out an orthodox succession from D major through D minor and A major back to D major. And though the Concerto for two pianos is certainly less straightforward than that (this was, after all, a new genre and not a quixotic intervention into an existing one), the lean, spruce harmony is of the 1930s. It went along with the wish to be functional, and with the sliding tendency towards abstract instrumental forms. In the decade after Dyagilev's death Stravinsky wrote only two works for the theatre, *Perséphone* and *Jeu de cartes*, even if the dramatic presentation of

117

two pianists, the atmosphere of game or duel, is written into the Concerto.

Jeu de cartes is a game too, of course, the second of three card games in Stravinsky's output, coming after the one in *Histoire du soldat* (though in this case the game comes in Ramuz's part of the proceedings) and before that in *The Rake's Progress*. Stravinsky was an active cardplayer himself, and at this time his favourite game was the one danced here: poker.[3] But more clues to *Jeu de cartes* come from these other dramatized card games than from his life, for both are jousts with the devil, with the human opponent's soul as prize, and in *Jeu de cartes* too the main agent is the malevolent Joker. Also, all three works are victories (in the case of *Histoire du soldat*, victory by defeat) for the hearts, with obvious symbolic meaning. *Jeu de cartes* is a dance in three 'deals', each introduced by fanfaring music that returns again to round off the piece, and each a sequence of short episodes planned to a scenario – but also planned, as they were not in *Perséphone*, to make a highly effective concert piece.

Indeed, the essential game is being played in the orchestra. It is not exactly clear how, when and by whom the scenario was written: Cocteau was involved, though the final result was attributed to the composer and a friend of his elder son's.[4] But the card game idea seems just a neat and colourful dress for an abstract parade of alliances and combats such as Stravinsky and Balanchine would offer openly in *Agon*. There is some presage of that later score, too, in the feeling of display, and not just the heraldic display of the introductory material but the exhibitionism of thought and scoring in all the linked sections that follow. The idea of instruments and groups on parade, or dancing, is stronger here than in any of Stravinsky's orchestral scores since *Pulcinella*. But there is also something new on show: a parodying not just of conventions from the past but of actual pieces, including most spectacularly a tune from *Il barbiere di Siviglia*. History is a pack of cards, to be reshuffled before each deal.

The first deal of *Jeu de cartes* is a sort of rondo, or a chain of refrains around two verses, as it might be better described in view of the flatness of Stravinsky's harmonic landscape, his typical way of avoiding bridges by using simple jumps, connections of pulse, or manifestly artificial framing devices. Cheekiest among the latter here are the prompt cadences that mark off the variations of the second deal – musical variations in that they all spring from this movement's march theme, and balletic variations in that they are danced by the

[3]See White, p. 393.   [4]See *SSC II*, pp. 312–22.

four queens in turn and then together. The angular variation for the Queen of Spades recalls the spiky music for the Joker in the first deal; then the combat of hearts and spades comes in the third deal, in quick music after a waltz-minuet that, in touching on Ravel, is a parody of parodies. Of course the hearts win through, but one may feel that this brilliant but nervy, brittle score was written under the sign of the Joker.

The appearance of the Praeludium at this point is a reminder that Stravinsky's output of short pieces had suddenly stopped after *Les cinq doigts*, except for arrangements of old miniatures and fragments for the pianola and then for Dushkin. This may have something to do with the creative dignity expected of an artist so publicly prominent, especially one who had taken the role of great composer as an extension of that of *grand seigneur* (life in Western Europe seems to have meant again what it had meant to him as a youth, when he had toured the spas and mountain resorts with his parents; and the patent artificiality of his post-*Pulcinella* music may convey this sense of permanent superior holiday). There were also all his proclamations about the need to be correct and canonical: proclamations which could be denied by the nature of the music (as by the comedy of the concertos for violin and for two pianos), but hardly by its scale. Even the Praeludium may have been meant as the first movement of a jazz suite, though the existing piece is barely more than the sketch of an opening, a little jazz fossil, with the glittering calcite of a celesta in its interstices.

The Praeludium was the first piece Stravinsky composed, or at least completed, in the United States, and the tours of 1935 and 1937 were accompanied by a westward turn in his output: *Jeu de cartes* was written for America; so were the next two major works, the Concerto in E flat and the Symphony in C. The former was commissioned by Mr and Mrs Robert Woods Bliss for performance at their house, Dumbarton Oaks, Washington, DC: hence the work's soubriquet. Presumably the circumstances of the commission dictated the use of a chamber orchestra, and hence, for Stravinsky at this point, an almost inevitable textural and thematic reference to the Brandenburg concertos: his own starts with a Bach tag, includes a good deal of fugato, and swivels from one texture to another in the manner of a concerto grosso with a flexible solo group. But of course a great deal else is going on in this music as well, including an almost Webernian game of imitation and flickering colour contrast in the second of the three short movements, the sudden swelling up of a gavotte as one of many episodes in the finale, and reminiscences of earlier Stravinsky, especially the Octet and *Apollo*. More surprising is the suggestion rather of the Symphonies of Wind Instruments, at least before the cadential fall, as the second movement comes to ground before the beginning of the third:

Ex. 18
Concerto in E flat: II–III

Continuity across the range from this to Bach seems to be maintained only by the tight instrumentation and consistency of pulse, and perhaps also by an atmosphere of showiness as Stravinsky works like a juggler, or like a cardplayer placing down one surprise after another on the green baize.

Symphony in C

The first movement of the Symphony in C was written in Paris in the autumn of 1938. On 30 November Stravinsky's daughter Lyudmila died: he had just started a concert tour in Italy, and hurried back to Sancellemoz before returning to fulfil his engagements the next month. Then in 1939 came two more deaths, that of his wife in Sancellemoz on 2 March (he was now living there, working on the second movement of the Symphony and on the lectures promised for Harvard in the autumn), and that of his mother, also in Sancellemoz, on 7 June. In May he had gone to conduct in Milan and Florence, but he did not attend the belated first performance of *Zvezdoliki*, given by Belgian Radio forces under Franz André in Brussels on 19 April.

In August he completed the second movement of the Symphony, still in Sancellemoz, before going back to Paris at the beginning of September and then leaving by ship for New York at the end of the month. In October and November he gave his Harvard lectures, published as *Poétique musicale*, and in December he conducted again in San Francisco and Los Angeles. In January 1940 he returned to New York, where Vera Sudeikina arrived from Europe on the 12th. They then went to Pittsburgh for concerts at the end of the month before going back to New York, and on 9 March they were married in Bedford, Massachusetts. More concerts followed in March and April in New York and Boston, as well as recordings in New York of the *Petrushka* suite and *The Rite of Spring*.

On 28 April, Russian Easter, Stravinsky finished the third movement of the Symphony. He and Vera then travelled in May–June from New York by boat to Galveston, and thence by train to Los Angeles, where they moved into 124 South Swall Drive, Beverley Hills, until November. In July–August he conducted in Mexico City, which fulfilled and fuelled his taste for Latin culture now that he was cut off from Italy and Spain. Also in August he completed the last movement of the Symphony (on the 19th) and conducted *The Firebird*, danced in Bolm's choreography, at the Hollywood Bowl, where he was to appear again several more times for summer concerts and ballet programmes in the 1940s and early 1950s. On 14 October he finished the Tango, in its piano version; also this month he began his next important work after the Symphony in C, *Danses concertantes*, and visited the Disney studios in the course of discussions about a cartoon version of *Renard*, never realized. On 7 November he conducted the Chicago Symphony in the first performance of the Symphony in C, staying on in Chicago for more concerts before leaving for New York towards the end of the month.

Another commission for an orchestral concert piece, another American orchestra's golden jubilee to be celebrated, and so another symphony. This time the placing of God before the music's human destination ('This symphony, composed to the Glory of God, is dedicated to the Chicago Symphony Orchestra on the occasion of the Fiftieth Anniversary of its existence') is not justified by the setting of sacred texts, but for Stravinsky there seems to have been a close connection between the religious and the canonical, and this four-movement symphony is in some respects one of his most canonical works. There is also a direct connection with the Symphony of Psalms, in that the prominent 'Laudate' motif of the last movement (D–E flat –B flat) becomes, transposed up a sixth, the basic cell of the Symphony in C (B–C–G). And finally, although Stravinsky writes here for an absolutely standard orchestra (as had been his inclination since his brush with the Tchaikovsky orchestra in *Le baiser de la fée*, the only exception to the correctness of this decade being *Perséphone*), nevertheless he treats the ensemble as one of soloists and choirs, and there is a particular suggestion of chant in the bassoon duet with low brass accompaniment that introduces the finale. As in the similar brief moment in the Concerto in E flat (Ex. 18), it is as if the litanies of the Symphonies of Wind Instruments are being recalled – if, indeed, they had ever really been forgotten.

The sense of one level being overlaid by, or usurped by, another is intensified by how in both these instances fast music comes rushing upon slow, rather as the climactic dances in each half of *The Rite of Spring* come rushing upon slow episodes that precede them, and in a way expect them. The great difference from the ballet, of course, is that now the fast music pretends, at least, to diatonic propriety, and the slow–fast dichotomy is also a distinction between ancient and modern, static and dynamic, modal and diatonic, rural and urban (it is also curiously often, as in Ex. 18, expressed in a difference of function between winds and strings, the former retaining the primality they had in *The Rite* or the Symphonies, while the strings come with the urgency of the new). Such splits between irreconcilable levels also suggest *Pulcinella*, as does the bright, alert tone of the piece, and its predominantly major-mode colouring.

However, there is now no borrowed material, and even the specific quotations, allusions and style imitations of the two immediately previous major works, *Jeu de cartes* and the Concerto in E flat, are gone. The Symphony may exist on split levels, but it has a stronger ego than anything in Stravinsky's output since the Violin Concerto, a more unified and confident feel. One symptom of that is the breadth of the outer movements, where, quite by contrast with the knotty time-signature changes of the Concerto in E flat, the bar remains one of four crotchets throughout (however, in a curious piece of fastidiousness, Stravinsky uses a 2/2 signature for the first movement and a ₵ for most of the finale).

Just as stable metre here provides a springboard for syncopations and cross-rhythms, so C major tonality can be distorted by modal gravitations. This is where the levels meet. It is not a case of face and mask, as in *Pulcinella*, but of separate faces, or of separate masks which have become indistinguishable from faces: if C major is a pose or a prison, it is one that Stravinsky has chosen and made his own, partly by changing its shape. The germinal motif of the work, the B–C–G it prolongs from the Symphony of Psalms, is in this abstract context not only a vestigial prayer but also a contortion of the simple cadential gesture G–B–C. It affirms, right from the start, the priority of the dominant (in this case G) that is almost ubiquitous in Stravinsky's diatonic music, and its extension into the first melodic subject re-emphasizes this while also showing that the basic chord is not the root-position triad C–E–G but the inversion E–G–C (see Ex. 19). The nominal keynote – the keynote declared in the title – is absent from the bass here, and present in the theme only as its precarious uppermost note, repeatedly placed in a rhythmically weak position and sliding down to the G.

As with the Serenade in A, the preposition in the title is highly charged with meaning, but differently. It is not that the specified note is an axis and final instead of a tonic, but rather that it is a tonic in an unconventional sense, an ironic tonic. Stravinsky's whole devotion to codes and canons, from *Mavra* onwards, was a devotion to things that had lost their original purpose: an exile's devotion to things of the past, but expressed with an eagerness and curiosity quite contrary to nostalgia. Forms and processes no longer arise from the material – and are not even made to seem as if they so arise, as in later Schoenberg – but instead are clamped on like moulds: Stravinsky's proud defences

Ex. 19
Symphony in C: I

[Moderato alla breve ♩ = 66]

of artifice and arbitrariness[1] are recognitions of that. So, once again, this is not a symphony in C in the way that Mozart's 'Jupiter', Beethoven's First or Schubert's Ninth are symphonies in C. It knows that the age of such symphonies is past (the whole game of neo-classicism depends on an unsentimental awareness and acceptance of separation from the past, or rather from that narrow part of the past represented by musical tradition, for a much larger past may be there in the background). The 'in C' is a little provocative, a little unreal, a little too emphatic.

The real title would have to be something more like 'Symphony in C with the first inversion as root chord and correspondingly with Phrygian leanings' – although any such qualifications apply only to

[1]See for example *Dialogues*, p. 33.

124

particular sections, so that even this title would have to flicker and change as the work proceeds. It is to this anti-systematic, and therefore anti-developmental, aspect of the music that Ansermet seems to be referring in describing the first movement as a 'portrait of a symphonic allegro',[2] perhaps a cubist portrait, done from different angles and in different perspectives, with the angle and the perspective of Ex. 19 as primary. In such a symphony consistency and cogency of movement are not to be expected: the work is as abruptly sectional as anything by Stravinsky. But the defining points of consistent, cogent symphonies are there. Just as a Picasso portrait will have eyes and nose in roughly the right places, so Stravinsky's portrait of a symphonic allegro has passages that demand to be identified as 'first subject' (Ex. 19, in which one can almost hear the demand being made), 'development section', or 'recapitulation of the second subject in the tonic'. Yet not only do the segments not fit smoothly together, but also each one is created with elements that are incompatible with its nominal function – elements like the harmonic levitation and the modality of Ex. 19. The quotation marks around the descriptions have to stay.

The use of anti-symphonic elements, as anti-symphonic as those of *The Rite of Spring*, might suggest the work of someone from another culture – an ancient Scythian no doubt – who had picked up a nineteenth-century handbook of symphonic form and followed its strictures. But then it would have to have been an ancient Scythian with a love of Tchaikovsky: as so often, Stravinsky's music is the collision site of many different times, where the only anathema is the orderly progress through time performed by traditional symphonies and more largely, by the whole history of traditional symphonies, in respect to which this work pokes out askew. And it does so all the more pointedly for being outwardly Stravinsky's most traditional piece, with the possible exception only of *The Rake's Progress*. Where the Symphony of Psalms had simply proposed a quite other way in which symphonies might be made (if not quite as radically other as that of the Symphonies of Wind Instruments, where the word's implications of form and scale are just discounted), the Symphony in C has the orthodox four movements in the most orthodox sequence: sonata allegro, slow movement, scherzo, finale.

There is, however, a gradual bending away from orthodoxy as the work proceeds: in that, too, *The Rake* will make a similar progress. Where the first movement acquires its stays and supports from the Viennese classics and from Tchaikovsky, the second movement,

[2]See White, p. 409.

Larghetto concertante, rather recalls Bach in its ornamented woodwind lines (the ancient Scythian is now having his pipes blow the tunes of eighteenth-century pastoralism, in the standard pastoral key of F), and the scherzo switches through time in the other direction, towards the instrumental brilliance and rhythmic agility of earlier Stravinsky, this being the only movement to abound in changes of time signature. Then the finale, in having to do more and more with the B–C–G motif of the first movement, acknowledges that the most persuasive past here is an internal one, and that the Symphony, so far from undertaking a journey or any much-favoured passage from doubt to certainty, is fated to remain on the spot. The only way to achieve an ending is, as in the Symphony of Psalms, with slow repetitions of the motif, repetitions that unloose the limits of the present, that bend all the arrows of symphonism round into circular ripples, in harmony (here white-note harmony) that knows there is nowhere else to go.

19

Symphony in Three Movements

From New York, in the winter of 1940–41, Stravinsky went to give concerts in Minneapolis, Baltimore, Washington, Cambridge and Boston. He also conducted the first performance, on 22 January in New York, of *Balustrade*, a Balanchine ballet to his Violin Concerto. In February he returned to Los Angeles for concerts with the Philharmonic, and on 6 April he and Vera moved into 1260 North Wetherly Drive, Hollywood, their home until 1964. On 12 May his brother Yuri died in Leningrad; his arrangement of the Bluebird Pas-de-deux from *Sleeping Beauty* may also date from this month. In July there was another visit to Mexico City, to finish the recording of the *Divertimento*, and on 14 October his arrangement of 'The Star-Spangled Banner' was heard for the first time, conducted by James Sample in Los Angeles.

After concerts in St Louis in December and in San Francisco at the beginning of the year, Stravinsky completed *Danses concertantes* on 13 January 1942 and a piano score of the *Circus Polka* on 5 February. The former work had its first performance on 8 February in Los Angeles, Stravinsky conducting the Werner Janssen Orchestra, who had commissioned it. Six days later there were discussions concerning 'a Donizetti ballet' at Massine's,[1] and the idea must have been alive for some while, since on 2 May Vera records having bought a score of *Lucia*. By then, though, Stravinsky was at work on the Symphony in Three Movements, begun on 4 April. In June and July there were film discussions with Louis B. Mayer and others, and on 19 July Stravinsky heard a radio broadcast of Shostakovich's 'Leningrad' Symphony. He completed the *Four Norwegian Moods* on 18 August, the full score of the *Circus Polka* on 5 October, and the first movement of the new Symphony on 15 October.

In January and February 1943 he conducted performances of *Petrushka* for Ballet Theater in San Francisco and Los Angeles, then wrote the second movement of the Symphony between 15 February

[1]See Robert Craft, ed.: *Dearest Bubushkin* (London, 1985), p. 125.

and 17 March. Later in March he went to New York for six weeks, conducting *Petrushka* at the Metropolitan Opera House, and *Apollo* and *Petrushka* in concerts. Back in Los Angeles he composed the orchestral *Ode* between 19 May and 25 June, and the outer movements of the Sonata for two pianos in September–October. The *Ode* had its first performance in Boston on 8 October under Koussevitzky, and in December Stravinsky made a revision of the 'Sacrificial Dance' from *The Rite*.

On 13 January 1944 he conducted the first performances in Cambridge, Massachusetts, of the *Circus Polka* and the *Four Norwegian Moods*; he then went on to Chicago for a lecture and a concert before returning to Los Angeles, where on 11 February he completed the middle movement of the two-piano Sonata. On 18 April Nathaniel Shilkret asked him to compose *Babel* for a multi-composer sequence of settings from Genesis, but it is not clear when this work was composed. The *Scherzo à la russe* was finished in June or July; *Scènes de ballet* followed between June and late August, and then the *Elégie* for viola solo (by November) and the Kyrie and Gloria from the Mass (by December). And all the while the symphony in two movements was waiting for its third.

February 1945 Stravinsky spent in New York. At the beginning of the month he conducted four New York Philharmonic concerts, and on the 5th recorded with them his recent orchestral pieces: the *Norwegian Moods*, *Circus Polka*, *Ode* and *Scènes de ballet*. He conducted *Apollo* for CBS radio on the 14th, lectured in Philadelphia on the 21st, and on 1 March went to Montreal for a concert, returning from there to Los Angeles. In April he made a new *Firebird* suite, which he conducted at the Shrine Auditorium in Los Angeles the next month. Then in August he completed the Symphony in Three Movements, two months after the end of the war.

Stravinsky suggested[2] that there was a difference between the European half of the Symphony in C (the first two movements) and the American half, but if so, it is hard to feel that this was due to a new musical environment. He had been exposed to the sound of American orchestras since his first tour in 1925 (maybe there was an echo of them carried over into *Oedipus rex*, in which, later that year, he returned to the full orchestra for the first time since 1918), had been writing for them since the Symphony of Psalms, and had probably, since his 1935 tour, been having more practical experience with

[2]See White, p. 404.

American than with European ensembles. The changes caused by emigration came later, and in several stages, of which one of the first was a curious reversal to something like the pattern of his output during his first wartime exile, in Switzerland.

Once again there was a big piece which, quite unusually, took some years to complete, and alongside which other smaller compositions were achieved. This new *Les noces* was the Symphony in Three Movements, begun within two years of the completion of the Symphony in C, but not finished for more than three years. Another link with the 1914–18 period, in contrast with the years since, is in the quantity of small pieces, though the most obvious reason was different. In the late 1930s and early 1940s Stravinsky was several times engaged on film projects, and though the only one to come to fruition was the use of some of *The Rite* in the Disney *Fantasia* (apparently done with his permission, though his European works were not protected by US copyright until 1941, except where he had taken the precaution of appointing a nominal American 'editor'), he did write various pieces of would-be movie music that found homes in the various orchestral works of this period.[3]

The predominance of orchestral music is of course another difference from the Swiss period, with other reasons than the enticements of the film industry. Conducting now provided Stravinsky with a ready source of income (his willingness to make the long rail journey from Los Angeles to St Louis for a single concert in December 1941 is symptomatic), to be boosted by the recordings he was making regularly for Columbia from 1940 onwards. The orchestra, much more than the piano, was now his instrument. Also, his renewed closeness to the ballet world meant, during this phase of at least surface conventionality, an engagement with orchestral music.

The stimulus here seems to have come from the opportunity, now that both were on the same side of the Atlantic, to work more regularly with Balanchine. After the première performances of the Symphony in C he went straight to New York for *Balustrade*. 'Balanchine composed the choreography as he listened to my recording, and I could actually observe him conceiving gesture, movement, combination, composition. The result was a series of dialogues complementary to and co-ordinated with the dialogues of the music.'[4] It was even, as Stravinsky said on the same occasion, 'one of the most satisfactory visualizations of any of my works'. During this same period he made a wartime economy version of a number from *The Sleeping Beauty* for

---

[3]See section 6 of Appendix A.   [4]*Dialogues*, p. 48.

Balanchine, wrote the clownish *Circus Polka* at his behest for an elephant ballet, and conducted for his Ballet Theater company in California and New York. He responded to a commission from a chamber orchestra with what is effectively a ballet score in advance, *Danses concertantes* (1940–42), his only work between the symphonies except for the Tango apparently written as a potboiler; Balanchine duly choreographed the *Danses* in 1944. There were also the discussions with another old Ballets Russes ally, Massine, about a 'Donizetti ballet', presumably a follow-up to their 'Pergolesi ballet', and an unrealized idea that may have laid the seed for *Scènes de ballet*, which, in a manner altogether more uncomplicated and cheerfully entertaining than *Le baiser de la fée*, is something of a Tchaikovsky ballet.

But much of the concert music of this period too, and not only the amphibious *Danses concertantes*, has the feel of classical ballet, for reasons that may have less to do with Stravinsky's current opportunities and tastes than with memories going back half a century to the Mariinsky, memories that might have surfaced after another dislocation, especially at a time when Russia was under threat, and that might have regained relevance from the particular state his music had reached. Given his predilections for ostinato basses played *détaché*, for open texture, for ideas with a strong gestural identity, and for movement propelled by rhythm while the harmony is stationary, the return to a greater harmonic and metrical regularity during the 1930s was almost bound to bring a greater nearness to Tchaikovsky. The balletic associations of large parts of the Symphony in C, for instance, may therefore be almost coincidental, arising unbidden from a process of clarification.

Those of *Danses concertantes* were obviously intended, but it is significant that Stravinsky was able to move straight from symphony to abstract ballet carrying some of the same material with him, for the theme of the new work's 'Pas d'action', the first of three dance sections, was an outgrowth, from the Symphony's finale.[5] In its classical ballet form, its sprightly display of quirks and its transparent self-awareness it is also almost a fourth deal for *Jeu de cartes*, while the chamber scoring and the delight in small groupings make it Stravinsky's second, more relaxed Brandenburg. These are the predecessors to which the piece looks: if the presence of a march to open and close should recall *Renard*, it would be with shock that so much has changed, at the jump from village to Imperial stage. The

[5]See *SPD*, p. 368.

1 Scene in Fyodor Stravinsky's library, early 1890s. The future composer and his father are looking at something together; his mother and his brothers Gury and Roman are also there.

2 The family at Morges, 1915. Catherine, the composer's first wife, is overseeing their younger son Soulima's piano practice; their two older children, Theodore and Lyudmila (the only one to have noticed the camera), are near an older lady who is perhaps the nanny, Berthe. Stravinsky at this time was working on *Les noces*.

3 The composer at work in *Les Diablerets*, 1917.

4 Drawing of the composer by Picasso, dated 24 May 1920, nine days after the first performance of their ballet *Pulcinella*.

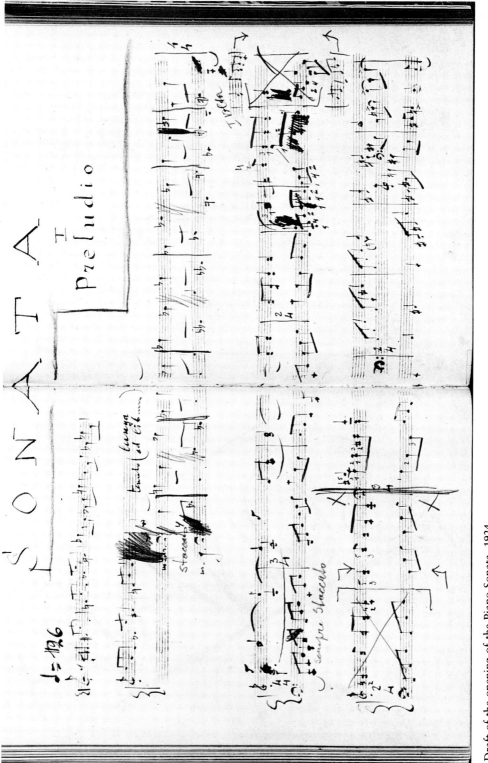

5 Draft of the opening of the Piano Sonata, 1924.

6 (*above*) Serge Lifar as Apollo and Alice Nikitina as Terpsichore in the first production of *Apollo*, 1928.

7 (*left*) The composer as gentleman, 1930s.

8 (*above right*) Tatiana Leskova, Marina Svetlova, Tamara Toumanova, Roman Jasinsky and Paul Patroff in *Balustrade*, the Balanchine ballet for which Stravinsky conducted his Violin Concerto, and which he described as 'one of the most satisfactory visualizations of any of my works'. New York, 1941.

9 (*right*) Nicholas Megallanes as Orpheus and Maria Tallchief as Eurydice, in the first production of *Orpheus*, New York, 1948.

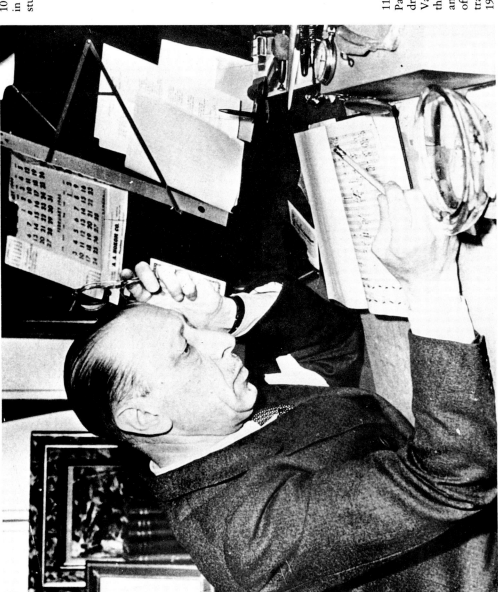

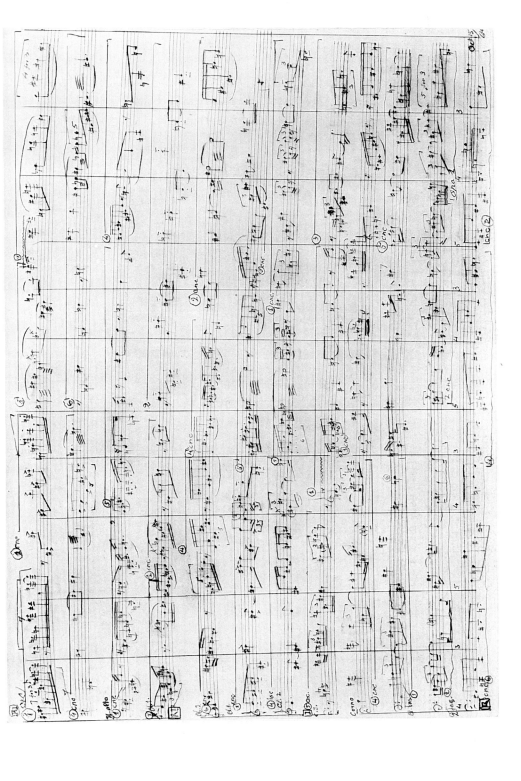

12 Rehearsing *Fireworks* at the Royal Festival Hall, London, during the 1960s

other dances concerted, after the lively 'Pas d'action', are a 'Thème varié' and a 'Pas de deux'. Once again as in *Jeu de cartes* the variations are musical and balletic at the same time: there are three quick sections between a slow theme and a slow coda, all essays in different kinds of movement. Then comes the 'Pas de deux', a form which had appeared in *Apollo* and *Le baiser de la fée*, and which Stravinsky approached with perhaps fewer misgivings, and certainly more affection, than the sonata allegro.

If Stravinsky was becoming more Tchaikovskian in the Symphony in C and *Danses concertantes* (though not as Tchaikovskian as he became in *Scènes de ballet*), he made Tchaikovsky a little Stravinskian in his crisp Bluebird arrangement, and in the same year of 1941 did something of the same for the US national anthem. On a scale of unlikelihood the *Four Norwegian Moods* are perhaps only a little further along: Norway was not so far away for one born on the Baltic, and of course there had been the Grieg arrangement of 1910. If, nevertheless, it is hard to imagine Stravinsky having embarked on this project without the incentive of a film commission, that only makes the unmistakable personality of the music the more remarkable. It is very much a choreographic personality, a matter of neatly executed metre, of ideas alive with movement, of melody cleanly set off against ostinato accompaniment, even of caesuras, in the first movement, to punctuate different episodes of dancing, all as if this were a suite from a lost *Peer Gynt* ballet. Besides that, the placing and scoring of chords, to achieve the utmost light, is completely characteristic, as is the diatonic dissonance, however mild the shock.

It was the mildness that so incensed Pierre Boulez and other young composers at the first Paris performance in 1945,[6] and maybe the work's title did not help, especially in its French form of 'Impressions norvégiennes', with its intimations of dawn mists over the fjord. Even by the time of the first performance Stravinsky was trying to mitigate this effect by saying that what he meant by 'mood' was 'a mode, a form or manner of style',[7] so that these are Norwegian pieces in the same ironic sense that the Symphony in C is a symphony in C. There may be a touch of special pleading here, though this and the *Circus Polka* were the first works he titled in English, and the slightly unfortunate result in the case of the *Moods* may also be a record of problems with what was his fourth language, after Russian, French and German. In any event, his judgement of his second great Parisian scandal seems just: 'once the *violent* has been accepted, the *amiable*, in turn, is no longer

[6]See *SSC II*, p. 347.   [7]See White, p. 415.

tolerable.'[8] But he refused to learn his lesson. Amiability, into which the frolicsomeness of the Capriccio and the Violin Concerto had turned to mark so much of the music of the early 1940s, remained strong right up to and into *Agon*.

The particular calmness of the Norwegian, or 'Norwegian', music may have been conditioned by its intended function as background, for there is a similar quality of grisaille in the *Ode* – a similar orchestral sound, too, with four horns prominent amid an otherwise completely standard ensemble. The horns have a picturesque utility in the middle movement of this triptych, apparently written for a hunting scene in a *Jane Eyre* film; they also contribute to the glow of the outer movements, which are closer to the solemn chants of 'Cantique' and the Symphonies of Wind Instruments, to which work this was a delayed successor in the line of Stravinsky's *tombeaux*, being dedicated to the memory of Natalie Koussevitzky, the conductor's wife. This time, though, the tribute was more professional than personal, having been commissioned by the widower, just as the viola *Elégie* – a two-part invention that makes a whole piece out of the spare, dark, low-voiced style that had appeared for instance in Ex. 17 and in the bassoon duets of the finale of the Symphony in C – was commissioned by Germain Prévost as a memorial to Alphonse Onnou (but again Stravinsky did at least know the object of his obsequies, since Onnou's Pro Arte Quartet had played his music).

The *Circus Polka*, proudly brazening out its associations in Stravinsky's version for full orchestra, in its quotation from circus repertory and in its inscription 'composed for a young elephant', is very different in style, though again written for a moderate ensemble: the Symphony in Three Movements is the only work from the two decades between *Perséphone* and *Agon* to be scored for an orchestra of more than classical proportions. The mere existence of the elephant polka illustrates Stravinsky's eagerness to make money, vouched for by so many anecdotes that one suspects a feint to draw attention away from other reasons why he might need to compose. The piece shows too, in such a different way from that of the *Norwegian Moods*, his equally celebrated inability not to leave a mark on whatever he touched. But it also suggests how quickly the patrician European composer, with his austere expression and his suits, was being overlaid by a rather different persona (this most photographed of composers seems to have been always smiling in his sixties, seventies and eighties, never in his thirties, forties and fifties), one ready to tackle all kinds of

[8] *SSC II*, p. 347.

commissions, responding to challenges, whether noble or not, with the same glee.

With the decisive exception of the *Circus Polka*, the works composed in 1940–43 – the *Danses concertantes*, *Norwegian Moods* and *Ode* – are among Stravinsky's most quiet-tempered, almost as if muffled, while their possible counterweight in the far more assertive, strenuous Symphony in Three Movements remained unachieved. The war may have been having an effect: an immediate practical effect in the depression of musical activity (Stravinsky's conducting appearances were rarer after the United States entered the war at the end of 1941, and both the *Norwegian Moods* and the *Circus Polka* had to wait for their first performances), and a personal effect on one who followed the events of the war closely and with renewed feeling for his home country.[9] That he should have listened to Shostakovich's 'Leningrad' Symphony, after writing off Soviet music in the 1920s and 1930s,[10] is one sign of the (temporary) change. Another was his wish – wholly extraordinary and uncharacteristic in the man whose most famous pronouncement was that music is 'essentially powerless to *express* anything at all'[11] – to associate the Symphony in Three Movements with 'this our arduous time of sharp and shifting events, of despair and hope, of continual torments, of tension, and at last cessation and relief'.[12] Yet another is the *Scherzo à la russe*, a cheer for the Red Army as the war began to go their way, if typically odd as it remembers the gasping accordions of *Petrushka*. This was another instance too of Stravinsky's financial astuteness, using music that had been written for a film to make a piece that could have a double life in jazz and symphony concerts.

Two other works of the later war years show, like this *Scherzo*, a livelier sort of gentleness: the Sonata for two pianos, and *Scènes de ballet*. The former, unlike all Stravinsky's other keyboard works since *Les cinq doigts*, was not written as repertory for himself, nor does it seem to have been commissioned, though that would be unusual. In tone, texture and scale it is a much lighter piece than the Concerto for the same duo, a play with Russian folk melodies (though the near-pentatonic music of the opening is Stravinsky's closest approach to gamelan). In *Scènes de ballet* the reference point is *The Nutcracker* rather than folksong: Stravinsky's wish to see it as 'a portrait of Broadway in the last years of the War'[13] is peculiarly, if not uniquely, wilful, despite the tango smooch at the start of the opening dance for

[9]See *SPD*, p. 556.   [10]See for example a 1935 letter to Ansermet in *SSC I*, p. 224.
[11]*An Autobiography*, p. 53.   [12]White, p. 430.   [13]*Dialogues*, p. 50.

the corps de ballet (Stravinsky himself devised an abstract scenario with male and female soloists). Like *Danses concertantes*, the piece is cast in conventional ballet forms and modes (even moods), and is seductive equally as ballet in the head.

The Symphony in Three Movements, finally emerging just after the end of the war to close this period, is not so much a matrix in the way of *Les noces* as an alternative world, just as distant from the superb frivolities of *Scènes de ballet* as it is starkly opposed to the tranquillity of the *Norwegian Moods* and *Ode*. It is also a quite different sort of symphony from the one in C. As the title may indicate, this is more a rhythmic than a tonal entity, its movements as much horological as chronological. This outbreak of dynamism, of jolting syncopations and metrical shifts, is quite unlike anything in Stravinsky's music since *Perséphone*, which the opening movement recalls too in its orchestral size and especially in its prominent piano part, another contribution to that particularly Stravinskian repertory, initiated by *Petrushka*, where the piano is not quite a soloist yet much more than another part of the orchestral machine.

There is again the sense of it as perpetuating the sound of the composer at work, as if there were a part of the score that has not yet been completed, even after three years, that remains in the composer's hands. Stravinsky's experience, as a ballet composer, of the piano as a rehearsal instrument is also at issue here, as in *Les noces*: every performance is a rehearsal, a making rather than a conveyance of something already made. At the same time the clangour of the piano within the tutti, most of all in the strident main material of the first movement, at once clenches the harsh metal sonorities and defines them as Stravinskian, as a Stravinskian return volley of a Soviet sound world (the recent listening to Shostakovich had not been for nothing: none of Stravinsky's listening was for nothing) that itself could not have existed without *The Rite of Spring*. The French qualities in Stravinsky now fall away, and if the language continues its sway over his titles for the moment, that is only because it was the lingua franca of well-born Eastern Europe: there is nothing very French musically in *Scènes de ballet*, not to mention the *Scherzo à la russe*. The works of the Second World War constitute rather another Russian period, beholden less to folksong (except in the Sonata) than to Soviet music and Tchaikovsky, to steel factories and the Mariinsky.

Both of these latter Russian aspects are represented in the Symphony, for its slow movement – the idea that it was written for the apparition of the Virgin in *The Song of Bernadette*[14] is almost unbelievable – is a

[14]See White, pp. 430–31.

gentle dance more on D major than in it, removing the heavier instruments (trumpets, trombones, timpani) as the Larghetto of the preceding symphony had done, and replacing the piano sub-soloist by a harp, in harmonies and cascades quite different from the dry monotones and recitatives the instrument was soon to bring to *Orpheus*. The other, internal contrast is with the speed, pulsation and tutti orchestration of the symphony's outer movements. Only *The Rite* is comparable in sustained instrumental density and clamour, and the fierce harmonic language is announced right at the beginning:

Ex. 20
Symphony in Three Movements: I

The opening gesture is like that of the Symphony in C in gathering an upsurge of energy – the earlier symphony does this by repeating a note in crescendo, the present one by its rampant glissando over-reaching the octave – to place what might have been, perhaps should have been, a tonal dominant on a high ledge. But this time the unstable equilibrium is even more hazardous: the A flat comes in a high register, awkward for the instruments, and what it instigates is not a melodic subject but a march of chords, an anti-tonal triumph of the octotonic scale (the main form here being A flat–B flat–B–D flat –D–E–F–G), the source of chords having a minor third in the treble and a major third duplicated in the bass to mimic the sound of bells,[15] though here they would have to be a ring of cracked bells. These few bars provide the basic material and the basic sound for both the outer movements, of which the first works more by alternation with less tempestuous music than by sonata rules, and the second, with both piano and harp, has a variety of episodes which seem to be there only to frustrate and delay the dinning close.

The Symphony in Three Movements may have had to be so noisy to shut out the curiosities that were contemporary with it: the elephant dance and the Russian jazzband scherzo, the Nordic modes and the Tchaikovskian ballet scenes. If ever there was a time – and if ever there was a composer – for a treatment of the Tower of Babel story, this was it, and this was him. Yet *Babel*, however apt the choice for his contribution to Shilkret's *Genesis* collection, is only a short sketch of a response to the task. It begins promisingly enough, with a reliving of the opening of *The Firebird* suitably joined by the rustic woodwind of *The Rite*, but the arrival of an orator (briefly displaced by a men's chorus chanting the words spoken by God) is no happier here than it was in *Perséphone*, of which this five-minute cantata forms a small male shadow. In both works there is a feeling that the music is not in touch with the words, not listening to them. Also, the choral writing does not spring the words alive by 'wrong' quantities and accentuations in Stravinsky's usual way, maybe because God sings a different song, maybe just because this was his (Stravinsky's) first setting in English. Nevertheless, he had, with Shilkret's help, stumbled on a genre (or perhaps remembered, after so many years since *Zvezdoliki*), a genre of musical icon distinct from the liturgies of psalms and mass, and one that was to grip most of the music of his last composing decade.

[15]See however Andriessen and Schönberger, p. 274.

20

The mass of *Orpheus*

In October 1945 Stravinsky played the *Duo concertant* with Szigeti in New York, and then returned to Los Angeles, where *Babel* had its first performance under Werner Janssen on 18 November. Thirteen days later he completed the *Ebony Concerto* for jazzband, and on 28 December he was granted US citizenship. During another month in New York, in January–February 1946, he conducted the New York Philharmonic in the first performance of the Symphony in Three Movements on 24 January, and made recordings of this work as well as *Fireworks*, the *Firebird* suite and the Pastorale (Szigeti plus wind). There were also concerts in Baltimore, Cambridge and Boston before he left for Miami, going from there by air to Havana to conduct. On the way home, in March, he gave further concerts in Dallas and San Francisco; he was not, therefore, at the first performance of the *Ebony Concerto*, given in New York on 25 March by Woody Herman's band under Walter Handl.

In July he conducted in Mexico City again, and on 8 August he completed the Concerto in D for strings; the same month he recorded the *Ebony Concerto* in Hollywood. In October he revised *Petrushka* for a slightly smaller orchestra, and on the 20th began a new ballet, *Orpheus*. In December he went to Montreal for concerts, going via Chicago, where he and Vera visited an exhibition of Turner, Hogarth and Constable on the 5th.[1] From Montreal they went to New York, where Stravinsky recorded the Symphony of Psalms, and at the end of the month they left for Cleveland. Concerts there, and in Philadelphia and Buffalo, followed, before Stravinsky returned to Los Angeles, and so missed another première, that of the Concerto in D in Basle under Paul Sacher on 27 January 1947.

Late in April he made a brief visit to New York for a performance (at Dumbarton Oaks) and recording of the Concerto in E flat. On 17 June, his sixty-fifth birthday, he went with Huxley to a performance of Britten's *The Rape of Lucretia*; eleven days later there came a

---

[1] So Vera's diary in *Dearest Bubushkin*, p. 138. In *SPD* (p. 396), however, the crucial encounter with Hogarth's *Rake's Progress* series is dated to 2 May 1947.

request from William Schuman for a quartet for the Juilliard.[2] He wrote a Little Canon for Nadia Boulanger's sixtieth birthday on 16 September 1947, and also that month made recordings of the Divertimento and *Danses concertantes*, besides completing *Orpheus* on the 23rd.

After the war the Stravinskys could have returned to Europe. But they had acquired a circle of friends in Los Angeles, including old Ballets Russes cronies (the Bolms, the Bermans), movie people (the Edward G. Robinsons) and social notables (Baroness d'Erlanger, Sir Charles and Lady Mendl: on 17 April 1946, according to Vera's diary, 'Lady Mendl comes with a child and a madman'),[3] a circle joined soon after the war by Aldous Huxley and his wife. Also, America was more conducive to composition: the Concerto in D for strings (1946) was Stravinsky's only European commission in the two decades between *Perséphone* and the *Canticum sacrum*, and by the mid-1940s he had taken on not only the outer dress of Americanism (the swing bands of the Praeludium, *Scherzo à la russe* and *Ebony Concerto*) but also some of the inner substance – though if his music of this period seems to come from the same new world as that written at the same time by Copland, Carter, Dahl and Berger, that is at least partly because their music, as much as that of Shostakovich, Prokofiev and Kabalevsky in the Soviet Union, had been born out of his, with of course, in the case of the American composers, the favour of Nadia Boulanger as midwife.

What was perhaps more important was that he had found, if not a home (there could be no home after 1917), then a comfortable resting place, and one that he could share, as had not been possible in France, with the woman he loved. America, perhaps, meant Vera, as France had meant a life of shuttling between wife and mistress, and his pleasure in America – as evidenced by the new friendliness to the camera, the musical amiability and the gift of the 'Star-Spangled Banner' arrangement – was in part his pleasure in her. There would be no return across the Atlantic until more than six years after the war, in 1951 for the première of *The Rake*. Meanwhile he and Vera took US citizenship, and there was another present to America in the *Ebony Concerto*.

These two adjacent concertos, in D and in ebony, are again on the scale of 'Dumbarton Oaks' and *Danses concertantes*, and are both in three short movements played fast–slow–fast. But there all re-

---

[2] See *SSC I*, p. 328.   [3] *Dearest Bubushkin*, p. 136.

semblances end. The *Ebony Concerto* is not so much a clarinet concerto as a swing concerto grosso with lead clarinet, the ensembles of saxophones and trumpets, the rhythm section and the duo of guitar and harp being just as energetically involved (the harp is a stranger here, though not in Stravinsky's music of this period, where it displays a range from hieratic Orphic lyre to impressionist fountain or belated recollection of the *gusli*, and this precise guitar–harp duo was to return in the Four Songs of 1953–4 to invoke the last association). Commissioned by Herman, the piece was Stravinsky's last salute to a musical world which, like his own, owed its existence to a mèsalliance of the primal and the sophisticated.

That is not quite the way of the Concerto in D. Unlike Stravinsky's only other piece for string orchestra, *Apollo*, it is laid out in the regular five parts, and though the music is characteristically sharp on choice textures, it is also drier in sound, extending the new chromatic language of the recent symphony. Each of its movements springs off from the abrasive discord of a minor ninth, located each time on one of the notes of the D major or minor triad (see Ex. 21). The opening movement delays the arrival of the keynote promised in the title until the very end of the wire-taut phrase, and then immediately re-linquishes it: as in the first movement of the symphony, though with a change from march to gigue (perhaps Stravinsky was remembering *Apollo* after all, its pervasive iambs turned alternately backwards into trochees), the music is rushed by the search for a tonic. The memory at the back of the rapturous Arioso is surely that of a balletic waltz, while the finale is a galop, and also Stravinsky's only designated rondo (though typically the form is more breached than observed, the piece being more a dance with trios).

But the references and the parodies (is the slow movement a parody or an affectionate homage?) are receding while the abstract creation of music out of intervals advances. Or even the creation of music out of single notes. The opening of the piece is a lesson in how Stravinsky can fire just one note with the energy to kick off a whole movement, giving it tension by means of accent, repetition and a characteristic yoking of arco and pizzicato tone. And as all these incipits show, repetition of crucial notes, of crucial intervals, becomes a recurrent way of lodging, implanting ideas that can then be subject to protraction and transformation. Once again the Concerto in D proposes a different sense of what it means musically to be 'in', pushing its notes into place against the jarring adversity of neighbours. It also affirms, as the Symphony of Psalms or the quartet pieces or so many other works had done, that Stravinsky's

Ex. 21

a) Concerto in D for strings: I

Ex. 21 cont.

b) Concerto in D for strings: II

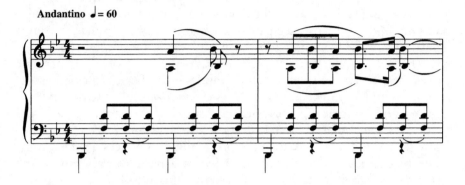

c) Concerto in D for strings: III

thinking was implicitly combinatorial and interval-based (rather than key-rooted) long before it became explicitly serial.

Orpheus, the next ballet for Balanchine after *Jeu de cartes*, continues these intimations. It does so, for example, in an angularity of melodic writing suggestive of Schoenbergian octave displacement (as already evident in Ex. 21a and b), in a bareness of texture, and in a concentration on small cells in processes of change: the trumpet solo at the end of the 'Dance of the Angel of Death', besides being a trailing fanfare, is a little serial invention on the A major or minor triad. That these had all been features of Stravinsky's Swiss–Russian music is occasionally brought right to the surface, as when, in the epilogue, one might begin to feel that the 1917 horn canons were not lost but entombed here. More generally, of course, the classical subject matter evokes returns to elements of classical style Stravinsky had developed in the 1920s and 1930s. The Phrygian E minor of the opening and closing sections (though the ballet ends, like its precedent Concerto, in D major) follows the same path into Hellenism that *Apollo* and *Perséphone* had taken, and Orpheus's solo to charm the furies, his 'Air de danse' for reeds, harp and strings, brings into a serene fusion the

141

composer's strain of Bachian *siciliana* slow movement and his inheritance from the Gallic muse.

Orpheus's journey is thus for Stravinsky a last lingering return to France – and to Cocteau in the device of the angel, inherited from his Orphic film. The work seems to exist in a twilight glimmer, coming partly from the dominance of harp and string tone, the harp being Orpheus's lyre-substitute. But gentleness comes too from the generally slow tempos, from the use of only a moderate orchestra (the orchestra of the Symphony in C and *Four Norwegian Moods*, but with just two horns) and from the high proportion of metrical regularity, not least in three passages placed in a stately 4/2, whose breves give a surely intentional antique look to the score. Only two dances are fast, and one of those, for the menacing furies, is a paradoxical 'agitato in piano', though the other, for the Bacchantes tearing Orpheus to pieces, is a decisive rupture to the muted, perhaps forcibly muted, fabric. The story unfolds as if in a dream, how Orpheus, lamenting over the death of Eurydice, is conducted to Hades by an angel and threatened there by the furies, how he seduces them with music and is granted Eurydice, how he takes off the bandage that has been placed over his eyes for the journey back to the earth, and how he thereby loses her, is violently dismembered, and then taken up to heaven by Apollo. This is not a rite of Orpheus but a remembrance, and at the end, when the return of the prelude counts for more than the new brass parts here and the easing into D, it seems that the dream could all slowly begin again.

Just before *Orpheus* Stravinsky had been practising something of the same orchestral restraint on his older music, making new versions of the *Firebird* suite and *Petrushka*, all of which activity, with the new ballet, interrupted the composition of what is very definitely a rite, and the story of a saving sacrifice foreshadowed by Orpheus and Persephone: the Mass for choir and a decet of reeds and brass (1944–8). This was the occasion for one of Stravinsky's best stories, that he discovered a pile of Mozart masses in a secondhand bookshop (useful places these: cf. *Oedipus rex* and St Francis) and decided to write something contrary to such 'rococo–operatic sweets of sin',[4] as contrary as his own mass undoubtedly is. Written for a church of which he was not a member (the text is in Latin), and for resources that would be rarely assembled for liturgical celebrations, this is though another rite for the concert hall, in the line of the Symphony of Psalms and the Symphonies of Wind Instruments, two other works in which winds are idealized voices making their own wordless chant.

[4]*Expositions*, p. 61.

The psalm symphony is a particularly near neighbour. The Mass similarly envisages children's voices in the upper parts, and similarly uses the instrumental complement as another, different choir, more often prompting, or punctuating, or adjacent to the voices than doubling and accompanying:

Ex. 22
Mass: Kyrie

This, from the opening, is perfect octotony, with only the cadential B flat in the tenor part foreign to the scale A flat–A–B–C–D–E flat–F –F sharp. But clearly it is octotony of a very different sort from that of the Symphony in Three Movements, or indeed anything earlier in Stravinsky's output. The initial wind chord, as much an image of resonance as a harmony, leaves the tonality ambiguous. The choir enters with rotations of the A flat major triad, but never with the tonic in the bass, then moves rather to C minor, but never with the fifth, which is absent from this form of the octotonic mode, and similarly the final hint that E flat after all might be the tonic cannot be ratified by the fifth. The music seems to exist both after the exact definitions of major–minor harmony have dissolved and before they have yet crystallized, to be contemporary at once with Schoenberg and with Josquin. That, along with the absence of any onward harmonic or

rhythmic urge, is its timelessness, that particularly exquisite achievement of the typically Stravinskian interfolding of ancient and contemporary. But if time is reversible, so too is space, as the perfect balancing
phrase slips the previous treble line down to the bass. There is a
stillness to this music, even when the singers are racing through the
items of the creed in bouncing triads (a direct return to the earlier
Credo of 1932), a glowing, open stillness quite unlike that of the
mummed *Orpheus* – something that might be grace.

21

An American opera

On 26 September 1947, three days after finishing *Orpheus*, Stravinsky wrote to his publisher Ralph Hawkes asking him to make contact with W. H. Auden as prospective librettist for an opera 'based on William Hogarth's famous masterpiece *The Rake's Progress*'.[1] Auden clearly responded at once and positively,[2] and by mid-November composer and librettist were sitting together at a performance of *Così fan tutte* in Los Angeles, during a week together working on a scenario (Stravinsky had earlier seen the other two Mozart – da Ponte comedies during this season given by the San Francisco Opera). He also completed a new version of the Symphonies of Wind Instruments on 25 November.

On 11 December he wrote the string quartet prelude to the graveyard scene in the third act, even though there was as yet no libretto and nothing else of the work was written until the following May. Possibly he was 'inspired by his vision of the drama';[3] but it is conceivable too that this was the failed beginning of a response to the Juilliard commission. On 30 January he conducted private readings of the new Wind Symphonies with film studio musicians, and in February he was in San Francisco and Mexico City for concerts. He finished the Mass on 15 March, shortly before more concerts with the Los Angeles Philharmonic. Then in April came a month in Washington and New York, including concerts in both cities. This was also an opportunity to consult with Auden, and with Kallman, who had joined the writing team. During the same visit Stravinsky conducted the first performance of *Orpheus*, given by Ballet Society at New York City Center on 28 April, in Balanchine's choreography and with Isamu Noguchi's designs.

The day after his arrival back in Los Angeles, on 8 May, he began work on *The Rake's Progress*, from the start of the first vocal number (the Prelude was added at the end). In July he conducted in Denver, and went there to performances of *Così* and *The Mother of Us All*,

[1] *SSC III*, p. 318.   [2] See *SSC I*, p. 299.   [3] *SPD*, p. 398.

the second opera by Virgil Thomson and Gertrude Stein. More operatic evenings followed in Los Angeles in October: *L'elisir d'amore* and *Don Giovanni*. Also this month, on the 27th, the Mass had its first performance, at La Scala, Milan, under Ansermet: this was another première Stravinsky missed.

He completed the first act of the opera on 16 January, and a week later left to prepare a concert in Houston, going on from there to New York, and another month on the east coast in February–March. During this period he conducted in Cambridge, Boston, New York, Newark, Brooklyn and Urbana, and made recordings of *Orpheus*, the Mass, the *Pater Noster* and the *Ave Maria*. There was another concert in Denver on the way home, and more visits to *L'elisir d'amore* and *Figaro* in Los Angeles in April–May.

On 1 June the Stravinsky household was joined by Robert Craft, who remained to the end, and whose function as the composer's musical assistant during these last twenty-two years was far-reaching. Craft's own successive memoirs[4] movingly suggest how the reasons for this have been a continuing, even deepening, mystery to the person who, apart from Stravinsky himself, was most closely involved. The two men had first met in the spring of 1948, when Stravinsky, following correspondence with Craft, had appeared at one of the aspiring young conductor's concerts, directing the new version of the Symphonies of Wind Instruments; thereafter there had been further meetings, leading to this point where Craft was invited to, in effect, join the family. Stravinsky had used other musicians as sounding-boards before: Lourié in the 1920s, Dahl in the earlier 1940s. But the relationship with Craft was personally closer, more long-lasting, and more various in its implications. Craft shared in the preparing and conducting of Stravinsky's concerts, shaped both voices contributing to their books of conversations, encouraged him on his serial path in the 1950s and 1960s, and even steered him towards particular creative projects. More immediately, with *The Rake* in progress, his role may have been to guide Stravinsky in his embrace of anglophone culture.

On 16 June Stravinsky conducted *Histoire du soldat* in Los Angeles. The next month he worked up the *Lied ohne Name* for bassoon duet from sketches of 1916; later in the year there was yet another visit to the San Francisco Opera *Don Giovanni* in Los Angeles, to Britten concerts and to Britten's *Albert Herring*, and to

---

[4]*Stravinsky: The Chronicle of a Friendship 1948–1971*; SSC I, pp. 327–70; *Stravinsky: Glimpses*.

another event with more distant repercussions in his output: 'Igor and I go to a beautiful concert of Medieval and Renaissance music'.[5]

Between February and May 1950 Stravinsky made an unusually prolonged stay in New York, with an excursion in late March for concerts in Urbana and St Louis. He also went to *The Beggar's Opera* at the Juilliard School and recorded *Apollo*. Act II of *The Rake* would seem to have been finished before this trip. The rest of the year he spent at home, except for concerts in Aspen in August and in San Francisco in December. In October he saw Menotti's *Medium* and *Telephone* in Los Angeles, and late in the month reached the end of the graveyard scene, leaving only the final madhouse scene and the epilogue to be done. These were duly completed by 7 April, after more concerts in Havana the month before.

In July, during the interim between the completion of the opera and its first performance, Stravinsky began a new work with a song for soprano and instruments that became the second movement of the Cantata. The next month he travelled by boat from New York to Naples on his first visit to Europe since 1939. From Naples he went to Milan for rehearsals of the opera, and from there to Venice, where the piece had its première at the Teatro La Fenice on 11 September, Stravinsky conducting. The director was Carl Ebert and the designer Gianni Ratto, with a cast comprising Robert Rounseville as Tom Rakewell, Elisabeth Schwarzkopf as Anne Trulove, Otakar Kraus as Nick Shadow, Jennie Tourel as Baba the Turk, Rafael Ariè as Trulove, Hugues Cuénod as Sellem, Nell Tangeman as Mother Goose, and Emanuel Menkes as the Keeper of the Madhouse.

The unique full-length operas of generalist composers – *Fidelio*, *Pelléas et Mélisande*, *Moses und Aron* – are often summations, if not consummations. But, whatever a Stravinskian summa would be, *The Rake's Progress* is not it. It is rather a particular answer to a particular puzzle, that of what it might mean to write a Mozartian opera bang in the middle of the twentieth century. It contains, of course, numerous traits having some correspondence in other works; it is also Stravinskian in every bar. But it is, as much as anything he wrote, one of a kind, and it leers out rather oddly from the chronological sequence of his works between two cool sacred pieces, the Mass and the Cantata.

There is no evidence that Mozart was in Stravinsky's mind before he wrote to Hawkes on 9 November 1947 asking for scores of the three

[5]*Dearest Bubushkin*, p. 147.

da Ponte comedies and *Die Zauberflöte*, the 'source of inspiration for my future opera'.[6] However, it is hard to believe that what he saw staring back at him from the walls of the Chicago Art Institute was not already a set of Mozartian characters and situations waiting dumbly. And perhaps he was looking for them – *The Rake's Progress* was one of his very few works not commissioned – under the spur of the growing reputation of Britten, with whom he shared a publisher after joining Boosey & Hawkes in 1947[7] (the company had recently acquired the Edition Russe de Musique catalogue), and whose reputation as an opera composer had rapidly established itself with *Peter Grimes* (1945), *The Rape of Lucretia* (1946) and *Albert Herring* (1947). Stravinsky had been to a performance of *Lucretia* (which harks back to Baroque opera and revives simple recitative, though accompanied by a piano), three months before announcing his own plans for an opera. *The Rake* could easily have started partly as a rejoinder to *The Rape*, rather as the Symphony in Three Movements could have been a rejoinder to Shostakovich: Schoenberg's remarks about *Oedipus rex* were truer than he probably knew, in drawing attention to a spirit of antagonism that had stimulated works since *Pulcinella*. But the intensest antagonism is addressed across the years to Mozart, and as in *Pulcinella* it is the antagonism of a passionate urge to possess, the motive force of a Don Giovanni (with a thousand and three musical conquests behind him) who has stepped outside his opera in order to have some sport with the characters who remain.

Only in a chronological sense can the opera be seen as a consummation even of Stravinsky's neo-classical period (or perhaps one might more justly call it his 'inverted-triad period'). Because it attaches itself so zealously to one particular work of the past, *Don Giovanni*, it is far more intimately enmeshed in that past than is anything else in Stravinsky's output. The orchestra is precisely the same, except for the very rare use of piccolo or cor anglais. The form, at the beginning, is a Mozartian sequence of concerted numbers and dry recitative with harpsichord accompaniment. The texturing of voices and orchestra begins Mozart-fashion too: the way the instruments, and especially the woodwind instruments, establish, support and curtail a musical–dramatic atmosphere. The work is also full of Mozartian clichés, such as the arpeggiating horns at the end of Tom's first aria.

And yet of course, as always with Stravinsky, the fake is clearly exhibited as a fake. Not only is the illusion limited once more by particular performing conventions of its time – modern harpsichord

[6]See *SPD*, p. 397.   [7]See *SSC III*, pp. 309–458.

and wind instruments, strict tempos – in ways Stravinsky is unlikely to have intended, but also – and this he surely did intend – the Mozart model is subject to distortion, and progressively so. The field of play is opened up to encompass all the time since Mozart, including especially the times of Rossini, Donizetti and early Verdi: the heroine Anne moves into their world, out of Mozart's, in her solo scene at the end of the first act, and Stravinsky himself drew attention, surely thinking of the introduction to Act II scene 2, to a crib from *Don Pasquale*.[8] He also pointed out self-references, to *Apollo* and *The Nightingale*,[9] and of course the whole piece is blatantly of the mid-twentieth century rather than the late eighteenth in its retroversion: like nothing else it exemplifies, and even celebrates, the central paradox in neo-classicism, that the reproduction of past manners is only very marginally a feature of classical style (in that respect it has less in common with *Don Giovanni* than with Mozart's strict imitations of Bach). Right at the start, too, there is a warning that Mozart's will not be the only past at issue here, for the work opens not with a Mozartian overture but with a single-page Prelude, mostly for brass quartet, suggesting much more the toccata from Monteverdi's *Orfeo*, and hinting that this will be another treatment of that myth.

Arcadia remains when the opera proper begins. The first ensemble comes by a correctly Mozartian settling from the E major of the Prelude into A major, and there are correctly eighteenth-century people on stage: Trulove (bass) in his garden, with his daughter Anne (soprano) and her intended husband Tom Rakewell (tenor). But the introductory music is a classicized symphony of wind instruments, for double-reed quartet, and when Anne and Tom begin to sing, they sound as if they are in a masque, recalling the Persephonic rite of spring. This fragile contrivance, of retroversion within retroversion (Stravinsky looking back to Mozart, Bach and Monteverdi; Tom and Anne looking back to the classical Golden Age; A major looking back to Mixolydian E), is disturbed when Trulove enters the ensemble, to voice doubts about the couple's sincerity. By extension he is also doubting the sincerity of the music, since this is what makes them – and him too, so the doubts are paradoxically self-undercutting, as they were in *Mavra*.

Then suddenly dry recitative arrives to bring this unease into the certainty, if illusory certainty, of a known world, that of *opera buffa*. Trulove has secured Tom a position; he, however, has other ideas, and in an accompagnato (more an arioso: Stravinsky, preferring dance to

---

[8]*Expositions*, p. 61.   [9]See *Dialogues*, p. 34.

pantomime in his ballets, similarly resists the rhetoric of eighteenth-century accompanied recitative) and aria he sings his credo. Human fortunes, being predestined (as indeed his seems to be, hurtling along the Mozartian railroad of related keys into F major), cannot be altered by effort, and so he will trust to luck. But not entirely: there is an anomaly – an effort at least of intention – in his exuberant passivity. 'I wish I had money,' he says, and this is an anomaly too in the musical text, since the line is spoken.

Here is the devil's opportunity, and the devil duly appears in the form of Nick Shadow (baritone). A harpsichord flurry introduces him and another passage of recitative, in which he announces that he comes with good news. But first Tom must call the others. When they have arrived, Shadow reveals in accompanied recitative (so marked in the score, though again this is almost an aria) that Tom has inherited wealth from an uncle. Everyone is grateful (B flat major quartet), and Anne and Tom rejoice that now their future together is sure (however, the tonality is becoming less certain), but Shadow advises that Tom must immediately accompany him to London in order to sort out his affairs, and everyone agrees, the ensemble thereupon ending in B flat. In a brief dry recitative Shadow takes Trulove aside, leaving Tom and Anne together for a farewell G major duettino, a gentle minuet. When Shadow returns, returning the music to recitative, Tom asks him to state what payment he will expect as his man, but Shadow puts off the settlement for a year and a day. Tom once more is compliant, and in arioso assures Trulove that he will send for Anne when his affairs are in order. A short orchestral link leads to the scene's closing terzettino, back in A major, with the same three characters as in the opening trio, but now all of them on separate tracks. Tom rejoices in his luck, Anne in her love; and Trulove is still doubtful.

By the beginning of the second scene, though, much has changed. After the country, town. This is Mother Goose's brothel in London, and an exuberant choral paean to violence and seduction, the parts taken in alternation by roaring boys and whores. There follows Tom's hedonistic catechism, in response to Shadow and for the madam's benefit, when he gives the right cynical answers to all questions until the mention of love sends him off in an anguished chromatic outburst. Now he wants to go, 'before it is too late', but Shadow shows that it need never be too late, that the hours can be made to wind backwards, and there is a short reprise of the opening chorus. Shadow then, in simple recitative, introduces Tom, who sings a C sharp minor cavatina, a prayer to love. The whores, touched, sing in the same key, but then bend aside as their interest turns from the song to the singer.

Mother Goose, however, exercises her 'elder right', and there is a mock nuptial chorus, with a childlike savagery under its A major lilt. After that the act ends back in the country with a solo scena for Anne, in the garden of the first scene but now under moonlight. Again there is a double-reed introduction, then a full Donizettian number of accompagnato–aria–accompagnato–cabaletta. Anne voices her rivalling concerns, for Tom and for her father, and resolves to go to London without waiting to be called.

In the first scene of the second act Tom, at home in London, sings a substantial ternary-form aria of dissatisfaction with the changeless pursuit of changeless pleasure. He then speaks his second wish, to be happy. Again, as in the first act, Shadow thereupon enters with the continuo, and makes the proposal that his master should marry a fairground novelty, the bearded lady Baba the Turk. Why? Because, as he explains in a short patter song, this will demonstrate his independence from both duty and desire. He leaves Tom to ponder this in an aria while studying her picture (a direct approach, dramatically if not musically, to Tamino's portrait aria in *Die Zauberflöte*). Tom laughingly accepts the idea, and in the big G major duet-finale he and Shadow prepare for the wooing.

The scene then shifts to the outside of the house. It is autumn, and dusk, and C minor. Anne enters alone, and sings of her anxieties in an accompagnato and arioso (as the muse of the piece she rarely, and only then at the end, acknowledges the possibility of dry recitative). She is puzzled by the arrival of servants with packages, and then by that of a sedan chair, out of which Tom steps. In the ensuing duet he tells her that she must go back, but she insists she has nothing to fear here if he still loves her. Baba (mezzo-soprano), with bassoons, interrupts, ill-tempered at the unaccustomed and unexplained delay. Now to Anne all is clear. She and Tom sing a threnody to their love, while Baba continues her complaining: a beautiful, wistful and funny number that finds Tom and Anne treading carefully around parodic cliches of love duet and lament, in harmony that wants to put off the cadence for ever, against Baba's efforts, on a quite different time scale, to thrust an ending on the music (see Ex. 23). This is only one tiny instance of how the words and dramatic situations are so aptly made for *opera buffa*, and of how Stravinsky's *opera buffa* drifts away from its archetypes. At this point, however, it suddenly goes the way of Baba and of artifice. Anne leaves, and there begins a finale in stately sarabande rhythm and solid D major. After Tom has at last escorted his new wife from her sedan, she grants the eager townspeople (and the audience) a sight of her luxuriant beard.

Ex. 23

The Rake's Progress: Act II Scene 2

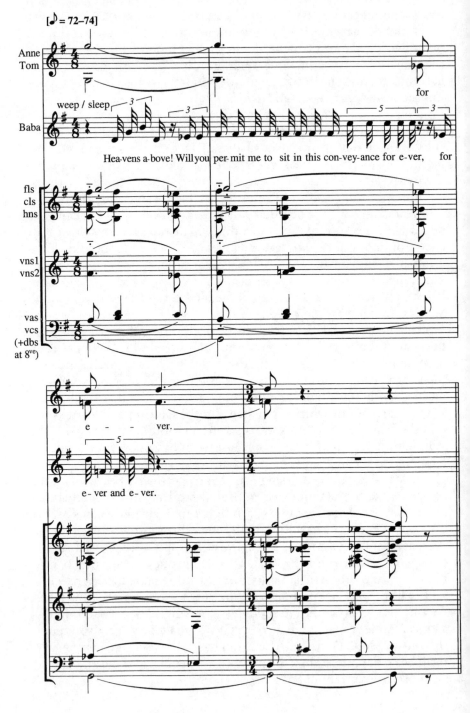

The last scene of the second act is set back inside the house, where Baba is gabbling away in an aria about all the trophies and curios she has accumulated during her theatrical career. Stopping to notice that Tom is not paying attention, she tries to coax him into life with a lumpish little unaccompanied ditty, then when that does not work storms into a big D minor aria of anger and frustration. After two strophes of this Tom places his wig over her face, silencing her, and then flings himself down on a sofa to sleep. Shadow wheels in a machine, to a toy-like G major accompaniment of ostinatos from a small orchestra of high clear woodwind and low horn and strings. Tom wakes, and speaks his third wish, that the dream he has just had may be true. Again the harpsichord cascade and Shadow, but the place of simple recitative in the opera is now lessening as the Mozartian pattern becomes one of the idylls that have been superseded. There is instead an excited passage of accompanied recitative and arioso in which Tom tells his dream of a machine that could make bread from stones. Sure enough, this is the very piece of gimcrack technology that Shadow has just brought in, and in a duet, more a non-duet, Tom exults in his contribution to philanthropy while Shadow makes sure the audience sees how easily fools may be hoodwinked. Shadow finally tells Tom they must go to demonstrate the machine to potential backers, and they cheerfully leave.

The cut to the third act, like that to the second scene, is abrupt. The setting is the same, and the silenced Baba is still in position, but now everything is covered with dust. The chorus have gathered here for a sale, since in the interim Tom has committed the capitalist sin of bankruptcy. Anne comes in, but nobody can tell her where Tom is. Then the auctioneer Sellem (tenor) arrives, a virtuoso of economics, and explains, with the exaggerated vocabulary of a music-hall master of ceremonies, that the auction will be a restoration of order. In his ensuing and wonderfully silly aria he sells three lots, of which the last is Baba, who, when he has pulled the wig from her head, sings the third strophe of her aria. Then Tom and his Shadow are heard singing a street cry from offstage; Anne's attention is caught, and the crowd prepare to be spectators at a new event, the confrontation of wife and betrothed. Baba tells Anne to take care of Tom; she will return to the stage. Tom and Shadow are heard again, and by now their street cry has become a nonsense song. In the stretto-finale (though there has been no break in the music since the preceding duet for Anne and Baba) Baba encourages Anne to go to Tom, and takes her leave. The scene then ends in the same bustling E major in which it began, in the same key and almost the same tempo as the Prelude. The entire auction scene has been a show within the show.

The quartet prelude to the next scene, slow and densely chromatic (more consistently so than anything hitherto in Stravinsky's output) could hardly be more different. It introduces a graveyard, at night. Tom and Shadow enter: Tom, in G minor, is fearful; Shadow, in the major, blithely singing to the ballad tune the two of them shared in the preceding scene, announces it is time for payment. Tom protests that he is penniless; Shadow counters that what he is after is not money but his master's soul, which will be forfeit on the stroke of midnight. But, showing again the devil's mastery of time, he stops the clock to allow Tom one last chance in a game of cards, played out over deceptive forking pathways in the harpsichord accompaniment's slow arpeggiations (and here suddenly the instrument has become something quite other than a continuo). As in *Histoire du soldat*, the hero cheats the devil with the assistance of the Queen of Hearts: it is hearing Anne's voice that reminds him of love – 'I wish for nothing else' is his fourth spoken desire – and so enables him to identify the card. It is Shadow who descends to hell, in an agitated B flat minor song, but as he goes he curses Tom with insanity. The Arcadian woodwind, an airy treble quartet, return as Tom duly sings his mad song, imagining himself Adonis.

The final scene is set in bedlam. Tom tells his fellow inmates that Venus is due to visit him; they respond with a chorus-minuet stating that hope, along with all other definitions, has been annihilated in the madhouse. Anne comes in, accepts from Tom her mythic role, and the two of them sing a love duet. She then gives him a lullaby, with just two flutes in accompaniment, charming the madmen too: from Venus she has turned into a female Orpheus. But she cannot bring Tom back. She leaves when her father comes for her, the two singing a duettino before they go. Tom wakes up, and in a florid lament at the loss of his beloved, briefly becomes Orpheus himself, then dies, and the madmen mourn him in A minor. Then, as in *Don Giovanni*, there is a sudden switch to the major for the epilogue, in which the five principals give the moral: 'For idle hands and hearts and minds the devil finds a work to do.'

Yet this is not the message of what has just been shown. The key words of the opera are those of return, of repetition, of restoration – words which are highlighted here almost as much as 'crossroads' is in *Oedipus rex*. Spring in the first scene is the renewal of the year. Shadow in the brothel scene has the knack of making time repeat itself. Tom advises Anne to go back from London. The bread-making machine will restore mankind's primal innocence. The auction is a mechanism to rectify imbalances in the orderly arrangement of wealth. Baba will return to the stage. Only Tom, the rake in progress, has no power of his own to go back, to make amends for the past: through his positivism, his belief only in hazard and money, he has lost that possibility. What could restore it to him is love, which is the devil's enemy precisely because it grants humanity supernatural power. Tom grasps failingly at love in the brothel scene, and it is his final hair's-breadth appeal to love that saves him his soul in the graveyard. Love can renew the initial state of affairs: the initial keys and luminous gentle wind colouring of the first scene, its classical metaphors, its enchanted family of father (unseen since that opening scene), daughter and son-in-law. But love acknowledged so late can only revivify an illusion, a madhouse facsimile. The rift of cynicism was too great to heal.

Artifice and illusion have, however, been the condition of the opera from the start, so that the message is repeated on this larger scale. The composer's passion for *opera buffa* comes too late, in the history of civilization, to create anything other than a replica. No secret has been made of this. In terms of form, the display of allusion and archaism is unusual even by Stravinsky's standards (a token is the presence of the harpsichord), and the libretto, like the music, is full of eighteenth-century phraseology and stock *opera buffa* motifs. As for the work's manner of expression, there is strangely little pleasure, strangely little Hogarthian relish and rollick, in an opera nominally about licentiousness. Tom never seems to be enjoying himself. Perhaps he is disqualified from doing so because he believes himself to be a pawn of fate: he has an inkling that words are being put into his mouth (the tragedy of Oedipus, of unawareness, has happened before this so-knowing opera begins). But the music too stifles rapture and sensuality: it is a parable, a sequence of painted scenes, at that distance from the flesh. It is too late for carnality. The tragedy of *The Rake's Progress* – and for all its wit and sprightliness it is a disturbing piece of theatre – is one that has affected its whole nature, that of having to strut out an existence in a world whose only beliefs are in facts, whose only judgements are validated by money. It is the tragedy of love disempowered.

22

New songs

After the first performance of *The Rake's Progress* Stravinsky went on to give concerts in Milan, Cologne (where he made his only recording of the Symphonies of Wind Instruments as well as his first of *Oedipus rex*), Baden-Baden, Munich, Geneva, Rome and Naples, the tour lasting until 21–2 November, when he flew from Rome to New York. Three days after landing he conducted *Le baiser de la fée* for New York City Ballet, and arrived back in Los Angeles only on 1 January 1952. There he resumed work on the Cantata with the sixth movement (the soprano–tenor duet) and then the fourth (for tenor solo), also in February attending Craft's rehearsals for a performance of the Schoenberg Suite for septet. There was a brief conducting visit again to Mexico City at the end of March, and in April he arranged the quartet Concertino for twelve instruments, before flying to New York and thence to Paris. There he conducted *Oedipus rex* with Cocteau narrating on 19 May; he also heard Boulez and Messiaen play the former's *Structures Ia* on 7 May, and gave other concerts in Paris and Brussels. In June he made his way back from Europe to Los Angeles by plane and car, and on 21 July he added the frame of the 'Lyke-Wake Dirge' to complete the Cantata.

The next day he began the Septet, of which the first movement was finished seventeen days later. In September he was present at more Schoenberg rehearsals under Craft, of the Serenade, and on 6 November he completed the second movement of the Septet, five days before conducting the first performances of the Cantata and the new Concertino in Los Angeles. In December he went to Cleveland and New York for performances, and to record the Symphony in C in the former city and the Cantata in the latter. The stay in the east was a long one. He finished the third movement of the Septet there, on 21 January, and attended the American première of *The Rake* at the Metropolitan on 14 February, recording the work in early March. Then, briefly back in Los Angeles, he rewrote for piano the cimbalom part in *Renard* for a performance on 30 March, leaving the next day for Havana and then Caracas. From there he went via New York to

Boston, arriving at the beginning of May to conduct *The Rake* at Boston University and to meet Dylan Thomas for talks about a new opera.

While awaiting the further development of this project, he wrote a set of three Shakespeare songs back in Los Angeles, the first finished on 7 September 1953 and the third on 6 October. But Thomas's death on 19 October put an end to the idea, and after being occupied with Los Angeles Philharmonic concerts in mid-November, Stravinsky sketched in early December a version of the fanfare for his next stage work, *Agon*. He then went again to the east, recording *Pulcinella* in Cleveland on 14 December, and the Octet, *Histoire du soldat* suite and Septet in New York on 26–7 January; he also conducted the first performance of the Septet at Dumbarton Oaks on 23 January. During brief periods back home – three weeks in February and a fortnight in March, interrupted by conducting engagements in Portland and Seattle – he composed the Song and the Prelude for a lapidary monument to the librettist he had lost, *In memoriam Dylan Thomas*. Meanwhile the Shakespeare songs had their first performance in Los Angeles under Craft on 8 March, during the time Stravinsky was in Oregon.

Between April and June 1954 he was again in Europe, conducting in Rome, Turin, Lugano, London (where he received the gold medal of the Royal Philharmonic Society after conducting – an odd choice – *Scènes de ballet* on 27 May) and Lisbon. Later in June, back home, he added the Postlude to the Thomas memorial, then went on to arrange the Balmont songs for the ensemble of the Japanese Lyrics in July, and the next month to make a decisive start on *Agon*. *In memoriam Dylan Thomas* and a new version of the Russian peasant choruses for female voices, with four horns added, had their first performances under Craft at the Monday Evening Concerts in Los Angeles on 20 September and 11 October respectively, though the Thomas piece had already been recorded a week before by Stravinsky, along with the Shakespeare songs. In October and December he took time off from *Agon* to conduct performances of *Petrushka* for Anton Dolin in Chicago, San Francisco and Los Angeles. By 23 December half the score had been written, up to the end of the 'First Pas-de-trois'.

Going in search of love, *The Rake's Progress* increasingly turns from Mozart not so much forwards as back: back to a Monteverdian masque of Orpheus and a more florid, ornamented vocal style, back to folksong and medieval lyric (part of the libretto's life and usefulness comes from its layers of delicate nonsense and wonder, along with

Beggar's Operaticks and Mozart-translationese), back to the tranquil modality that *Orpheus* and the Mass had also reached. And this movement backwards continued as Stravinsky progressed from *The Rake* to his next work, again with words in English, the Cantata of love song, prayer, 'sacred history' and dirge based on poems of the fifteenth and sixteenth centuries, which he began with three songs for voices similar to those of Tom and Anne (the Stravinsky tenor, in particular, is a being with a strong individuality, identifiable all the way from the Cock and the Fox through the Hussar, Oedipus, Eumolpus, Tom Rakewell and the anonymous singer of the Cantata into the later works: a bright, edgy voice, centred in the upper half of the stave and rarely going above, daring in ornament more than range).

'The maidens came', dating from the summer of 1951, was written before the arrival of another 'Elizabeth, our quen princis', as the acclamation in the song has it, though this is not to discount a curious Englandward quality in Stravinsky's music from *The Rake's Progress* to the Shakespeare songs, in definite contrast with the Americanism of the works of the early 1940s. Perhaps this was a matter of responding to Britten; perhaps it came from the interest in Byrd and Purcell sparked off by *The Rake*.[1] The second movement to be composed, the duet 'Westron Wind', was apparently written first as a purely instrumental number.[2] Then came the tenor solo 'Tomorrow shall be my dancing day', followed by the stanzas of the 'Lyke-Wake Dirge' set for female chorus (the dully chanting madwomen of bedlam, perhaps) as frame and interludes to give the whole work a simple verse–refrain form that is repeated in more intricate ways within the solo songs and the duet.

The closeness to *The Rake's Progress* is not just a matter of language, modality and vocal tessitura, but also of scoring, since the ensemble of flutes, oboes (plus cor anglais) and cello recalls the high woodwind profile of the opera. However, this is a different world. The word-stressing, unusually proper for Stravinsky in *The Rake*, is full of corrugations, and there is no eighteenth century here, nothing between the 1950s and about 1600. This may have something to do with the revival of interest in medieval and renaissance music at the time, for Stravinsky always had a nose for musical news and had been to that rediscovery concert in November 1949. But the wind blowing him backward may have come from a nearer quarter, for what is most medieval about the Cantata, apart from its texts, is the open

[1]See *SSC III*, p. 319.   [2]See *SPD*, pp. 421–2.

constructivism, more evident than in anything since *Les cinq doigts*, and generally attributed to a renewed curiosity about Schoenberg.

Various events could have facilitated this turn. One was Schoenberg's death, in July 1951, the very month when the Cantata was begun: not only did this remove a psychological obstacle, it also placed Schoenberg in the past, and thereby brought him into Stravinsky's field of study. Another was his relationship with Robert Craft, who was maybe the first person he had found to be passionate about his own music and (rather than 'or') Schoenberg's, and whose Schoenberg rehearsals he was attending. He could also have been shaken by the evidence that his music of the 1940s was *vieux jeu* in Paris, and that serialism was where all the action was for the liveliest minds in Europe (Boulez: he heard *Structures Ia* while at work on the Cantata) and America (Babbitt). Equally there were the tendencies towards chromaticism, spruceness and wide-angled lines in *Orpheus* that could have propelled Stravinsky's music towards serialism from within.

Though the Cantata is not a twelve-note piece, nor serial, it does begin the journey along the path from ostinato-harmonic to imitative texture, and from a world centred, or off-centred, on keys to one of autonomous pattern. The tenor solo, the 'sacred history' of Christ voiced in the first person, strikes furthest along this path, with luminous modal blocks of burden ('To call my true love to my dance') as illuminated letters in a text of canons and other manifest constructions, such as in Ex. 24. The brackets, repeated here from the published score, show how the three phrases of the vocal line (the verbal rough-riding is typical) are echoed instrumentally in inversion, then retrogression, then prime form (slightly adjusted), but all with rhythmic changes, octave jumps and note repetitions that recess the architecture, especially when there is so much smaller-scale imitation going on in the music. Also characteristic of this piece is the limited vocal range, of just a minor sixth, which again looks both distantly backwards and sideways, suggesting folksong while also holding on to an Ariadne's thread of pitch limitation during the passage into total chromaticism: the cello part, too, is constrained to a nine-note chromatic mode, but over two octaves.

Once begun, the move towards serialism seems to have been unstoppable, and after a long period conditioned at once by consistency and improvisatory flexibility (so that, for example, if the dates of the Octet or *Scènes de ballet* were unknown, it would not be easy to place them correctly in sequence), Stravinsky's music suddenly acquires a directional urge. The first movement of the Septet, composed so soon after the Cantata, is Stravinsky's last original piece with a key signature, though the three sharps of A major here are applied only intermittently and hold any reality only for the first subject and its recapitulation in this compact quasi-sonata form. The scoring of the piece, for wind and string trios with piano, has suggested comparisons with Schoenberg's Suite, which Stravinsky had so

Ex. 24
Cantata: Ricercar II

Ex. 24 cont.

recently been hearing Craft rehearse, though the fact that he was again
writing for Dumbarton Oaks might have revived memories of his own
Concerto in E flat: the Septet is similarly in three short movements
placed fast–slow–fast, and its ensemble is that of the earlier piece, but
with a piano substituting for the missing flute, horn and extra strings.

Even in the opening movement, though, the Bach clichés have been
replaced by an order of contrapuntal writing that is both older and
newer, and this process continues in the following Passacaglia and the
final Gigue in canons. The Passacaglia has a ground theme in a highly
chromatic mode (E–F sharp–G–G sharp–A–B–C–C sharp), a theme
that at first trails through different instrumental colours in a manner
suggesting Webern (Webern's op. 22 quartet was also something
Craft had been rehearsing), but also recalling 'Dumbarton Oaks'.
Later the theme is normally carried by cello and piano beneath canonic
variations. The Gigue is based on this same mode and its inversion
(E–D–C sharp–C–B–A–G sharp–G), but it is still a mode and not a
row, despite Stravinsky's use of the word 'row' in the score to show its
appearances: the order of notes is not defined except as an expression
of thematic shape (which is a strong definer, nonetheless, in music
which is such a canonade of canons), and there is a remnant of A-
centredness, affirmed by the close on a chord which contains six notes
of the inverted mode but with only those of the A major triad repeated
in different registers.

Chords of such density are effectively ruled out from Stravinsky's next opus, the Three Songs from William Shakespeare, set in a skittish, bass-free sound world for voice (thus the score, though a mezzo-soprano would seem the only possibility), flute, clarinet and viola, and cast in a wispy counterpoint of usually just two or three parts. All this suggests an increasing turn from Schoenberg towards Webern, but Stravinsky's fussy vocal writing, ticking with mannerisms like a disordered machine, is nothing like Webern's, and his intervallic world is quite different, with no shame in thirds and fifths. Also, the music is essentially still modal. The opening song has, for the first time, an ordered set, but one of only four notes (B–G–A–B flat), a quiver into chromatic space, and the other numbers are based on reorderings of the notes of G flat and A flat major (later C major) scales respectively. Serialism, as Stravinsky understood it, was a way of rehearing old means (major scales, for example), and the Shakespeare texts make the point in connecting together to execute a fable rather like that of the Symphony of Psalms. 'Musick to heare' is an admonition, which might well be needed in a context startlingly fractured by comparison with the Cantata finished only a year before, that if 'the true concord of well tuned sounds, / By Unions married do offend thine eare' the fault is thine (the period spelling is the expression of a collector's antiquarianism; others are the use of the bare fifth as consonance, here as in the Mass, and the large rhythmic values that had entered *Orpheus*). 'Full fadom five' then executes a sea-change on the declamatory three-part G flat major canon of its opening line into the pearles and corall of chromatic counterpoint. And 'When Dasies pied' is a song, inevitably a spring song, presupposing both the warning and the demonstration of change: a new song, but one entirely Stravinskian in its repeated figures, its verse-refrain form, its peasant closeness to nature and its fresh, piping ensemble, the viola here being used exclusively in high harmonics and, less commonly, pizzicatos. The whole little triptych is a beautiful testimony to the self-reinvention it proposes.

The sea-change going on within Stravinsky's music at this time has unavoidably lost some of the shock effect it had, on supporters and on opponents, when it was happening. The decades have mollified the astonishment, and allowed the threads of continuity to be perceived: the fact that conscious cellular working is present as much in the Symphony in C as in the Septet, or that automations of the compositional process began in the quartet pieces if not the piano studies, or that the Shakespeare songs are fundamentally as modal as *Petrushka*, or that precision of dissonance, harmonic or metric, is a principle in all Stravinsky, the placing of emphases to irregularize the rhythmically regular, or the enlivening of wide-spanned concords with just the right wrong notes. Perhaps most of all, self-remaking had always been his way, and in that respect the springtime Shakespeare triptych directly echoes the springtime Japanese triptych of forty years before. The only difference, and a real cause for continued surprise, was that now the change was being achieved by a man in his eighth decade.

To paraphrase what he said at the earlier period, when he was working on *The Rite*, it is as if twenty and not two years had passed since *The Rake's Progress* was composed, for all that one may occasionally feel the Shakespeare songs are being sung by Baba the Turk. Stravinsky was teaching himself to compose again, ordering the world of sound anew, and it was a dramatization of this process that should have been his next large-scale work. Leaving aside the Auden–Kallman *Delia* – 'a celebration of Wisdom in a manner comparable to Ben Jonson's Masques',[3] which might have been imaginable at any point in the 1930s or 1940s but was now hopelessly out of date – he moved on to the Dylan Thomas project, to be 'about the rediscovery of our planet following an atomic misadventure. There would be a recreation of language, only the new one would have no abstractions; there would be only people, objects and words.'[4]

The 'recreation of language', of course, was what he was musically about, and the hazardousness of the enterprise may account for the lean output of 1953 – though this was also a time when he was clearing the decks, making versions of unfinished or unsatisfactory old works, including the Tango, the Praeludium, the new grouping of Four Songs with flute, harp and guitar, and the Four Russian Peasant Songs with added horns, that would be suitable for the Los Angeles chamber concerts at which most of his compositions were having their first performances. Possibly it was the convenience of the Evenings on the Roof, later the Monday Evening Concerts, that brought about the move to small formations: throughout the twelve years from the start of the Symphony in C to the completion of *The Rake's Progress* Stravinsky had been working almost non-stop on an orchestral scale; the works of 1951–4 come as close-ups. But equally the concentration could have been part of the re-education, the 'recreation of language' that never found its dramatic expression because of Thomas's death.

In memoriam Dylan Thomas, the first of Stravinsky's late funerary steles, is perhaps an elegy not only for the poet but for the aborted collaboration. Setting Thomas's memorial to his father as a song for tenor and string quartet framed by 'dirge canons' for the latter in

[3]Ibid., p. 205.   [4]*Conversations*, p. 78.

antiphony with trombones, this was Stravinsky's first fully serial piece, his first new naming of the world of notes and intervals. The process gains an elemental evidence and gravity from the use of a row of just five notes: its pathways are clear, and they proceed cautiously through twelve-note space, both because the set consists of two abutting fragments of the chromatic scale (E–E flat–C–C sharp–D), always sounded in close position by the trombones and often too by the voice, and because Stravinsky generally links set forms by contiguity, so that the gathering of new notes into play is slow. The song's vocal refrain (it also has an instrumental one) shows this:

Ex. 25
In memoriam Dylan Thomas

The reiteration of this refrain is a repeated naming of an object – a musical object: the five-note set – that was heard in the Prelude and will be heard again in the Postlude, so that when the trombones take it up there it will seem to have a verbal halo, 'Rage, rage against'. The form is not, then, as monumentally symmetrical as it might appear: the song impinges words on what was at first a purely musical idea. What this example also shows is the residual tonality in Stravinsky's five-note serialism: the bold octaves and fifths, and even a D minor triad in the second bar, as well as the sense of a chromatic wobble of pitch centre from E flat through this D to E (the first two trombone canons ended on E/F flat minor chords; the last two string ones will end on D minor and major). As Stravinsky acknowledged: 'The intervals of my series are attracted by tonality; I compose vertically, and that is, in one sense at least, to compose tonally.'[5]

[5]Ibid., p. 24.

164

This first serial composition is also entirely characteristic in its avid gestures, these including a good deal of not so characteristic word-painting, of which the outburst of *forte* in Ex. 24 and the rare melisma for 'dying' are only two momentary instances. Others include the 'W' of sevenths and ninths at the mention of forked lightning, or the arrival at last of the G needed to complete the chromatic total as the voice in the sixth bar sings 'at close of day'. Also very Stravinskian, and not at all Schoenbergian, is the high incidence of repetition, brought about not only by the canons and refrains but also by the use of the row so often in one of a few rhythmic forms and registral placings. But perhaps what is most typical, most cherishing of displaced continuity, is the way serialism provides a new way of singing a very old idea, the three-note chromatically descending *lamento*.

23

Ag—Canticum sacrum—on

In January 1955 Stravinsky fairly quartered the United States, conducting concerts in Portland, Salem, Birmingham and Atlanta. Back in Los Angeles he wrote the *Greeting Prelude* for Monteux's eightieth birthday in early February, and attended the first performance of the Four Songs under Craft on the 21st. Early the next month he went to Pittsburgh for concerts, and then on to Madrid, by way of New York and Lisbon, to begin a European tour that lasted until early May and took in concerts in Madrid, Rome, Baden-Baden, Lugano, Mannheim and Copenhagen. During this tour he also visited Venice and tested the acoustics in the Salute and Frari churches with an ear to his new commission for the 1956 Venice Biennale (this was on 18 April); he went too, six days later, to Webern's grave at Mittersill. Late in May he conducted the Los Angeles Philharmonic at Ojai.

Not until June this year did he have a prolonged period for composition, and now, putting aside *Agon*, he embarked on the Venice commission, the *Canticum sacrum*, on which he proceeded steadily until it was finished on 21 November. During this time, on 28 July, he made recordings in Hollywood of his recently revised songs (the Balmont pair, the Four Songs, and the women's choruses with horns), as well as the Three Japanese Lyrics and Three Little Songs. At the beginning of December he went to Cleveland for concerts, and from there to New York, where he worked on his adaptation of the Bach canonic variations on *Vom Himmel hoch*. These were completed in Los Angeles on 27 March (he had gone back home in mid-January), and first performed at Ojai on 27 May 1956, on a programme with *Les noces*.

The next month Stravinsky sailed from New York for Patras by way of Lisbon, Barcelona, Naples (from which port he drove to Gesualdo: a pious visit like that to Mittersill) and Palermo. He visited Athens, Mycenae and Istanbul, and then went to Venice, where the *Canticum sacrum* had its first performance under his direction in San Marco on 13 September. Concerts in Montreux and Berlin followed, and then a period of five and a half weeks in hospital in the latter city in

October–November. Once discharged he went on to Munich, Rome, Paris and London before returning to New York just before Christmas.

In January 1957 he conducted the New York Philharmonic in *Petrushka* and *Perséphone*, recording the latter, and then returned to Los Angeles after an absence of more than seven months. He attended the Monday Evening Concert at which Boulez conducted *Le marteau sans maître* (11 March), and completed *Agon* on 27 April. After that he turned to completing Gesualdo's *Illumina nos*, writing two parts to substitute for those missing; this work was finished on 5 May. The first performance of *Agon*, as a concert piece, conducted by Craft, took place in Los Angeles on 17 June, Stravinsky's seventy-fifth birthday. He then recorded the work the next day, and *Canticum sacrum* the day after that.

The temptation would be to see the four small works of 1951–4 (the Cantata, Septet, Shakespeare songs and Thomas memorial) as making possible the four large works of 1954–7 (the *Greeting Prelude*, Bach arrangement, *Canticum sacrum* and new ballet), and indeed there is much that is retained in terms of compact form (the Monteux prelude, a snazzy little contrapuntal invention on 'Happy birthday to you' playing for forty seconds or so, must be one of the tiniest pieces in the orchestral repertory, along with the decade-later *Firebird* canon), compartmented structuring and sharply outlined polyphony. At the same time, Stravinsky pauses to recuperate a solider harmony. The *Canticum sacrum* for the first time includes twelve-note sets, notably in the tenor solo 'Surge, aquilo' (again, as in the Cantata, Stravinsky moves forward on the voice of a tenor), but the serial control is less exacting than in 'Musick to heare' and *In memoriam Dylan Thomas*, and in all these works the starkly uttered counterpoint has a strong tonal grounding, as well as a set of more precise echoes in history – though in a more distant history than was plumbed in the works from *Pulcinella* to *The Rake's Progress*.

The resonances in the *Canticum sacrum* are very obviously with Venetian music, and in particular with the antiphonal motets of Giovanni Gabrieli or the vespers of Monteverdi, which were being heard in the building for which this piece was written, San Marco, three hundred and fifty years before. Like Gabrieli, Stravinsky writes for choirs of instruments and voices: woodwind (solo flute with oboes and bassoons), trumpets and trombones, harp and strings (violas and basses only), organ, and chorus. Like Monteverdi, he interleaves full numbers with more intimate, virtuoso music for soloists. But the scoring and the form and the tone of the piece also look back to a work of his own, the Symphony of Psalms. Once again, this is an invented liturgy, and not so much a liturgy of St Mark (though the complete title is *Canticum sacrum ad honorem Sancti Marci nominis*) as a liturgy of faith.

The liturgy begins with a sung dedication, given out by the tenor and baritone soloists with trombones, and standing rather at the doorway to the work, just as the sung title of *Zvezdoliki* is both part of the composition and separate. The first movement proper, and the last, are both loud, shuddering choruses concerned with Christ's commission to the disciples to 'go . . . into all the world and preach the gospel to every creature' and with their execution of that commission, set to almost the same music, with organ verses that seem to be listening to the same harmonies from a greater distance (this was Stravinsky's only use of an instrument associated so much with the Western church). The second and fourth movements are solo pieces, for tenor and baritone respectively, the former singing of spiritual gifts in the sensuous imagery of the Song of Songs, the latter relating an incident from St Mark (the first and last movements also take their words from the gospel of Venice's patron), in which Christ says that 'all things are possible to him that believeth' and a man replies: 'Lord I believe; help thou my unbelief'.

Belief is also the ultimate subject of the middle movement, whose sections devoted to charity, hope and faith (with apposite fragments of scriptural text) are each as long as any of the other movements. They are also marked off as a trinity by organ intonations and instrumental frames in chant-like style (altogether there is a striking confluence with Messiaen in this Venetian–Byzantine icon). The fierce symmetry, so unlike the progressive extension of the Symphony of Psalms, has been associated with the domescape of San Marco – five cupolae, the central the largest[1] – so that the form of the piece adds to the acoustic and historical qualities that fit the piece for its first and ideal habitation.

The Bach arrangement, though made for the same place to complete the programme, and scored for almost the same forces (the principal absentee is the organ of Bach's original), could scarcely be more different: lucid diatonic counterpoint instead of darkly resplendent chromatic–modal litanies. The five variations are prefaced by a setting of the chorale for brass sextet, in a Bach harmonization from the *Christmas Oratorio*; thereafter the text is followed scrupulously (one

[1]See White, pp. 482–3.

might remember Stravinsky's comment about *Pulcinella*: 'the remarkable thing . . . is not how much but how little was added or changed'),[2] but with octave doublings, changings of key, the choral singing of the melody in all but the first variation, and the interposing of trumpet and trombone counterpoints in the second and third variations. The great difference from *Pulcinella* – and this was Stravinsky's first big work based wholesale on existing music since *Pulcinella* and *Le baiser de la fée* – is the relaxation, the fondness. This is more a meeting than a contrariety, a meeting for which the invitation had been accepted in the Concerto in E flat, and it prepared the ground for the meetings soon to happen with Gesualdo, and then with Sibelius and Wolf.

Meanwhile the new ballet for Balanchine was waiting. The original idea, emanating from Balanchine and Kirstein in the summer of 1953, had been for a work to complete a triple bill with the two earlier Stravinsky–Balanchine Greek episodes *Apollo* and *Orpheus*; they had suggested the subject of 'Apollo Architectons: builder of shelters and bridges'.[3] Stravinsky, giving his reason that the third part of the trilogy ought to counterweight the predominant slowness of *Apollo* and *Orpheus*, suggested instead 'the Nausicaa episode of *Odyssey*',[4] which had been the intended subject of a film project that had some fitful life in 1952–3, at one point with Thomas as potential librettist.[5] One can understand why Stravinsky should now have cherished this particular story, as a motif of recommencement, but in the event it was decided that the third Greek ballet should be abstract, an agon, or 'public celebration of games'.[6]

This made it possible for Stravinsky, as with the fair of *Petrushka* or the sacrifice of *The Rite of Spring*, to work with a stage image matching what was going on in the music, for the score of *Agon* is a gymnastic display by teams of instruments and intervals, freed from each other and also marshalled by the new serial principles that were growing in his music even while the score was in progress. And it is by this point decisively Webern, rather than Schoenberg, who is the presiding authority, honoured here in the strict counterpointing of wide-angled lines, the disjunct colour, the grace notes (previously rare in Stravinsky), the momentary ormolu of mandolin and guitar, and the restriction of unpitched percussion, represented only, but crucially, by the ticking castanet timekeeper in one number, the 'Bransle Gay'. But, as this title serves to remind one, *Agon* is at least as much about the French renaissance as it is about the Second Viennese School. The

[2]*Expositions*, p. 113. [3]*SSC I*, p. 285. [4]Ibid., p. 286.
[5]See *SSC III*, pp. 353, 372 and 374. [6]OED.

music looks back to a rather earlier period in the history of the *ballet de cour* than that glimpsed in *Apollo*, and includes examples of three bransles, a galliard and a sarabande, created after the prescriptions in de Lauze's *Apologie de la danse* of 1623, and sometimes after the music examples (from Mersenne) in the modern edition Stravinsky used. Also, in its exuberant and colourful cross-cutting of times, the music takes up essentially Stravinskian ideas, including not only the paralleling of dramatic and musical actions but also the use of instrumental choirs with their own repertories of intervals (as in the Symphonies of Wind Instruments), or the presence of the orchestral piano as athletic pseudo-soloist (as in *Petrushka*, *Perséphone* and the Symphony in Three Movements), or the dominance of brass and strings (as in the Symphony of Psalms and *Canticum sacrum*, though this is a quite different sort of piece), or the collision of old and new (as in *Pulcinella*).

Just as the musical games are being played with an assembly of twelve notes, so the dances are to be executed by twelve people, and this is even directed in the score. First comes a Pas-de-Quatre for the men, a lively responsory of different groupings: the trumpet-led brass, and then woodwind, low strings and a luminous ensemble of mandolin, harp, double-bass harmonics and muffled low tollings. Then comes an agitated Double Pas-de-Quatre for the eight women, leading, without change of the hurrying tempo, into a Triple Pas-de-Quatre for all twelve dancers which completes the first trio of numbers. There is then a fanfaring Prelude to the First Pas-de-Trois, which consists of a male solo Saraband-Step for solo violin (suggesting Apollo more than the Soldier) with trombones and xylophone, a Gailliarde for the two women (the harp and the mandolin are now refractions of a lute, heard in a harmonic echo chamber of flutes and low strings), and a Coda for the threesome, and for solo violin again (now more Soldierly, in a 6/8 rag), this time with flutes, trumpets, trombones, mandolin, harp, piano and solo cello.

An Interlude, effectively a later view of the Prelude, introduces the Second Pas-de-Deux, made up of the three bransles. The Bransle Simple, for two men, is dominated by a rivalling canonic pair of trumpets in another close complementation of music to choreography, as with the violin and male soloists of the First Pas-de-Deux. The solo female dance is the Bransle Gay, its characteristic pattern of two light beats followed by two accented beats is played in syncopation by woodwind couples and harp against the castanet. The Bransle Double then for the first time presents twelve-note successions, in a strenuous line for the violins in octaves that has a trumpet–trombone counterpoint on each of its appearances before more dissolved static verses. After another Interlude, again looking back to the Prelude, wide-spanning melody continues in the Pas-de-Deux, an Adagio for strings with solo violin followed by more active variations for the man (horns and piano) and the woman (flutes and strings), and a coda for strings, brass and tuned percussion. The following Four Duos is a dance for four couples to a twelve-note invention for low strings and trombones. Then the final Four Trios – the twelfth dance, for all twelve dancers – sets itself the problem of moving smoothly from the score's most atonal music, recalling the style and instrumentation of the Bransle Double but with a different row, into its most tonal, that of the opening Pas-de-Quatre. This is a magical moment. The four-part serial polyphony, on a row made up exclusively of semitones and minor thirds and their transpositions, is halted by an echo of horn calls from the first dance, but the notes of the first horn chord are precisely those required by the serial unfolding:

Ex. 26
Agon: Four Trios

Stravinsky's tonality turns out to be required by his new serial practice. *Agon* has created a field of action in which everything from the past fifty years can be at play.

24

Threnodies, movements and monuments

Stravinsky spent the middle part of July 1957 in Santa Fe, where Craft was conducting *The Rake's Progress*, then travelled to New York to take the boat for Plymouth at the start of August. There followed one of his longest stays in England, of more than a fortnight, during which he visited many of the sights: Tintagel, Wells, Stonehenge, *The Mousetrap*. He went on to Venice, where he started *Threni* on the piano of his hotel's nightclub on 29 August. At the end of September he left for Munich, and then for Baden-Baden, to rehearse the Südwestfunk Symphony Orchestra in *Agon* for performances in Paris, Donaueschingen and Rome. At the end of October he sailed from Le Havre back to New York, and left by train for Los Angeles without staying for the stage première of *Agon* by New York City Ballet at New York City Center, on 1 December.

With a break for concerts in Houston in early January, he completed *Threni* on 21 March 1958 (his diary, confined almost exclusively to medical affairs, records for this date only: 'Dr Knauer, bursitis treatment, new hernia belt.')[1] On 7 April he attended Craft's recording of Stockhausen's *Zeitmasze*, leaving three days later for concerts in San Francisco; he also conducted *Mavra* and *The Faun* at UCLA in mid-June. On 9 July he finished the first of the Movements for piano and orchestra, and soon after left for another summer and autumn in Europe, beginning with six weeks in Venice, where he completed the second part of Movements on 7 September, and where he conducted the first performance of *Threni*, in the Scuola di San Rocco, after a performance of the Symphonies of Wind Instruments, on 23 September. During the next seven weeks he conducted his latest work in Basle, Zurich, Berne, Hamburg and Paris; he also conducted in Vienna (including *Oedipus* at the Vienna State Opera), Florence, Rome and London before taking the boat back to New York in mid-December.

He stayed in New York to attend the American première of *Threni*, under Craft on 4 January 1959, and to record the work over the next

[1] *A Stravinsky Scrapbook*, p. 161.

two days. Then he returned to Los Angeles, where he finished the third and fifth Movements in February and March before making his only journey to Japan, by way of Honolulu, Manila and Hong Kong. He was in Japan for five weeks, from early April to early May, conducting in Osaka and Tokyo, and attending performances of Japanese theatre, puppet plays and court music. After only ten days at home (presumably it was during this part of May that he wrote the *Epitaphium*) he went to Copenhagen to receive the Sonning Prize and conduct a concert. He was then at home until the end of June, when he went to Santa Fe again, conducting *Threni* there. Back home he completed the fourth Movement on 30 July and the interludes for the work in the middle of August, then flew to New York and on to London at the beginning of September.

During this visit to Britain he went to Stratford (*Coriolanus* with Olivier) and Edinburgh, before his usual early-autumn stay in Venice, where he wrote new completions for two more Gesualdo motets and also composed a Double Canon for string quartet. He then visited or revisited other favourite places in Italy – Rome, Gesualdo, Paestum, Naples, Bologna, with concerts in the last two cities – and so did not attend the Donaueschingen Festival (as he had in each of the preceding two years), where the *Epitaphium* in memory of the Donaueschingen prince and patron Max Egon zu Fürstenberg had its first performance on 17 October. From Italy he went to London for more than a fortnight, during which time he conducted *Oedipus rex*, and sailed back to New York in mid-November. There, on 20 December, he conducted *Les noces* at a concert which also included the first performance of the Double Canon; he recorded *Les noces* the next day. He also made a television recording of *Firebird* extracts in early January, and a new recording of *The Rite*, his third and last.

On 10 January 1960 he conducted the first performance of Movements in New York, with Margrit Weber as soloist (the work had been commissioned for her by her husband);[2] the Gesualdo completions were also heard for the first time. Stravinsky then returned to Los Angeles, where he made a new recording of *Petrushka* (as with *The Rite*, the last one was twenty years old) and transcribed three Gesualdo madrigals for instruments to create the *Monumentum* for this lately chosen musical godfather's quartercentenary. In June he recorded this new work, in advance of its official Venetian première, and also the Mass, and he visited the Monet exhibition at the Los Angeles County Museum. In July there was another prolonged visit to

[2]See *SPD*, p. 452.

Santa Fe, where he conducted *Oedipus rex* and the Symphony of Psalms, and then after a few days at home he made a five-week tour of Latin America, with concerts in Mexico City, Bogotá, Lima, Santiago, Buenos Aires and Rio de Janeiro: this was his first tour of South America since the visit of 1936. He left there for New York, and then in mid-September for his much more regular staging post, Venice, where he remained until early November. He conducted the first performance of the *Monumentum* – the third of his Biennale commissions, after the *Canticum sacrum* and *Threni* – on a programme with *Orpheus* at the Palazzo Ducale on 27 September.

Threni, the second of these Venetian pieces, is a liturgy like the first, and like the Symphony of Psalms and the Mass, and more like the Mass in setting liturgical texts, from the Lamentations of Jeremiah used in the tenebrae offices of Holy Week. In this case, though, no liturgical performance is conceivable: the church in which these chantings take place is provided by the lines, harmonies and colours of the orchestra, or rather of the small ensembles chosen from the orchestra to surround what is essentially a sequence of chants. It is also essentially a sequence of canons. In what was his first completely twelve-note composition, Stravinsky lays out combinations of serial forms in segments that often make up larger patterns of verse and chorus, and because the series is composed exclusively of semitones, thirds and fifths – because, too, Stravinsky frequently repeats particular intervallic patterns (such as the motif of falling semitone, falling fourth, rising major third at the start of the solo soprano line in the example below) – there is a solemnity of affirmation and reaffirmation about the music, a ritual–repetitive quality that strikes back to *Les noces*, as Walsh has observed,[3] for all the difference of languages (musical and verbal), speed and tone. The primacy of the voice is important to this affinity too, as in this element from the long centrepiece of the triptych, an element heard three times here as a refrain (see Ex. 27).

The atmosphere of lament, which necessarily predominates here and throughout the work, certainly has its parallels in moments of *Les noces*, and there are drones and intimations of ostinato, as well as less blatant means of creating harmonic stasis. Not content with the thirds and fifths already present in the series (E flat–D–A–C sharp–G sharp –B–F sharp–A sharp–G–E–F–C is the form presented here, with the men soloists taking up from the women the last three notes and

[3]See pp. 242–3.

Ex. 27

Threni: De elegia tertia: Sensus spei

[Mine eye trickleth down, and ceaseth not, without any intermission.]

then the first three, while the oboes project the chorus's Hebrew letter and another set form), Stravinsky draws other means of pitch centring out of the twelve-note substance: octaves and double octaves, repetitions of fragments, and arrangements of events in the interests of tonal coincidence: here a concluding fifth, where in the example from *Agon* it was a recollected horn call.

This persistency of modality is one feature that distances *Threni* from the sacred cantatas of that other master of serial canon, Webern, as far as the Byzantine mosaics of San Marco are distant from the flowers and mineral crystals of the Carinthian alps. There is also the heavy weighting of the music, not wholly suggested by Ex. 27, towards the bass, accomplished partly by the use of unusual low-register instruments: alto as well as bass clarinet, and sarrusophone (a sort of brass contrabassoon). And there is the way the music is not so much song as incantation. There are very few phrasing marks in *Threni* (or in *Les noces* for that matter), and no instances of rubato, just a hieratic pronouncement of notes and syllables. This is all very characteristic of Stravinsky, if extreme, but what is less characteristic is the lack of global rhythm. Partly because so much of the music is canonic, each voice appears to be pronouncing at its own pulse, and there is not the customary kicking of verbal stress against musical

Ex. 28
Movements I

176

metre. The barlines in Ex. 27 seem to be there simply as a relic and a help in rehearsal; where the texture is even more austere, reduced to unaccompanied vocal monody or bicinium, they are indeed omitted.

If all the literature of serial technique were to be lost (what a thought), it would be possible to reconstruct the basic rules of twelve-note ordering and set transformation from *Threni* alone. But what of Stravinsky's next work (see Ex. 28)? Here in Movements one can identify a twelve-note succession in the piano and clarinet parts (E flat–A–G–A flat–D flat–D–C–F–G flat–F flat–C flat–B flat), but the derivation of the flute part from that series is by no means easy or unequivocal. There are motifs that match, like the initial G–C sharp–B–C (the first four notes of the set for piano and clarinets, up a major third), but there are others that do not, like the B flat–G–A flat–A in the second bar, which contains one interval, the minor third, foreign to both the piano–clarinets series and to the twelve-note statement at the start of the work, in each of which major and minor thirds (and therefore minor and major sixths) are excluded.

Where the emphatic canonic textures of *Threni* positively demand that twelve-note melodies be explained in terms of each other, in a closed network of self-reference, there is no such invitation in Movements. For instance, analysis of the flute part in Ex. 27 along the lines of the opening twelve-note set has to be implausibly ramshackle;[4] one might better look for arrows of likeness pointing outwards, to the writing for alto flute in *Le marteau sans maître*. Stravinsky had heard Boulez conduct that work in Los Angeles in 1957; he also heard Boulez's Third Piano Sonata and Stockhausen's *Gruppen* for three orchestras during his visits to Baden-Baden and Donaueschingen in 1957 and 1958 respectively, and Stockhausen's *Zeitmasze* in Los Angeles in 1958. This was the repertory that enabled him to jump from the stationary, bass-heavy solemnities of *Threni*, a work solidly embedded in his own forty-year tradition of choral rites, to the airy agility of Movements, whose newness remains fresh and astonishing. In describing the rhythmic language of Movements as his most advanced,[5] Stravinsky was drawing attention perhaps not only to the conflicts of basic unit – present almost throughout Ex. 28, as generally when the counterpoint is in two parts (and it is rarely in more) – but also to the larger disparities of motion which those conflicts produce and which the title may punningly imply.

In Ex. 28, for example, barring the occasional accidents of grace notes, the flute part is in entirely regular values, while the other line

---

[4]See White, p. 506.   [5]*Memories*, p. 106.

wobbles among units of pulsation related to the flute's in proportions of ¾, 1½, 2, ⅘ and ⅔. This could be interpreted as a superposition of the rationally related tempos laid out alongside each other in *The Rite*, *Les noces* and the Symphonies of Wind Instruments, but it is hard not to see the new viewpoint as backed too, and more so, by what Stravinsky had been hearing from Boulez and Stockhausen. After all, it is not just different tempos that are overlaid but different kinds of tempo, as in *Zeitmasze*, while the creation of a line from abutting and overlapping cells is something that loops out from *The Rite* through Messiaen and Boulez to its place back in Stravinsky's music here.

Different kinds of tempo. The flute's is stable, of course, and tending too towards a stability of metre, towards a 7/16 of three plus two plus two beats (the pattern is substantiated by the similar pitch contours, not always with exactly the same intervals, in the last two bars). The piano–clarinets line, by contrast is unstable, ametric (with ties over three of the four interposed barlines) and lacking in any such progressiveness. And there are other obvious antinomies: of instrumentation (again stable and unstable: perhaps one could hear the clarinet tone as springing out from the piano, like a shoot from a seed; there is a lot of such nimble movement of ideas between soloist and ensemble in the work), of register, of interval content, of line. The piano–clarinets part suggests an upward urge that rapidly starts to collapse back on itself in the perfect retrograde of the last bar, while the flute part continues upwards to the end, on a succession of energies injected by minor ninths (cf. the opening of the Symphony in Three Movements): B–C in the first bar, then A flat–A at the end of the second and again B–C in the third, then a double leap C–D flat–D, a third B–C at the same level as the other two (but now spelt C flat–C) and finally A–B flat) to the nearly final apex.

not in his example it isn't

Not at all an interlocking grid system like *Threni*, Movements is a loose shuffle of vectors through these various dimensions – and the thinking in terms of separate dimensions, or parameters, is not the least of Stravinsky's debts here to his musical grandsons. In this multidimensional space the same object can have different profiles in different dimensions: the flute part in Ex. 28, for example, is level in pulse, interval content and colour, increasingly regular in metre, and increasingly extreme in register. No doubt it would be possible to see the piece more conventionally as a pocket concerto, with a first movement (there is even a repeat of the 'exposition'), three slow movements of different type (like the arias of the Violin Concerto perhaps) and a finale. There are also many instrumental gestures strongly reminiscent of known Stravinsky: the little echoes of repetition, the clarinet tremolando coming to the end of the middle movement out of the first of *Pribautki*, the cimbalom-style piano writing in the second movement. But the memories are buoyed up by the arrows operating in a new high, clear air; all the old gravities are counterbalanced by centrifugal musical thought that spins the material around and away from the piano. This is a concerto for soloist as lepidopterist, trying to catch into the keyboard the profusely varied figures of the surrounding instruments and ensembles. Or one might think of a shadowplay, moving towards a climax just ten bars before the end (again a nearly final apex), when the celesta finally enters, briefly tries to replace the suddenly silenced piano, and lets the shadows dissolve into the dark.

This lively, fantastical piece stands on the threshold of a last decade in which Stravinsky was preoccupied by Biblical parables and monuments, the latter beginning with the two instrumental miniatures of 1959. The *Epitaphium* has something of the rhythmic flexibility of Movements, being composed at the same time, but frozen into a ceremonial antiphony of twelve-note statements between treble woodwind and bass-register harp, the latter like dampened bells. The Double Canon is more completely a pendant to *Threni*, an interlocking of twelve set forms.

Canons are found too, though more sporadically, in the completing parts for the Gesualdo motets – an instance of subsumed creativity equalled only by *Le baiser de la fée* – and the recomposition of three Gesualdo madrigals for blocks of instruments. Some of these blocks, such as the quintet of trumpets and trombones or the quartet of cellos, have their direct equivalents in Movements; but of course Gesualdo's harmony, even Gesualdo's, is only a little lifted from the ground by comparison with Stravinsky's, and the music's facture asks for dialogue within and between blocks rather than for the complex cross-currents of Movements. But *Monumentum* too seems to be addressing a new generation. Boulez had included Dufay as well as Webern in his early Paris concerts,[6] and Davies and Birtwistle were learning from plainsong and polyphony as much as from Nono. Stravinsky's transcription, wholly lacking in the satires and anxieties of his earlier retrogressions, belongs with these endeavouring to find a mirror in the past, while the particular fascination with Gesualdo was perhaps prompted not only by Craft's interests but also by the fact that here was a composer who broke the rules, as Stravinsky was breaking Schoenberg's.

[6]See Antoine Goléa: *Rencontres avec Pierre Boulez* (Paris, 1958), p. 187.

25

Stories from the Bible

As Stravinsky neared and passed his eightieth birthday, in 1962, there was no let-up in his foreign travels, but rather the reverse. The 1956–60 pattern of spending several autumn weeks in Venice came to an end, but the journeys to Japan in 1959 and Latin America the next year were followed by a tour to New Zealand and Australia in 1961 and then, in the octogenary year itself, by visits to South Africa, Rome, Hamburg, Israel, Russia, Caracas and Toronto. There cannot now have been any financial imperative to take on conducting engagements (by this point he was usually on the podium for just one item in a programme otherwise left to Craft): he was travelling rather as a living monument, the only composer alive whose works made an unbroken span of masterpieces back to the first decade of the century, and who was still – though this may have been less important in public consciousness – active. Four new works had their first performances in 1962 alone.

In November 1960 he left Venice for Genoa, Rome and Paris, then went by ship back to New York, and so on to Washington to conduct and record *The Nightingale* at the end of the year. Early in January he recorded the Octet and visited the Columbia–Princeton Electronic Music Center in the company of Milton Babbitt. He then flew back to Los Angeles, recorded the complete *Firebird* (the *Epitaphium* and Double Canon were also recorded on this occasion), and completed a new work for Sacher, *A Sermon, a Narrative and a Prayer*, on 31 January. A week later he began *The Flood*, commissioned by CBS television, and also in February recorded the Symphony in Three Movements, the *Histoire du soldat* suite and Movements. In early April he made a brief visit to Mexico City, where he conducted *The Rite* for the last time, and in June he recorded the Symphony of Psalms in Los Angeles. In July–August he was in Santa Fe again, conducting *Oedipus rex* and *Perséphone*. He then sailed to Europe at the beginning of September, conducting in Helsinki, Stockholm (where he also saw Ingmar Bergman's production of *The Rake*), Berlin, Belgrade, Zurich and London, before going on via Egypt to Auckland,

Wellington, Sydney and Melbourne in November. Early in December he arrived back in Los Angeles via Tahiti, and later that month arranged the tango finale of *Les cinq doigts* for a *Monumentum*-like ensemble of double reeds, trumpets and trombones.

The annus mirabilis began with the completion of the Anthem, to words from Eliot's 'Little Gidding', on 2 January, with conducting engagements in Los Angeles and Toronto, and with dinner at the White House with the Kennedys on 18 January, followed by performances of *Oedipus rex* in Washington. After a short stay in New York, where he recorded *Renard* and *Rag-time*, Stravinsky returned to Los Angeles to hear the first performance of the Anthem, under Craft on 19 February, and to work at *The Flood*, which was completed on 14 March and recorded for television on the last two days of the month: it was broadcast on 14 June, three days before the birthday, by which time Stravinsky was in Rome. He also missed the first performance of *A Sermon*, given by Sacher in Basle on 23 February; he himself recorded the work on 29 April, along with the Eight Instrumental Miniatures, ensemble scorings of *Les cinq doigts* that had not been heard before.

The world tour began with three weeks in South Africa in May–June 1962, including concerts in Johannesburg, the black township of Springs, and Pretoria. Stravinsky then flew to Rome and, on his birthday, on to Hamburg, where there were five performances of his Greek–Balanchine trilogy in the order *Orpheus–Agon–Apollo*, the last with him conducting. At the end of June he flew to New York and, after stopping for a concert in Chicago, returned home, though only briefly, because in late July he went again to Santa Fe, where he began his next work, *Abraham and Isaac*, on 2 August. Near the end of that month he flew to Tel Aviv to conduct at the Festival of Israel, which had commissioned the new work, and to see the Holy Land sites.

After a week in Israel he took a short holiday in Venice before his return to Moscow on 21 September. During three weeks in Russia he conducted in both Moscow and St Petersburg, and visited Khrushchev. He then went back, via Paris and Rome, to New York, from where he made a short visit to Caracas for two concerts in early November, and another to Toronto for recordings of *Zvezdoliki*, the Four Studies, *Babel*, the *Scherzo fantastique* and the Symphony in C. After these few days in the studios he flew back to Los Angeles in early December, and completed *Abraham and Isaac* on 3 March 1963. More recordings in Toronto followed at the end of that month: *Scènes de ballet*, the two suites for small orchestra, the *Circus*

Polka, the *Four Norwegian Moods*, the Symphony of Psalms and the varied Bach variations.

The next month Stravinsky sailed to Hamburg, where *The Flood* had its first stage performance on the 30th, Craft conducting. After that came visits to Budapest, Zagreb, Paris, London (fiftieth anniversary performance of *The Rite* under its original conductor in the Royal Albert Hall on 29 May), Dublin, Stockholm and Milan, before the flight back to Los Angeles via New York as June turned into July. On 10 July he completed his arrangement of Sibelius's *Canzonetta*, prompted by the award of the Wihuri–Sibelius prize, and on 12 August, during another visit to Santa Fe, he finished drafting the variation for twelve violins that was to find a place in his next major work, the Variations for orchestra. Early in September he gave two concerts in Rio, and in mid-November he made a brief visit to Rome and Sicily, returning from there to New York, where he recorded *Fireworks*, the *Scherzo à la russe*, the Concerto in D and the *Greeting Prelude* in mid-December.

Stravinsky's identification in Movements with the European avant-garde adventure was not maintained, perhaps partly because that adventure itself was not. Movements belongs, alongside Boulez's Third Sonata and Stockhausen's *Gruppen*, to a brief heroic age, after which the younger composers began to go in different directions. Stravinsky remained a concerned observer, as witness his interest in Stockhausen's *Momente*[1] or Babbitt's electronic studio, but his first works of the 1960s suggest a city street after the parade has passed by. There are the discards of what went before – notably the complex rhythmic superpositions – but not the energy.

There is a return too in these pieces, *A Sermon* and *The Flood*, to the didactic manner of *Babel*, which is one cause of the flatness; another is the episodic character, the absence of frame and wholeness. There is a *Canticum sacrum* sound world; there is a *Threni* sound world; but the same cannot be said of these two later works. Nor do they impose themselves as rituals: the use of a non-sacred language, English, and of speech, directly following *Babel*, goes along with the apparent wish to instruct rather than to show. The speaking voice fixes attention on narrative, rather than on the way in which narrative is being presented, and the reasons why these stories are being told – the story of Stephen's stoning in *A Sermon* and of Noah in *The Flood* – are not so clear. The vernacular and the expository plainness make these

[1]See *SSC II*, p. 356.

disconcertingly Protestant achievements for a composer so musically Orthodox, even though *A Sermon* is a linked triptych like the Symphony of Psalms and a document on faith like the *Canticum sacrum*.

The Flood was Stravinsky's largest piece after *Threni* and his last dramatic work, another mixing of genres incorporating choral prayer, spoken narration, sung dialogue (with God's voice a duplet of basses and the human characters speaking) and dance. Written for television, it perhaps awaits a worthy production, though both these works appear as successions of treasurable moments (the last appearances of the Stravinsky tenor as Stephen and Satan; the setting of *A Prayer* with the deep resonances of tam tams reinforced by pizzicato basses and harp and piano in their bottom-most register; the few bars of watery imagery as Noah surveys the inundated world) with others less treasurable. The arbitrariness – not the precise resolve of inchoate possibility, as arbitrariness had been in works from the piano studies to Movements, but rather a haphazardness of form and diffuseness of structural motivation – could be a symptom of age. It could also be a response to the same pressures – including the dissolution of the unified avant garde of the 1950s – that led to the unfixed concatenation of events in such contemporary works as *Momente* or Boulez's *Pli selon pli* (the tam tams, surely remembered from *Le marteau*, are evidence that Boulez was still in Stravinsky's thoughts). The looseness, however untypical, can therefore be understood. But the naivety, in Stravinsky, is almost shocking.

Abraham and Isaac is a sudden gust of life. Again a biblical story is being told, and again it is one that Britten had told shortly before (his *Noye's Fludde* dates from 1957, his *Abraham and Isaac* from 1952), but now there is everything that was clamorously absent in Stravinsky's two preceding works: frame and wholeness, a special sound world and a sacred language. The Genesis text is delivered in Hebrew as melodic declamation by a high baritone, a new kind of Stravinsky voice and one suggestive of a synagogue cantor, singing almost continuously (there is a midpoint interlude of pacing figures to separate the preparation from the sacrifice) against the barest accompaniment. In this instrumental landscape of flickerings, abrupt chords and brief contrapuntal inventions, all tight-drawn, melodic efflorescence from the instruments is as rare as vegetation in the desert, and when it comes it has a momentous effect, as here, where the flute line seems to be introducing the voice of the angel before the heavenly messenger speaks in the text:

Ex. 29
Abraham and Isaac

[And the angel of the Lord called unto him out of heaven, and said,
Abraham, Abraham: and he said, Here am I. And he said, Lay not]

This example also shows how Stravinsky's twelve-note working,
though still looser than in *Threni*, has pulled back towards canonic

obedience. The flute sings a retrograde of the voice's opening twelve-note series, but in precise rhythmic canon, while the tuba unfolds the retrograde inversion from the same note in doubled rhythmic values. Harmony in the simple sense is hardly an issue here when the parts are so widely separated in register and colour, but the harmony of the tireless vocal melody is, clearly, beautifully composed. The work's series is made up almost entirely from minor and major seconds (there is just one exception, a major third), and this comparative featurelessness becomes a positive advantage: it makes possible a lot of fluent scalar motion, and it also allows Stravinsky to repeat motifs, which gain a signature rather as neumes in plainsong do. One example is the E–F sharp–F grouping that appears twice in Ex. 29: it is normally in close position, so that the unusual high E in the first bar here (the upper limit of the vocal compass) is specially emphatic.

Since the voice is limited to a range of an octave and a fourth (vocal exhibitionism is certainly not the intention), the notes from F to A sharp have only one possible register, and so passages of contiguous motion like that in the third bar of Ex. 29 arise inevitably from the system. But of course they do so only because of the composition of the row, just as Stravinsky's serial engineering later in this example seem designed to throw up useful constancies and correspondences. The final note of the set, C sharp, becomes the first in a rotation of the second hexachord (A–G–G sharp–A sharp–B sharp–C sharp) up a step (hence A sharp–G sharp–A–B–C sharp–D); then comes a reversal of the first hexachord just as it was, and a rotation of this hexachord down a major third. The steps between serial statements – a semitone, a major third – are the same as the steps within them. More than that, the particular choices here enable Stravinsky to, for example, return to the E–F sharp–F neume, or to dose the line heavily with Ds (and dramatically with high Ds), or to end on the voice's lowest note.

The repetitive elements in the vocal line, the little melismas, the ululations and the iterated notes all evoke religious chant, and in particular Jewish chant, but the ritual aspect of the piece is joined by a compulsion that seems to come from within the voice. As Stravinsky pointed out: 'The verbal and musical accentuation are identical . . . which is rare in my music.' The rarity is significant, provoking an unusual sense of natural delivery, which the ease of the melody does not impede. For a composer whose music had seemed for sixty years to have its essential sources in rhythm, bodily gesture and movement, this sudden access to the voice, to the lone narrating voice, is remarkable. *Abraham and Isaac* is like nothing else he wrote, which is to say it is like every great pinnacle in his output from *The Firebird* onwards.

26

Memorials

Stravinsky remained on the east coast for the first five weeks of 1964, giving concerts in Philadelphia, New York and Washington, and recording *Apollo* (the great round of re-recording in the 1960s was occasioned partly by the arrival of stereo technology). In March he made a brief visit to Cleveland for more concerts and recordings, of *Jeu de cartes* and *Ode*; on 1 April he completed the *Elegy for J.F.K.*, which had its first performance under Craft five days later at the Monday Evening Concerts. The première of the *Fanfare for a New Theatre* followed on 19 April at the New York State Theater, Lincoln Center, in Stravinsky's absence. The next month he conducted *Perséphone* at Ann Arbor, recorded a number of previously unrecorded works in Toronto (*The Faun*, *Mavra*, *The Star-Spangled Banner*) and made a new recording of the Piano Concerto in New York. In June he was in England to record *The Rake* and conduct the Symphony of Psalms in Oxford, and in July he recorded *Orpheus* in Chicago.

In mid-August he went by air to Israel for just a few days, for the first performance of *Abraham and Isaac*, sung by Ephraim Biran and conducted by Craft, in Jerusalem on the 23rd and Caesarea the next day. The programme also included the Capriccio under Craft, and the Symphony of Psalms and Bach variations, both sung in Hebrew, under Stravinsky. The following month he made another long but brief ?
journey by air, to Berlin, returning in early October to a new home at 1218 North Wetherly Drive. There, on 28 October, he completed the Variations for orchestra dedicated to the memory of Aldous Huxley. Then in late November he went to New York for concerts and more recordings, of various smaller vocal works including (the childhood memories, *Pribautki*, *Cat's Cradle Songs*, Shakespeare set and *Elegy for J.F.K.*).

He returned to Los Angeles in the new year and wrote the *Introitus* in memory of Eliot between 14 January and 17 February, then began the Requiem Canticles in March. At the end of that month he flew to Texas, and in mid-April on to Chicago, where the Variations and

Introitus had their first performances under Craft on 17 April. After more recordings in New York (the Praeludium, Tango and Ebony Concerto), he sailed to Göteborg in early May, making his last sea crossing of the Atlantic. He was filmed revisiting the Théâtre des Champs-Elysées, where *The Rite* had had its first performance fifty-two years before, and also Clarens, where much of that work had been written. He also conducted the *Firebird* suite in Warsaw and attended a triple bill at the Paris Opéra of *The Rite*, *Les noces* and *Renard*, conducted by Boulez and choreographed by Maurice Béjart. In mid-June he returned home, but was soon making conducting appearances in Indianapolis, Ravinia and Vancouver.

In August 1965 there were more recordings in Hollywood: *Le baiser de la fée*, *Pulcinella* (both complete score and suite), the new Variations, and choral items (the Four Russian Peasant Songs and the Slavonic Credo). In mid-September he made a brief visit to London, his last, to conduct the *Firebird* suite; in October he conducted in Cincinnati and made yet more recordings in Hollywood (the Pastorale, Concertino and Septet), followed by another batch in late November (the Cantata and *In memoriam Dylan Thomas*). The next month he went to New York, and from there to Toronto (first performance of a tiny new Canon for orchestra on the finale theme from *The Firebird*, conducted by Craft on 16 December) and Minneapolis (in January).

He returned to the west coast in late January 1966 and conducted the Symphony of Psalms in Los Angeles at the end of that month and in San Francisco the next. In May he recorded the early Symphony and *Perséphone* in Hollywood before going to Europe for concerts in Athens and Lisbon, returning home for the first fortnight of July. He was then in New York for ten days, conducting the psalms again and a performance of *Histoire du soldat* with Elliott Carter as Narrator, Aaron Copland as Soldier and John Cage as Devil. Then it was back home, where he completed the Requiem Canticles on 13 August. In September he conducted the *Firebird* suite in Louisville, and in October he attended the first performances of his last two original works: the Requiem Canticles under Craft at Princeton on the 8th, and *The Owl and the Pussy-Cat*, with Peggy Bonini singing to Ingolf Dahl's accompaniment, at the Los Angeles Monday Evening Concerts on the 31st.

After a rather barren period in Stravinsky's output, between Movements and *Abraham and Isaac*, the works of 1963–6 – three of substantial proportions on the miniaturized scale of late Stravinsky (the Variations, *Introitus* and Requiem Canticles), four of lesser size (the *Elegy for J.F.K.* setting four haiku verses by Auden for baritone and clarinets, the fanfare for Balanchine's new theatre, the *Firebird* canon and the Edward Lear song) – suggest the creative variety and vitality he had known fifty years before. Of course the moment was brief: he was over eighty. And of course even this least autobiographical of composers was writing against the imminence of death: four of these last works were explicitly made as memorials, and the Requiem Canticles, though dedicated to the memory of Helen Buchanan Seeger in obedience to the commission, have generally been interpreted as the composer's funerary monument for himself. But *The Owl and the Pussy-Cat* is a serial nursery rhyme for voice in canon and piano octaves, looking straight back to the Russian animal songs (the vocal line is confined to just over an octave: it could well be sung by a child); the Canon is a brave burst of splendour for full orchestra; and the Variations are not at all elegiacal in tone.

Their aura is rather of lightning energy, though of a more crystalline, geometrical sort than in Movements. Once again the orchestra is used as a pool of small groupings, but the form is more that of a responsory – of 'verses for ensembles', to quote a Birtwistle title – and there are stronger groundings in repetitions and chord progressions. Double bars divide the five-minute work into eleven sections, of which the second, fourth and penultimate are counterpoints of twelve rhythmically diverse parts, set for violins (suggesting a kinship to the simultaneous birdsongs of the 'Epode' from Messiaen's *Chronochromie*), for violas and double basses, and for woodwind and horn. The outermost sections use the most various formations; the others are more confined in colour, the ninth being a fugato for strings. There are connections with the instrumental litanies of the Symphonies of Wind Instruments, and even with that work's wordless modal chants, within a form strongly articulated by the duodecaphonic refrains, where the splintered, zig-zagging ideas are suddenly muffled in a continuum.

The muffling is more pervasive in the four-minute *Introitus*, dedicated to the memory of T. S. Eliot, of whose *Four Quartets* Stravinsky had set a fragment in his unaccompanied Anthem of 1962. The quite individual sound of this piece comes by way of a further passage into the world of *A Prayer*, with men's voices chanting in the gloom of low resonances from harp and piano, viola and double bass, tam tams and shuddering timpani. For the first time among Stravinsky's serial works, the texture is predominantly block-chordal rather than canonic or kaleidoscopic, but the implied harmonic fundamentals are in an extreme bass beyond hearing.

One testimony to Stravinsky's continuing fertility is the fact that he could move from this immediately to an entirely different set of funeral prayers, the Requiem Canticles, setting short extracts from the Latin mass for the dead (or, as perhaps one should put it, from the librettos of the Mozart and Verdi requiems) in six vocal segments with a Prelude, halfway Interlude and Postlude. The varieties of the Variations are now brought to an emphatic, rudimentary simplicity, with orchestral groupings maintained through whole sections (the Prelude for strings, the Interlude for flutes, bassoons, horns and timpani, the Postlude a final apotheosis of bell sounds), a large-scale symmetry over the fifteen-minute composition (enforced not only by the placing of the instrumental movements but also by the presence of a solo movement in each vocal half: first a 'Tuba mirum' for bass with trumpets followed by bassoons, then a 'Lacrimosa' for contralto with flutes, harp and strings, and trombones to punctuate), the presence of smaller-scale verse-response forms, and a further move towards chordal texture and harmonic encompassing.

Ex. 30, from the 'Exaudi', the opening choral imprecation, may illustrate these traits. This is a sequence of seven hexachords, all related to one another by transposition, inversion or rotation, but the chords are such as might have appeared in Stravinsky's music of an earlier period – the one with string harmonics, in particular, is a last echo of a momentous image going back to the appearance of the Sage in *The Rite* – and the choral announcement of the six notes makes them into a cadential gesture that might have been found in the Mass. Other things here too have long Stravinskian histories: the bass remembers that he was once Creon, the orchestral piano bursts in as it has been doing since *Petrushka*, and solo strings, wailing against the throbbing mass in the Prelude, recall the ritual keenings of *Les noces*. Such recollections help substantiate this as the great endstop to Stravinsky's output, but it would not be a Stravinskian masterpiece if it did not also find new ways of speaking musically, as in the final vocal movement, the 'Libera me' for murmurous speaking chorus around a singing quartet supported on horns.

Ex. 30
Requiem Canticles: Exaudi

Ex. 30 cont.

27

Silence

The four and a half years after the Requiem Canticles were a postlude of miserable ill health and – what seems to have made the composer even more miserable – creative desertion. In November–December 1966 he conducted in Pasadena, Honolulu, Columbus and Portland; at the turn of the year he was conducting in Chicago. Then came the last recording, of the *Firebird* suite in Hollywood on 18 January, and the last conducting appearance, performing the *Pulcinella* suite in Toronto on 17 May. After that his travels were limited and occasional. He attended concerts in Oakland in February 1968, and performances of *The Rake* in Phoenix and Los Angeles the next month. On 23 April comes a poignant note in his diary: 'Asked Bob [Craft] to compose opera libretto for me. He agreed.'[1] But there was to be no opera, and no further new work. Instead, in the summer, because he 'wanted to say something about death and felt that he could not compose anything of his own',[2] he instrumented two Wolf songs.[3] In the autumn he made a visit to Zurich and Paris; *The Rite* at the Paris Opéra was the last of his works he attended. In April 1969 he flew to New York, where he was admitted to hospital early in May; arrangements of four preludes and fugues from Bach's forty-eight, made during these two months, have not been published. He was released from hospital in mid-June, and returned to Los Angeles the next month, but in mid-September he went back to New York, and a month later moved into the Essex House there. He remained in New York until the end of his life, except for an eleven-week stay in Evian during his last summer. On 29 March 1971 he and Vera moved into a new apartment, and he died there on 6 April, to be buried on the cemetery island of San Michele in Venice nine days later, after a

---

[1]*A Stravinsky Scrapbook*, p. 179.   [2]Craft, quoted in White, p. 551.
[3]There is some doubt about just when the work was achieved. The published score is dated 'May 1968' for each song, and Craft's footnote in *Dearest Bubushkin*, p. 227, gives further precision to the period as that of 15–17 May. But the caption to Plate 26 in *SPD* states that the second song was finished on 28 June. The two songs had their first performance, once more at the Monday Evening Concerts, on 6 September, with Christina Krooskos singing (not Marilyn Horne, to whom they are dedicated) and Craft conducting.

funeral at Santi Giovanni e Paolo, at which the Requiem Canticles had what was perhaps their destined performance.

It is not at all untoward that Stravinsky's creative life, which was so much a re-creative life, should have ended with acts of instrumentation. But in every other respect his last publication, the pair of Wolf songs with the accompaniment arranged for three clarinets, two horns and solo string quintet, perplexes. Here, right at the end, Stravinsky suddenly goes deep into the Austro-German tradition to which his whole output had seemed to offer a set of contraries. And as he does so, he leaves no doubtless trace that the one making this last journey is Stravinsky. The music is neither hailed from a position of nearness, as Musorgsky, Tchaikovsky, Bach, Gesualdo and Sibelius had all been hailed, nor ravished, as 'Pergolesi' had been ravished. The use of the winds and strings as antiphonal choirs, exclusively so in the first song, is perhaps a Stravinskian feature, and perhaps too there is a faint echo of the Symphonies of Wind Instruments as clarinets and horns take up the repeated little cadence with which the first song begins. But far, far louder in this opus is the self-effacement, and if we want to hear Stravinsky saying 'something about death', we have to listen to the posthumous blankness.

There are, too, larger implications of this opus ultimum. To search it for 'Stravinskian' aspects of scoring is to subscribe to a notion of closed, definable personality that his whole output calls into question. Of course there are links, as we have seen, between works of different periods: between *Threni* and *Les noces*, between *The Firebird* and the Requiem Canticles, between *Histoire du soldat* and *Agon*. But if links are our concern, we will find many works by Copland, Carter and Poulenc more 'Stravinskian' than Movements, and certainly far more so than the Two Sacred Songs. The lesson of Stravinsky's output is rather one of widening disparity, reaching ever outwards until this final meeting – more bewildering than the meetings with Bach, Lully, Tchaikovsky, Mozart, Webern or Boulez – with Hugo Wolf. Who but a splintered man – peasant and sophisticate, classicist and iconoclast, believer and mercenarian, modalist and serialist – should have been the dominant, emblematic musician of the twentieth century?

Appendix A

Calendar

Year	Age	Life	Contemporary musicians and events
1882		Igor Fyodorovich Stravinsky born on 5 Jun* in Oranienbaum, on the coast forty kilometres to the east of St Petersburg	Births of Malipiero, 18 Mar, Grainger, 8 Jul, Szymanowski, 6 Oct, and Kodály, 16 Dec. Bartók 1, Borodin 49, Brahms 49, Busoni 16, Debussy 20, Dukas 17, Dyagilev 10, Falla 6, Glazunov 17, Ives 8, Janáček 28, Liszt 79, Lyadov 27, Mahler 22, Medtner 2, Myaskovsky 1, Puccini 24, Rakhmaninov 9, Ravel 7, Rimsky-Korsakov 38, Roslavets 1, Roussel 13, Ruggles 6, Satie 16, Schoenberg 8, Sibelius 17, Skryabin 10, Strauss 18, Tchaikovsky 42, Verdi 69, Wagner 69
1883	1		Births of Shteynberg, 4 Jul, Casella, 25 Jul, Ansermet, 11 Nov, Webern, 3 Dec, and Varèse, 22 Dec; death of Wagner (69), 13 Feb.
1884	2	Birth of his brother Gury. Summer in the country, as in most succeeding years until he left Russia.	Birth of Asaf'yev, 29 Jun.
1885	3	First summer on his uncle Yelachich's estate at Pavlovka.	Births of Berg, 7 Feb, Monteux, 4 Apr, and Klemperer, 14 May.
1886	4		Death of Liszt (74), 10 May.
1887	5		Birth of Nadia Boulanger, 16 Sep; death of Borodin (53), 27 Feb.
1888	6		

1889	7		Births of Cocteau, 5 Jul, and possibly of Nijinsky, 17 Dec.
1890	8		First performance of Tchaikovsky's *Sleeping Beauty* (Mariinsky, 15 Jan).
1891	9	First piano lessons. Also first meeting with Catherine Nossenko, later his wife.	Births of Roland-Manuel, 22 Mar, and Prokofiev, 23 Apr.
1892	10		Births of Honegger, 10 Mar, Lourié, 14 May, and Milhaud, 4 Sep; first performance of Tchaikovsky's *Nutcracker* (Mariinsky, 18 Dec).
1893	11	Glimpse of Tchaikovsky at the Mariinsky.	Death of Tchaikovsky (53), 6 Nov.
1894	12		First performance of Debussy's *Prélude à l'apres-midi d'un faune* (Paris, 22 Dec).
1895	13	Visit to Homburg with parents.	Births of Massine, 8 Aug, and Hindemith, 16 Nov.
1896	14	First holiday at Ustilug, henceforth his regular summer retreat.	Births of Thomson, 25 Nov, and Sessions, 28 Dec.
1897	15	Return to Homburg with parents. Death of the eldest Stravinsky son, Roman.	Death of Brahms (63), 3 Apr.
1898	16	First surviving composition, a Tarantella for piano.	Birth of Gershwin, 26 Sep.
1899	17		Births of Poulenc, 7 Jan, and Chávez, 13 Jun.
1900	18		Births of Weill, 2 Mar, Antheil, 8 Jul, and Copland, 14 Nov.
1901	19	Begins law studies in St Petersburg.	Births of Crawford Seeger, 3 Jul, and Partch, 24 Jun; death of Verdi (87), 27 Jan.
1902	20	A song, 'Storm Cloud', and a piano scherzo. In Germany with his parents, he called on Rimsky-Korsakov. His father died on 21 Nov*.	Birth of Wolpe, 25 Aug; first performance of Debussy's *Pelléas et Mélisande* (Paris, 30 Apr).
1903	21	Piano Sonata begun at Pavlovka.	Births of Nicolas Nabokov, 17 Apr, and Adorno, 11 Sep.
1904	22	Cantata for Rimsky's 60th birthday. Completion of the Sonata at Pavlovka.	Births of Balanchine, 22 Jan, and Dallapiccola, 3 Feb; first performance of Puccini's *Madama Butterfly* (Milan, 17 Feb).
1905	23	Engagement to Catherine Nossenko (1 Aug)*. Around the same time he began the Symphony in E flat.	Birth of Tippett, 2 Jan; troops fired on demonstrators in St Petersburg.

1906	24	Marriage (11 Jan)*. The orchestral Pushkin song cycle *The Faun and the Shepherdess*, and a comic song, 'Conductor and Tarantula'. Graduation from the university in May.	Birth of Shostakovich, 25 Sep; first performance of Mahler's Sixth Symphony (Essen, 27 May).
1907	25	Birth of the Stravinskys' first child, Theodore (17 Feb)*. Performances in St Petersburg of the middle movements of the Symphony and of the first Gorodetzky song. Work at Ustilug on completing the Symphony and on the *Scherzo fantastique*.	Birth of Auden, 21 Feb; first performance of Rimsky-Korsakov's *The Legend of the Invisible City of Kitezh* (Mariinsky, 20 Feb).
1908	26	First complete performance of the Symphony and of *The Faun*. Completion of the *Scherzo*. Work at Ustilug on a *Chant funèbre* for Rimsky, the Four Studies for piano, a second Gorodetzky song, and *Fireworks*. First stage work, *The Nightingale*, begun (16 Nov)*. Birth of the Stravinskys' second child, Lyudmila.	Births of Messiaen, 10 Dec, and Carter, 11 Dec; death of Rimsky-Korsakov (64), 8 Jun*; first performance of Schoenberg's Second Quartet (Vienna, 21 Dec).
1909	27	First performances of the *Scherzo fantastique* and *Fireworks* (6 Feb?)*. Unique performance of the *Chant funèbre* (13 Feb?)*. Opening of *Les sylphides* in Paris (2 Jun), with two numbers reorchestrated by Stravinsky for Dyagilev's company. He was at Ustilug finishing the first act of *The Nightingale*. Work on that broken off for *The Firebird* in Nov.	First performance of Strauss's *Elektra* (Dresden, 25 Jan).
1910	28	First vision of *The Rite*. Completion of *The Firebird* in St Petersburg (18 May?)*, and its first performance in Paris (25 Jun). First sketches for *The Rite* made on holiday in Brittany; energies transferred to *Petrushka* in late summer, when the family moved to Switzerland. Second son, Sviatoslav Soulima, born in Lausanne (23 Sep).	

1911	29	Christmas in St Petersburg, planning *Petrushka*. To Rome with the Ballets Russes (Apr); completion of *Petrushka* (26 May), and its first performance in Paris (13 Jun). Summer in Ustilug: Two Balmont Poems and *Zvezdoliki*. Return to Clarens (Sep) and beginning of *The Rite* in earnest.	Death of Mahler (50), 18 May; first performance of Strauss's *Der Rosenkavalier* (Dresden, 26 Jan) and Mahler's *Das Lied von der Erde* (Munich, 20 Nov).
1912	30	Completion of the first part of *The Rite* (7 Jan). In Paris for the Ballets Russes productions of *L'après-midi d'un faune* (29 May) and *Daphnis et Chloé* (8 Jun). First visit to England for the London première of *The Firebird* (18 Jun). Then to Ustilug, to finish *Zvezdoliki*; trip to Bayreuth with Dyagilev (*Parsifal*, 20 Aug). Return to Clarens (Oct); completion of *The Rite* in sketch score (17 Nov). With the Ballets Russes to Berlin; at performance of *Pierrot lunaire* under Schoenberg (8 Dec). Back in Clarens worked on Three Japanese Lyrics.	Births of Markevich, 27 Jul, Cage, 5 Sep; first performance of Schoenberg's *Pierrot lunaire* (Berlin, 16 Oct).
1913	31	With the Ballets Russes to Budapest, Vienna and London. Completion of *The Rite* (8 Mar), then work with Ravel on *Khovanshchina*. First performance of *The Rite* in Paris (29 May). To Ustilug, to resume *The Nightingale* (Jul). Back to Clarens (Sep).	Birth of Britten, 22 Nov; first performance of Debussy's *Jeux* (Paris, 15 May).
1914	32	First performance of the Three Japanese Lyrics in Paris (14 Jan). Birth of fourth and last child, Maria Milena, the next day in Leysin. Completion of *The Nightingale* (27 Mar). First concert performance of *The Rite* in Paris (5 Apr). Back in Leysin first of Three Pieces for quartet completed (26 Apr). First performance of *The Nightingale* in Paris (26 May). Second quartet piece finished in Salvan (2 Jul). Then a	Birth of Mellers, 26 Apr.

quick visit to Ustilug and Kiev
for volumes of Russian folk
verse, the last return to Russia
until 1962. Third quartet piece
(25–6 Jul), *Pribautki* (Aug–Sep),
Polka and March for piano duet
(Nov–Dec), beginning of Four
Russian Peasant Songs for
women's chorus (Dec).

1915	33	Encounter with cimbalom (28 Jan). Visit to Dyagilev in Rome to play *Les noces* (Feb). Waltz for piano duet (6 Mar). *Cat's Cradle Songs* (May–Nov). Move to Morges (Jun). Public débuts as conductor with *Firebird* suite in Geneva and complete ballet in Paris (Dec).	Birth of Perle, 6 May; death of Skryabin (43), 27 Apr; first performance of Sibelius's Fifth Symphony (Helsinki, 8 Dec).
1916	34	*Renard* (Jan–Aug), beginning of *Three Tales for Children* (Jan). Visit to Spain (May).	Birth of Babbitt, 10 May.
1917	35	Five Easy Pieces for piano duet (Jan–Apr), completion of set for female chorus (Jan) and *Chant du rossignol* (4 Apr). Visit to Italy to conduct *The Firebird* and *Fireworks* for the Ballets Russes, meeting with Picasso. Completion of *Three Tales* (May–Jun). Summer in Diablerets, meeting with Gide. Completion of *Les noces* in sketch score (11 Oct), *Etude* for pianola (Nov).	Bolshevik Revolution (7 Nov); first performance of Satie's *Parade* (Paris, 18 May).
1918	36	Completion of piano *Rag-time* (25 March) and beginning of *Histoire du soldat* (Apr). First performance of latter in Lausanne (28 Sep). Three Clarinet Pieces (Oct–Nov), first of Four Russian Songs (Dec).	Births of Bernstein, 25 Aug, and Zimmermann, 20 Mar; death of Debussy (55), 25 Mar; first performance of Bartók's *Bluebeard's Castle* (Budapest, 24 May).
1919	37	Completion of Four Russian Songs (Jan–Feb) and new *Firebird* suite (Feb). First performances of *Pribautki* and *Cat's Cradle Songs* in Vienna (6 Jun). Completion of *Piano-Rag-Music* (28 Jun) and beginning of *Pulcinella* (Sep). Chamber concerts in Switzerland (Nov–Dec) and first	Birth of Kirchner, 24 Jan.

		performance of *Chant du rossignol* in Geneva (6 Dec).
1920	38	First stagings in Paris of *Chant du rossignol* (2 Feb) and *Pulcinella* (15 May). Holiday in Brittany, where Symphonies of Wind Instruments completed (2 Jul) and Concertino begun. Family in Paris, Stravinsky with Coco Chanel. Instrumentation of Symphonies finished (30 Nov).	First performance of Milhaud's *Le boeuf sur le toit* (Paris, 21 Feb).
1921	39	Completion of *Les cinq doigts* (18 Feb) and beginning of ultimate instrumentation of *Les noces*. Move into apartment at Maison Pleyel (Apr), family to Anglet (May). First performance of Symphonies in London (10 Jun). Beginning of affair with Vera Sudeikina (24 Jul). Three Movements from *Petrushka*, start of *Mavra*. Family to Biarritz (autumn). Opening of Ballets Russes *Sleeping Beauty* in London (2 Nov).	Death of Saint-Saëns (86), 16 Dec; first performance of Janáček's *Katya Kabanova* (Brno, 23 Nov) and Prokofiev's *The Love for Three Oranges* (Chicago, 30 Dec).
1922	40	Completion of *Mavra* in Biarritz (9 Mar). First performances in Paris of *Renard* (18 May) and *Mavra* (3 Jun). In Berlin awaiting arrival of mother (Aug –Nov).	Birth of Xenakis, 1 May.
1923	41	Completion of *Les noces* (6 Apr) and Octet (20 May), first performances of both in Paris (13 Jun and 18 Oct). First recording, of the Octet (Nov.)	Birth of Ligeti, 28 May; first performances of Varèse's *Hyperprism* (New York, 4 Mar) and Milhaud's *La création du monde* (Paris, 25 Oct).
1924	42	Concerts in Brussels (Jan) and Spain (Mar). Completion of Piano Concerto (21 Apr) and first performance in Paris (22 May). Trip to Copenhagen (Jul). Family to Nice (25 Sep), where Piano Sonata completed (Oct). Concert tour through the Netherlands, Switzerland, Germany, Poland and Czechoslovakia (Oct–Dec).	Birth of Nono, 29 Jan; deaths of Busoni (58), 27 Jul, Fauré (79), 4 Nov, and Puccini (65), 29 Nov; first performances of Poulenc's *Les biches* (Monte Carlo, 6 Jan) and Janáček's *The Cunning Little Vixen* (Brno, 6 Dec).

1925	43	First American tour (Jan–Mar). Beginning of Serenade, Suite after *Pulcinella* for violin and piano. Appearance at ISCM Festival in Venice (8 Sep). Completion of Serenade (9 Oct) and proposal of *Oedipus rex*. Concert tour including first performances of Serenade and violin–piano Suite in Frankfurt (25 Nov).	Births of Berio, 24 Oct, and Boulez, 25 Mar; first performances of Ravel's *L'enfant et les sortilèges* (Monte Carlo, 21 Mar) and Berg's *Wozzeck* (Berlin, 14 Dec).
1926	44	Beginning of *Oedipus rex* (2 Jan). Conducted *Rite* for first time (Amsterdam, 28 Feb) during concert tour. Spiritual epiphany in Padua (Mar), setting of Lord's Prayer. Performances in Milan (May–Jun). Concentration on *Oedipus* from Aug.	Births of Feldman, 12 Jan, Henze, 1 Jul, and Kurtág, 19 Feb; first performances of Puccini's *Turandot* (Milan, 25 Apr), Shostakovich's First Symphony (Leningrad, 12 May), Hindemith's *Cardillac* (Dresden, 9 Nov) and Bartók's *The Miraculous Mandarin* (Cologne, 27 Nov).
1927	45	Completion of *Oedipus* in sketch score (14 Mar) and first performance in Paris (30 May). Beginning of *Apollo* in Nice (16 Jul).	Birth of Donatoni, 9 Jun; first performance of Berg's Lyric Suite (Vienna, 8 Jan).
1928	46	Completion of *Apollo* in Nice (9 Jan). Conducted first full concert: *Chant du rossignol*, *The Rite*, *Petrushka* (Paris, 10 Feb). First stagings of *Oedipus* (Berlin, 25 Feb) and *Apollo* (Washington, 27 Apr). *Apollo* in Paris (12 Jun). *Le baiser de la fée* (Jul–Oct) and its first performance in Paris (27 Nov). Completion of Four Studies (Oct) and beginning of Capriccio (Dec).	Births of Barraqué, 17 Jan, and Stockhausen, 22 Aug; death of Janáček (74), 12 Aug; first performance of Weill's *Die Dreigroschenoper* (Berlin, 31 Aug).
1929	47	Concerts in Dresden (Feb), Paris (Mar), London (Jun) and Berlin (Jun). Completion of Capriccio (9 Nov) and first performance in Paris (6 Dec).	Death of Dyagilev (57), 19 Aug; first performance of Bartók's Fourth Quartet (Budapest, 20 Mar).
1930	48	Beginning of Symphony of Psalms (6 Jan). Concerts in Germany, Bucharest, Prague and Barcelona (Jan–Mar). Completion of Symphony of Psalms (15 Aug). Concert tour	First performance of Shostakovich's *The Nose* (Leningrad, 18 Jan) and his Third Symphony (Leningrad, 21 Jan).

through Switzerland, Germany
and Vienna (Oct–Dec).
First performance of Symphony of Psalms in Brussels
(13 Dec).

1931	49	Concerts in London. Completion of Violin Concerto (Sep) and first performance in Berlin (23 Oct) during concert tour with Dushkin (Oct–Dec). Beginning of *Duo concertant* (27 Dec).	Births of Bussotti, Gubaydulina, 24 Oct, Kagel, 24 Dec, and Lumsdaine, 31 Oct; death of Nielsen (66), 3 Oct; first performance of Webern's Quartet op. 22 (Vienna, 13 Apr).
1932	50	Completion of *Duo concertant* in Voreppe (15 Jul), where family then living. First performances of *Duo concertant* and *Suite italienne* with Dushkin in Berlin (28 Oct). Beginning of Concerto for two pianos (14 Nov).	Births of Castiglioni, 17 Jul, and Goehr, 10 Aug; first performance of Ruggles's *Suntreader* (Paris, 25 Feb).
1933	51	Recital tour with Dushkin (Feb–Mar). Beginning of *Perséphone* (May).	Birth of Penderecki, 23 Nov; first performances of Varèse's *Ionisation* (New York, 6 Mar) and Strauss's *Arabella* (Dresden, 1 Jul).
1934	52	Completion of *Perséphone* (24 Jan) and first performance in Paris (30 Apr) after recitals in England with Dushkin (Feb). More recitals with Dushkin in Belgium and France (Dec).	Births of Birtwistle, 15 Jul, Davies, 8 Sep, and Schnittke, 24 Nov; deaths of Delius (72), 10 Jun, Elgar (76), 23 Feb, and Holst (59), 25 May; first performance of Shostakovich's *The Lady Macbeth of the Mtsensk District* (Leningrad, 22 Jan).
1935	53	Second American tour (Jan–Apr). Concerts in Copenhagen and Italy (May), and Scandinavia (Sep–Oct). Completion of Concerto for two pianos (9 Nov) and first performance in Paris (21 Nov). Beginning of *Jeu de cartes* (1 Dec).	Births of Rands, 2 Mar, and Young, 14 Oct; death of Berg (50), 24 Dec; first performance of Gershwin's *Porgy and Bess* (New York, 10 Oct).
1936	54	Concerts in Milan, Rome, Barcelona and Bournemouth (Feb–Mar). Tour of South America (Apr–Jun). Completion of *Jeu de cartes* (6 Dec) and beginning of Praeludium before departure for third American tour.	Birth of Reich, 3 Oct; death of Glazunov; first performance of Rakhmaninov's Third Symphony (Philadelphia, 6 Nov).

1937	55	Completion of Praeludium (6 Feb) and first notation for Symphony in C (3 Mar). First performance of *Jeu de cartes* in New York (27 Apr). Return to Paris (May). *Jeu de cartes* in Venice (Sep) and London (Oct). *Petit Ramusianum harmonique* (Oct).	Deaths of Gershwin (37), 11 Jul. Ravel (62), 28 Dec, Roussel (68), 23 Aug, and Szymanowski (54), 29 Mar; first performances of Bartók's Music for Strings, Percussion and Celesta (Basle, 21 Jan) and Shostakovich's Fifth Symphony (Leningrad, 21 Nov).
1938	56	Completion of Concerto in E flat (29 Mar). First movement of Symphony in C (autumn). Death of daughter Lyudmila (30 Nov).	First performances of Hindemith's *Mathis der Maler* (Zurich, 28 May) and Prokofiev's *Romeo and Juliet* (Brno, 30 Dec).
1939	57	Death of wife in Sancellemoz (2 Mar). Move there to work on Symphony and Harvard lectures. Death of mother (7 Jun). Completion of second movement of Symphony (Aug). Move to New York (Sep). Harvard lectures (Oct–Nov). Concerts in Los Angeles and San Francisco (Dec).	Birth of Holliger, 21 May; death of Schmidt (64), 11 Feb.
1940	58	Return to New York (Jan). Marriage to Vera in Bedford, Massachusetts (9 Mar). Concerts in New York and Boston, and completion of third movement of Symphony (28 Apr). Move to Los Angeles (Jun). Concerts in Mexico City (Jul–Aug). Completion of fourth movement of Symphony (19 Aug). Completion of Tango (14 Oct) and beginning of *Danses concertantes*. First performance of Symphony in C in Chicago (7 Nov).	First performance of Schoenberg's Violin Concerto (Philadelphia, 6 Dec).
1941	59	Concerts on east coast (Jan) and Los Angeles (Feb). Bluebird Pas-de-deux arrangement. Concerts in Mexico City (Jul) and St Louis (Dec).	First performance of Messiaen's *Quatuor pour la fin du temps* (Görlitz, 15 Jan).
1942	60	Concerts in San Francisco (Jan). Completion of *Danses concertantes* (13 Jan) and first performance in Los Angeles (8 Feb). Beginning of Symphony in Three Movements (4 Apr).	Deaths of Rakhmaninov (69), 28 Mar, and Zemlinsky (70), 15 Mar; first performances of Shostakovich's Seventh Symphony (Kuibishev, 5 Mar) and Strauss's

		Completion of *Four Norwegian Moods* (18 Aug), *Circus Polka* (5 Oct) and first movement of new symphony (15 Oct).	*Capriccio* (Munich, 28 Oct).
1943	61	Conducted staged *Petrushka* in San Francisco and Los Angeles (Jan–Feb). Second movement of Symphony in Three Movements (15 Feb–17 Mar). New York (Mar–May). *Ode* (19 May–25 Jun). Outer movements of Sonata for two pianos (Sep–Oct). Revision of 'Sacrificial Dance' (Dec).	Births of Bryars, 16 Jan, Ferneyhough, 16 Jan, and Hopkins, 5 Jun; first performance of Webern's Orchestral Variations (Winterthur, 3 Mar).
1944	62	First performances of *Norwegian Moods* and *Circus Polka* in Cambridge, Massachusetts (13 Jan). Completion of Sonata for two pianos (11 Feb). Commissioning of *Babel* (Apr), beginning of *Scènes de ballet* (Jun) and completion of *Scherzo à la russe* (Jun or Jul). Completion of *Scènes* (Aug), *Elégie* (by Nov) and Kyrie and Gloria of Mass (Dec).	Birth of Tavener, 28 Jan; first performance of Copland's *Appalachian Spring* (Washington, 30 Oct).
1945	63	New York (Feb). New *Firebird* suite (Feb). Completion of the Symphony in Three Movements (Aug). First performance of *Babel* in Los Angeles (18 Nov). Completion of *Ebony Concerto* (1 Dec). Granted US citizenship (28 Dec).	Deaths of Bartók (64), 26 Sep, and Webern (61), 15 Sep; VJ Day, 8 May; first performances of Messiaen's *Vingt regards sur l'Enfant Jésus* (Paris, 26 Mar) and Britten's *Peter Grimes* (London, 7 Jun).
1946	64	First performance of Symphony in Three Movements in New York (24 Jan) and other concerts on east coast and in Havana, Dallas and San Francisco. Concerts in Mexico City (Jul). Completion of Concerto in D (8 Aug), revision of *Petrushka* (Oct) and beginning of *Orpheus* (20 Oct). Visit to Chicago, Montreal, New York and Cleveland (Dec–Jan).	Birth of Matthews, 13 Feb; first performances of Prokofiev's *War and Peace* (Leningrad, 12 Jun)and Britten's *The Rape of Lucretia* (Glyndebourne, 12 Jul).
1947	65	New York (Apr–May). To *The Rape of Lucretia* with Huxley (17 Jun). Completion of *Orpheus* (23 Sep) and proposal	Birth of Adams, 15 Feb; first performance of Carter's *The Minotaur* (New York, 26 Mar).

of *The Rake's Progress*. Visit from Auden (Nov). String quartet prelude to graveyard scene of *The Rake* (11 Dec).

1948	66	Concerts in San Francisco and Mexico City (Feb). Completion of Mass (15 Mar). First performance of *Orpheus* in New York (28 Apr), discussions with Auden. Beginning of *The Rake* (8 May).	First performance of Schoenberg's *A Survivor from Warsaw* (Albuquerque, 4 Nov).
1949	67	Completion of first act (16 Jan). New York (Feb–Mar). Craft joined household (1 Jun). *Lied ohne Name* (Jul). Attendance at *Don Giovanni*, early music concert, *Albert Herring* and Britten evenings (Oct–Dec).	Death of Pfitzner (80), 22 May; first performance of Messiaen's *Turangalîla-Symphonie* (Boston, 2 Dec).
1950	68	New York (Feb–May). Concerts in Aspen (Aug) and San Francisco (Dec).	Death of Weill (50), 3 Apr; first performances of Boulez's Second Piano Sonata (Paris, 29 Apr) and Strauss's Four Last Songs (London, 22 May).
1951	69	Concerts in Havana (Mar). Completion of *The Rake* except for Prelude (7 Apr) and beginning of Cantata (Jul). First voyage to Europe since 1939 (Aug). First performance of *The Rake* in Venice (11 Sep), followed by concerts in Germany, Geneva and Italy. Return to New York (Nov).	First performance of Britten's *Billy Budd* (London, 1 Dec).
1952	70	Return to Los Angeles (1 Jan). At Craft's rehearsals of Schoenberg Suite, continuation of Cantata. Arrangement of Concertino for twelve instruments (Apr). Paris (May–Jun). Completion of Cantata (21 Jul) and beginning of Septet (22 Jul). At Craft's rehearsals of Schoenberg Serenade (Sep). First performances of Cantata and new Concertino in Los Angeles (11 Nov). To Cleveland and New York (Dec).	Birth of Rihm, 13 Mar; first performance of Cage's *4'33"* (Black Mountain College, North Carolina).
1953	71	Completion of Septet (21 Jan). *The Rake* in New York (Feb –	Death of Prokofiev (61), 5 Mar; first performances of

Mar) and Boston (May), meeting with Thomas on latter occasion. Shakespeare songs (Sep–Oct). Concerts in Los Angeles (Nov). First sketch for *Agon* (Dec). To Cleveland and New York (Dec).

Stockhausen's *Kontra-Punkte* (Cologne, 26 May) and Shostakovich's Tenth Symphony (Leningrad, 7 Dec).

1954 72 First performance of Septet at Dumbarton Oaks (23 Jan). Song and Prelude of Thomas memorial (Feb–Mar). European tour (Apr–Jun). Postlude for *In memoriam Dylan Thomas* (Jun), new versions of Balmont songs and female choruses, and decisive start on *Agon* (Aug). Conducted staged *Petrushka* in Chicago, San Francisco and Los Angeles (Oct–Dec). Completion of first half of *Agon* (23 Dec).

Birth of Weir, 11 May; Death of Ives (79), 19 May; first performances of Schoenberg's *Moses und Aron* (Hamburg, 12 Mar) and Varèse's *Déserts* (Paris, 2 Dec).

1955 73 Concerts in Portland, Salem, Birmingham and Atlanta (Jan), *Greeting Prelude* (Feb). European tour (Mar–May). *Canticum sacrum* (Jun–21 Nov). To Cleveland and New York (Dec). Beginning of Bach variations.

Deaths of Enescu (73), 3/4 May, and Honegger (63), 27 Nov; first performance of Boulez's *Le marteau sans maître* (Baden-Baden, 18 Jun).

1956 74 Return to Los Angeles (Jan), completion of Bach variations (27 Mar) and first performance at Ojai (27 May). To Venice via Mediterranean ports (Jun). First performance of *Canticum sacrum* in Venice (13 Sep), followed by concert tour interrupted by period in hospital in Berlin (Oct–Nov). Return to New York (Dec).

First performances of Messiaen's *Oiseaux exotiques* (Paris, 10 Mar), Stockhausen's *Gesang der Jünglinge* (Cologne, 30 May) and *Zeitmasze* (Paris, 15 Dec).

1957 75 Return to Los Angeles (Jan). At *Le marteau* under Boulez (11 Mar). Completion of *Agon* (27 Apr) and Gesualdo *Illumina nos* (5 May). Santa Fe (Jul), England (Aug), Venice (Aug–Sep). Beginning of *Threni* (29 Aug). Performances of *Agon* in Paris, Donaueschingen and Rome (Oct). Return to Los Angeles.

Birth of Tan Dun, 18 Aug; death of Sibelius (91), 20 Sep; first performance of Boulez's Third Piano Sonata (Darmstadt, Sep).

1958 76 Concerts in Houston (Jan). Completion of *Threni* (21 Mar). Concerts in San Francisco (Apr)

Deaths of Schmitt (87), 17 Aug, and Vaughan Williams (85), 26 Aug; first and Los Angeles (Jun). Completion of first of Movements (9 Jul). Venice (Aug–Sep), including first performance of *Threni* (23 Sep), followed by European concert tour (Oct–Dec). Return to New York.

performance of Stockhausen's *Gruppen* (Cologne, 24 Mar).

| 1959 | 77 | Return to Los Angeles. Japan (Apr–May). *Epitaphium* (May). Sonning Prize ceremony in Copenhagen (May). Santa Fe (Jun-Jul). Completion of Movements (Aug). Britain (Sep), Venice (Sep–Oct). Two more Gesualdo completions and Double Canon (Sep). Concerts in Italy and London (Oct–Nov). Return to New York. | Deaths of Martinů (68), 28 Aug, and Villa-Lobos (72), 17 Nov. |

| 1960 | 78 | First performance of Movements in New York (10 Jan). Return to Los Angeles. *Monumentum* (Mar). Santa Fe (Jul). Tour of Latin America (Aug–Sep). Venice (Sep–Nov), including first performance of *Monumentum* (27 Sep). Return to New York. | First performances of Barraqúe's . . . *au delà du hasard* (Paris, 26 Jan) Boulez's *Pli selon pli* (Cologne, 13 Jun), Shostakovich's Eighth Quartet (Leningrad, 2 Oct) and Messiaen's *Chronochromie* (Donaueschingen, 16 Oct). |

| 1961 | 79 | Return to Los Angeles (Jan). Completion of *A Sermon* (31 Jan). Concerts in Mexico City (Apr). Santa Fe (Jul–Aug). European tour (Sep–Oct). Australasian tour (Nov–Dec). Return to Los Angeles. | First performances of Nono's *Intolleranza* (Venice, 13 Apr) and Carter's Double Concerto (New York, 6 Sep). |

| 1962 | 80 | Completion of Anthem (2 Jan). East coast (Jan–Feb), including White House dinner (18 Jan). Completion of *The Flood* (14 Mar). Concerts in Seattle and Toronto (Apr). South African tour (May–June). Rome and Hamburg (Jun). Return to Los Angeles via New York and Chicago, Santa Fe (Aug), beginning of *Abraham*. Israel (Aug–Sep). Russia (Sep–Oct). Concerts in Rome (Oct) and Caracas (Nov). Recordings in Toronto | First performances of Stockhausen's *Momente* (Cologne, 21 May), Britten's *War Requiem* (Coventry, 30 May) and Shostakovich's Thirteenth Symphony (Moscow, 18 Dec). |

		(Nov–Dec). Return to Los Angeles.	
1963	81	Completion of *Abraham* (3 Mar). Recordings in Toronto (Mar). European tour (Apr–Jun). Santa Fe (Jul–Aug). Concerts in Rio (Sep) and Italy (Nov). Return to New York.	Deaths of Cocteau (74), 11 Oct, Hindemith (68), 28 Dec and Poulenc (64), 30 Jan.
1964	82	Concerts in Philadelphia, New York and Washington (Jan). Return to Los Angeles (Feb). Concerts in Cleveland (Mar) and Ann Arbor (May), recordings in Toronto (May). England (Jun), Chicago (Jul). First performance of *Abraham* in Jerusalem (23 Aug). Paris and Berlin (Sep). Completion of Variations in Los Angeles (28 Oct). To New York (Nov).	First performances of Messiaen's *Couleurs de la Cité Céleste* (Donaueschingen, 17 Oct) and Stockhausen's *Mikrophonie* 1 (Brussels, 9 Dec).
1965	83	Return to Los Angeles. *Introitus* (14 Jan–17 Feb), beginning of Requiem Canticles (Mar). Texas-Chicago-New York (Mar–May). European tour (May–June). Concerts in Vancouver (Jul) and recordings in Hollywood (Aug). Concerts in London (Sep) and Cincinnati (Oct), more recordings in Hollywood (Oct–Nov). To New York (Dec).	Deaths of Cowell (68), 10 Dec, and Varèse (81) 6 Nov; first performances of Ligeti's Requiem (Stockholm, 14 Mar) and Boulez's *Eclat* (Los Angeles, 26 Mar).
1966	84	Concerts in Minneapolis (Jan), Los Angeles (Jan), St Louis (Feb), San Francisco (Feb) and Rochester (Mar), recordings in Hollywood (May). European tour (May–Jun). New York (Jul). Completion of Requiem Canticles in Los Angeles (13 Aug). Concert in Louisville (Sep). At first performance of Requiem Canticles in Princeton (8 Oct). Concerts in Pasadena, Honolulu, Columbus, Portland and Chicago (Nov–Dec).	Death of Lourié (74), 12 Oct; first performance of Barraqué's *Chant après chant* (Strasbourg, 23 Jun).
1967	85	Last recording: *Firebird* suite (Hollywood, 18 Jan). Last concert: *Pulcinella* suite in	First performance of Stockhausen's *Hymnen* (Cologne, 30 Nov).

		Toronto (17 May).	
1968	86	Instrumentation of Wolf songs (summer). Switzerland and Paris (Sep–Nov).	First performance of Birtwistle's *Punch and Judy* (Aldeburgh, 8 Jun) and Berio's *Sinfonia* (New York, 10 Oct).
1969	87	To New York (Apr), in hospital (May–Jun). Return to Los Angeles (Jul). Back to New York (Sep).	Deaths of Adorno (65), 6 Aug, and Ansermet (85), 20 Feb; first performances of Davies's *Eight Songs for a Mad King* (London, 22 Apr) and Shostakovich's Fourteenth Symphony (Leningrad, 29 Sep).
1970	88	Evian (Jun–Aug).	Deaths of Gerhard (73), 5 Jan, and Zimmermann (52), 10 Aug; first performance of Stockhausen's *Mantra* (Donaueschingen, 28 Oct).
1971	89	Death in New York (6 Apr), funeral in Venice (15 Apr).	Adams 24, Babbitt 54, Barraqué 43, Berio 45, Bernstein 52, Birtwistle 36, Boulez 46, Britten 57, Bryars 28, Cage 58, Carter 62, Castiglioni 38, Chávez 71, Copland 70, Dallapiccola 67, Davies 36, Donatoni 43, Feldman 45, Ferneyhough 28, Goehr 38, Gubaydulina 39, Henze 44, Holliger 31, Hopkins 27, Kagel 39, Kirchner 52, Kurtág 45, Ligeti 47, Lumsdaine 39, C. Matthews 25, Mellers 56, Messiaen 62, Nono 47, Penderecki 57, Perle 55, Rands 36, Reich 35, Rihm 19, Schnittke 36, Sessions 74, Shostakovich 64, Stockhausen 42, Tan Dun 13, Tavener 27, Thomson 74, Tippett 66, Weir 17, Xenakis 48, Young 35.

Why do we keep having to have a minor composer like Tan Dun repeatedly rammed down our throats? It couldn't possibly, could it, have anything to do with the fact that Griffiths is writing an opera libretto for him, so can't pass up any occasion to overstate his importance?
(A book like this ought to be a serious academic endeavour, not a subliminal advertising opportunity)

Appendix B
List of works

This list is, as near as possible, complete, and includes some or all of the following information for each work: title (plus other forms, date of composition, author of text, note of derivation from other work), scoring, publishers, extracts available for separate performance and subsidiary or associated works. Details of scoring use common conventions: abbreviations are as in *The New Grove*, and orchestral ensembles are given in the order woodwind (flutes, oboes, clarinets, bassoons) – brass (horns, trumpets, trombones, tubas) – percussion (including timpani, keyboards and harp) – strings (violins I, violins II, violas, cellos, basses). Where the instrumentation is straightforward, some or all departments may simply be enumerated. Elsewhere doublings are indicated inside brackets, so that, for example '3 cl (1st + E flat, 3rd + b cl)' means that there are three clarinettists, of whom the first doubles on E flat clarinet and the third on bass clarinet.

1 DRAMATIC WORKS

1.1 Complete items

The Firebird (Zhar'-ptitsa, L'oiseau de feu; 1909–10)
Ballet in two scenes to a scenario by Michel Fokine
2 pic (2nd + fl), 2 fl, 3 ob, cor anglais, 3 cl (3rd + D), b cl, 3 bn (3rd + dbn), dbn – 4.3.3.1 – timp, perc, bells, xyl, cel, pf, 3 harps – 16.16.14.8.6 (plus 3 tpt, 2 t tubas and 2 b tubas behind the scenes)
Jurgenson, Schott, Broude; *see also* 2.2, 4.4, 5.2, 5.4

Petrushka (Pétrouchka; 1910–11)
Ballet in four scenes to a scenario by the composer and Alexandre Benois
4 fl (3rd and 4th + pic), 4 ob (4th + cor anglais), 3 cl, b cl, 3 bn, dbn – 4 hn, pic tpt in D, 2 tpt (both + cornets), 3 trbn, tuba – timp, perc, xyl, 2 cel, pf, 2 harps – strings
Edition Russe de Musique; *see also* 2.2, 4.4, 5.1, 5.4
rev. for 3 fl (3rd + pic), 2 ob, cor anglais, 3 cl (3rd + b cl), 2 bn, dbn – 4.3.3.1 – timp, perc, xyl, cel, pf, harp – strings (1946)
Boosey

The Rite of Spring (Vesna svyashchennaya, Le sacre du printemps; 1910–13)
Ballet in two parts to a scenario by the composer and Nicolas Roerich
pic, 3 fl (3rd + pic), a fl, 4 ob (4th + cor anglais), cor anglais, cl in D + E flat, 3 cl in A + B flat (3rd + b cl), b cl, 4 bn (4th + dbn), dbn – 8 hn (7th and 8th + t tubas), pic tpt in D, 4 tpt (4th + b tpt), 3 trbn, 2 tubas – timp (2 players), perc – strings
Edition Russe de Musique, Boosey, *see also* 2.2, 5.1, 5.4
Sacrificial Dance rev. 1943: Associated

The Nightingale (Solovey, Le rossignol; 1908–14)
Opera in three acts to a libretto by Stepan Mitusov
The Nightingale (S), The Emperor (Bar), The Fisherman (T), Death (A), minor
roles for STBBB, SATB chorus
pic, 2 fl, 2 ob, cor anglais, 3 cl (3rd + b cl), 3 bn (3rd + dbn) – 4.4.3.1 – timp,
perc, bells, cel, pf, 2 harps, mandolin, guitar – strings
Edition Russe de Musique, Boosey; *see also* 2.1, 2.2, 3.6, 4.4, 5.2

Renard (Bayka; 1915–16)
'A burlesque in song and dance' on Russian folk verse
TTBB soloists – pic + fl, ob + cor anglais, cl in E flat + B flat + A, bn – 2.1.0.0
– timp, perc, cimbalom – 1.1.1.1.1
Henn, Chester; also version with pf replacing cimbalom and fragment with
instruments replacing voices;[1] *see also* 3.6

Les noces (Svadebka, The Wedding; 1914–17)
Ballet in four scenes on Russian folk verse
SATB soloists, SATB chorus – 3.3.3.2 – 4.4.3.1 – timp, perc, harmonium,
cimbalom, harpsichord, pf, 2 harps – 3.0.2.2.1 (1917, almost complete)
rev. SATB soloists, SATB chorus, timp, perc, harmonium, 2 cimbaloms,
pianola (1919, scenes 1–2 only)
rev. SATB soloists, SATB chorus, timp, perc, xyl, 4 pf (1922–3)
Chester; *see also* 3.6, 5.4

Histoire du soldat (The Soldier's Tale; 1918)
'To be read, played and danced', words by C. F. Ramuz
3 actors, dancer – cl in A, bn, cornet, trbn, perc, vn, db
Chester; *see also* 4.1, 4.2, 5.2

Pulcinella (1919–20)
Ballet in one act after the commedia dell'arte and music by 'Pergolesi'
STB soloists – 2 fl (2nd + pic), 2 ob, 2 bn – 2.1.1.0 – 1.1.1.1.1 (concertino),
4.4.4.3.3. (ripieno)
Edition Russe de Musique, Boosey; *see also* 2.3, 3.6, 4.4, 5.4

Mavra (1921–2)
Opera buffa in one act to a libretto by Boris Kochno after Pushkin
Parasha (S), The Hussar/The Cook (T), The Mother (A), The Neighbour (Mez)
3 fl (3rd + pic), 2 ob, cor anglais, cl in E flat, 2 cl in B flat + A, 2 bn – 4.4.3.1 –
timp – 1.1.1.3.3
Edition Russe de Musique, Boosey; *see also* 2.1, 3.6, 4.4

Oedipus rex (1926–7)
'Opera–oratorio' in two acts to a libretto by Jean Cocteau and Jean Daniélou
after Sophocles
Oedipus (T), Jocasta (Mez), Creon (BBar), Tiresias (B), The Shepherd (T), The
Messenger (BBar), The Speaker
3 fl (3rd + pic), 2 ob, cor anglais, 3 cl in B flat + A (3rd + E flat), 2 bn, dbn –
4.4.3.1 – timp, b drum, pf, harp – strings

[1]See *SSC* I, p. 415.

Stravinsky

Edition Russe de Musique, Boosey; *see also* 2.1, 3.6

* *Apollo* (Apollon musagète; 1927–8)
  Ballet in two scenes
  strings with divided cellos: 8.8.6.4.4.4.[2]
  Edition Russe de Musique, Boosey; *see also* 5.2

* *Le baiser de la fée* (The Fairy's Kiss, 1928)
  Ballet in four scenes after Hans Christian Andersen and music by Tchaikovsky
  3 fl (3rd + pic), 2 ob, cor anglais, 3 cl (3rd + b cl), 2 bn – 4.3.3.1 – timp, b drum, harp – strings
  Edition Russe de Musique, Boosey; *see also* 2.2, 4.4, 5.2

  Perséphone (1933–44)
  'Melodrama' in three scenes to a libretto by André Gide
  narrator, T soloist, SA children's chorus, SATB chorus – 3 fl (3rd + pic), 3 ob (3rd + cor anglais), 3 cl (3rd + b cl), 3 bn (3rd + dbn) – 4.3.3.1 – timp, perc, pf, 2 harps – strings
  Edition Russe de Musique, Boosey; *see also* 3.6

* *Jeu de cartes* (A Game of Cards, The Card Party; 1936)
  Ballet 'in three deals' to a scenario by the composer and Nikita Malayev
  2 fl (2nd + pic), 2 ob (2nd + cor anglais), 2 cl, 2 bn – 4.2.3.1 – timp, b drum – 12.10.8.6.6.
  Schott; *see also* 5.2

  Scènes de ballet (1944)
  Short ballet for a revue
  2 fl (2nd + pic), 2 ob, 2 cl, 2 bn – 2.3.3.1 – timp, pf – strings
  Chappell, Schott

* *Orpheus* (Orphée; 1947)
  Ballet in three scenes to a libretto by the composer and George Balanchine
  pic, 2 fl, 2 ob (2nd + cor anglais), 2 cl, 2 bn – 2.2.2.0 – timp, harp – strings
  Boosey

* *The Rake's Progress* (1947–51)
  Opera in three acts to a libretto by W. H. Auden and Chester Kallman
  Tom Rakewell (T), Anne Trulove (S), Nick Shadow (Bar), Baba the Turk (Mez), Sellem (T), Trulove (B), Mother Goose (Mez), Keeper of the Madhouse (B), SATB chorus
  2 fl (2nd + pic), 2 ob (2nd + cor anglais), 2 cl, 2 bn – 2.2.0.0. – timp, harpsichord – strings
  Boosey; *see also* 2.1, 4.3

* *Agon* (1953–7)
  Ballet 'for twelve dancers'
  3 fl (3rd + pic), 2 ob, cor anglais, 2 cl, b cl, 2 bn, dbn – 4.4.3.0 – timp, tom toms, xyl, castanet, mandolin, pf, harp – strings
  Boosey; *see also* 5.1

* *The Flood* (1961–2)
  'A musical play' to a libretto by Robert Craft after Genesis and English miracle plays

[2]See *An Autobiography*, p. 142.

Noah, Noah's Wife, Noah's sons, Narrator, Caller (spoken roles), Lucifer/ Satan (T), God (2 B), SAT chorus
3 fl (3rd + pic), a fl, 2 ob, cor anglais, 2 cl, b cl, db cl, 2 bn, dbn – 4 hn, 3 tpt, 2 t trbn (2nd + a trbn), b trbn, tuba – timp, tom toms, cymbal, b drum, xyl + mar, pf + cel, harp – strings
Boosey

1.2 Contributions

Les sylphides
Orchestrations of Chopin's Nocturne in A flat and Valse brillante in E flat for Dyagilev (1909)

Les orientales
Orchestration of Grieg's 'Kobold' for Dyagilev (1910)[3]

Khovanshchina
Orchestrations and finale, in collaboration with Ravel, for Dyagilev (1913)

The Sleeping Beauty
Orchestrations of the 'Variation d'Aurore' and 'Entr'acte symphonique' for Dyagilev (1921)

The Sleeping Beauty
Orchestration of the 'Bluebird Pas-de-deux' for Balanchine (1941)
1.1.2.1 – 1.2.2.0 – timp, pf – strings
Schott

2 ORCHESTRAL WORKS

2.1 Works with voices

The Faun and The Shepherdess op. 2 (Favn' i pastushka, Faune et bergère; Pushkin; 1906–7)
Mez – 3.2.2.2 – 4.2.3.1 – timp, perc – strings
Belaieff, Boosey; *see also* 3.6

Two Songs of the Flea (Goethe; 1909; after Beethoven and Musorgsky)
Beethoven's arranged for B – 2.2.2.2 – 2.0.0.0 – strings
Musorgsky's arranged for Bar/B – 3.2.2.2 – 4.2.3.1 – timp, harp – strings
W. Bessell, Boosey

Zvezdoliki (Star-Faced, Le roi des étoiles, The King of the Stars; Balmont; 1911–12)
TTBB chorus – pic, 3 fl, 4 ob (4th + cor anglais), cl in E flat, 3 cl, 3 bn, dbn – 8.3.3.1 – timp, b drum, tam tam, cel, 2 harps – strings
Jurgenson; *see also* 3.6

The Nightingale (1908–14: *see* 1.1)
extracts: Song of the Fisherman (T), Song of the Nightingale (S)[4]

---

[3]Craft in *Glimpses*, p. 11, suggests that Stravinsky also orchestrated music by Sinding for this ballet.

[4]These extracts were not separately published, but Stravinsky included them in his concert repertory.

Stravinsky

Mavra (1921–2: *see* 1.1)
extract: Chanson de Paracha (Parasha's Aria) (S)
Boosey; *see also* 3.5, 4.4

Tilimbom (1923; after Three Tales for Children no. 1; *see* 3.5)
S – 3.2.2.0 – 2.1.0.0 – timp – strings
Chester

Oedipus rex (1926–7: *see* 1.1)

Three Little Songs (1929–30: *see* 3.5)
S – 2.2.2.2 – 0.0.0.0 – strings without dbs
Edition Russe de Musique, Boosey

Symphony of Psalms (Symphonie de psaumes; Vulgate; 1930)
SATB (preferably with children in upper parts) – 5 fl (5th + pic), 4 ob, cor anglais, 3 bn, dbn – 4.5.3.1 – timp, b drum, pf, 2 harps – cellos, basses
Edition Russe de Musique, Boosey

Perséphone (1933–4: *see* 1.1)

Babel (Genesis 11:1–9; 1944)
narrator, TB chorus – 3 fl (3rd + pic), 2 ob, 2 cl, b cl, 2 bn, dbn – 4.3.3.0 – timp, harp – strings
Schott; *see also* 3.6

The Rake's Progress (1947–51: *see* 1.1)

Two Poems of Verlaine (1951: *see* 3.5)
Bar – 2.0.2.0 – 2.0.0.0 – strings
Boosey

Canticum sacrum ad honorem Sancti Marci nominis (Vulgate; 1955)
tenor, baritone, SATB chorus – fl, 2 ob, cor anglais, bn, dbn – 3 tpt, b tpt, 2 t trbn, b trbn, db trbn – harp, organ – violas, basses
Boosey; *see also* 3.6

Choral-Variationen über das Weihnachtslied 'Vom Himmel hoch da komm Ich her' (1955–6; after J. S. Bach)
SATB chorus – 2 fl, 2 ob, cor anglais, 2 bn, dbn – 3 tpt, 3 trbn – harp – violas, basses
Boosey

Threni: id est lamentationes Jeremiae prophetae (Vulgate; 1957–8)
SATTBB soloists, SATB chorus – 2 fl, 2 ob, cor anglais, 2 cl (2nd + a cl in F), b cl, sarrusophone – 4 hn, flugelhorn, a trbn, t trbn, b trbn, tuba – timp, tam tam, pf, cel, harp – strings
Boosey

A Sermon, a Narrative and a Prayer (Authorized Version, Dekker; 1960–61)
speaker, AT soloists, SATB chorus – fl, a fl, 2 ob, cl, b cl, 2 bn – 4.3.3.1 – 3 tam tams, pf, harp – 8.7.6.5.4
Boosey

The Flood (1961–2: *see* 1.1)

214

, *Abraham and Isaac* (Hebrew Bible; 1962–3)
Bar – 2 fl, a fl, ob, cor anglais, cl, b cl, 2 bn – 1.2.2.1 – strings
Boosey

, Requiem Canticles (Latin Requiem; 1965–6)
AB soloists, SATB chorus – 3 fl (3rd + pic), a fl, 2 bn – 4.2.3.0 – timp (2 players), xyl, vib, bells, pf, cel, harp – strings
Boosey

2.2 Works for full orchestra

Symphony in E flat op. 1 (1905–7)
pic, 2 fl, 2 ob, 3 cl, 2 bn – 4.3.3.1 – timp, triangle, cymbals, b drum – strings
Jurgenson, Forberg

Scherzo fantastique op. 3 (1907–8)
pic, 3 fl (3rd + a fl), 2 ob, cor anglais, 3 cl, b cl, 2 bn, dbn – 4.3.0.0 – cymbals, cel, 3/2 harps – strings
Jurgenson, Schott

Fireworks op. 4 (Feu d'artifice, Feuerwerk; 1908)
pic, 2 fl, 2 ob (2nd + cor anglais), 3 cl (3rd + b cl), 2 bn – 6.3.3.1 – timp, triangle, cymbals, b drum, bells, cel, 2 harps – strings
Schott

Orchestrations of Chopin and Grieg (1909–10: *see* 1.2)

The Firebird (1909–10: *see* 1.1)
suite for same orchestra without stage instruments (1911): Jurgenson
Berceuse with reduced wind (?1911): Jurgenson
Finale with reduced wind (1915)
suite for 2 fl (2nd + pic), 2 ob (2nd + cor anglais), 2 cl, 2 bn – 4.2.3.1 – timp, triangle, cymbals, tambourine, b drum, xyl, pf, harp – strings: Chester
extended version of 1919 suite for same orchestra (1945): Leeds

Petrushka (1910–11: *see* 1.1)
suite[5]

The Rite of Spring (1910–13: *see* 1.1)
concert ending after introduction to second part (?1923): ?lost[6]

Chant du rossignol (Pyesnya solov'ya, The Song of the Nightingale; symphonic poem, 1916–17; after *The Nightingale*: *see* 1.1)
2 fl (2nd + pic), 2 ob (2nd + cor anglais), 2 cl (2nd + E flat), 2 bn – 4.3.3.1 – timp, perc, cel, pf, 2 harps – strings
Edition Russe de Musique, Boosey; *see also* 5.2, 5.4

, Four Studies (nos. 1–3, 1914–18 after Three Pieces: *see* 4.2; no. 4 1928 after Etude: *see* 5.4)

[5]The score includes concert endings for the 'Russian Dance' and for the entire work omitting the final drama. Stravinsky's own concerts included a suite far more often than they did the complete work, the omissions including, besides the last pages, the whole of the third scene and sometimes the opening of the first, with the start made at fig. 58 in the revised version. See *SPD*, p. 68.
[6]Made for Ansermet. See *SSC II*, p. 432.

3 fl (3rd + pic), 3 ob (3rd + cor anglais), cl in E flat, 2 cl, b cl, 2 bn – 4.3.2.1 – timp, pf, harp -- strings
Edition Russe de Musique, Boosey

The Sleeping Beauty extracts (1921: *see* 1.2)

Le baiser de la fée (1928: *see* 1.1)
Divertimento, suite from above for same orchestra (1934)
edition Russe de Musique, Boosey; *see also* 4.4

Capriccio (1928–9)
pf solo – 3 fl (3rd + pic), 2 ob, cor anglais, 3 cl (2nd + E flat, 3rd + b cl), 2 bn – 4.2.3.1 – timp – 1.0.1.1.1 (concertino), ripieno strings
Boosey; *see also* 5.1

Concerto in D (1931)
vn solo – pic, 2 fl, 2 ob, cor anglais, cl in E flat, 2 cl, 3 bn (3rd + dbn) – 4.3.3.1 – timp – 8.8.6.4.4
Boosey; *see also* 4.4

Jeu de cartes (1936: *see* 1.1)

Symphony in C (1938–40)
pic, 2 fl, 2 ob, 2 cl, 2 bn – 4.2.3.1 – timp – strings
Schott

The Star-Spangled Banner (after John Stafford Smith; 1941)
3.3.2.2 – 4.3.3.1 – timp – strings
Mercury

Circus Polka (1942)
pic, fl, 2 ob, 2 cl, 2 bn – 4.2.3.1 – timp – strings
Associated, Schott; *see also* 5.2

Four Norwegian Moods (Quatre pièces à la norvégienne; 1942)
2 fl (2nd + pic), 2 ob (2nd + cor anglais), 2 cl, 2 bn – 4.2.2.1 – timp – strings
Associated, Schott

Ode (elegiacal chant, 1943)
3 fl (3rd + pic), 2 ob, 2 cl, 2 bn – 4.2.0.0 – timp – strings
Schott

Scherzo à la russe (1943–4)
pic, 2 fl, 2 ob, 2 cl, 2 bn – 4.3.3.1 – timp, perc, xyl, pf, harp – strings
Chappell, Schott; *see also* 2.6

Symphony in Three Movements (1942–5)
pic, 2 fl, 2 ob, 2 cl, b cl, 2 bn, dbn – 4.3.3.1 – timp, b drum, pf, harp – strings
Associated, Schott

Orpheus (1947: *see* 1.1)

Greeting Prelude (1955)
pic, 2 fl, 2 ob, 2 cl, 2 bn, dbn – 4.2.3.1 – timp, b drum, pf – strings
Boosey

Agon (1953–7: *see* 1.1)

216

Movements (1958–9)
  pf solo – 2 fl (2nd + pic), ob, cor anglais, cl, b cl, bn – 0.2.3.0 – cel, harp –
  6.6.4.5.2
  Boosey; *see also* 5.1

Variations (1963–4)
  2 fl, a fl, 2 ob, cor anglais, 2 cl, b cl, 2 bn – 4.3.3.0 – pf, harp – 12.0.10.8.6
  Boosey

Canon (on a Russian popular tune, 1965)
  pic, 2 fl, 2 ob, cor anglais, 2 cl, b cl, 2 bn, dbn – 4.3.3.1 – timp, b drum, pf, harp
  – strings
  Boosey

2.3 Works for chamber orchestra

Rag-time (1918)
  fl, cl, hn, cornet, trbn, cimbalom, perc, 2 vn, va, db
  Sirène, Chester; *see also* 5.2, 5.4

Pulcinella suite (?1922: *see* 1.1)
  for same orchestra as the ballet but without voices
  Edition Russe de Musique, Boosey

Suites nos. 1–2 (no. 1 1917–25 after Five Easy Pieces nos. 1–4: *see* 5.1; no. 2 1921
  after Three Easy Pieces and Five Easy Pieces no. 5: *see* 5.1)
  2 fl (2nd + pic), ob, 2 cl, 2 bn – 1.2.1.1 – perc, pf – strings
  Chester

Concerto in E flat 'Dumbarton Oaks' (1937–8)
  fl, cl, bn, 2 hn, 3 vn, 3 va, 2 vc, 2 db
  Schott; *see also* 5.1

Bluebird Pas-de-deux (1941: *see* 1.2)

Danses concertantes (1940–42)
  1.1.1.1 – 2.1.1.0 – timp – 6.0.4.3.2
  Associated, Schott

Concertino (1952: *see* 4.2)
  fl, ob, cor anglais, cl, 2 bn, 2 tpt, 2trbn, vn, vc
  Hansen

Monumentum pro Gesualdo di Venosa ad CD annum (1960; after Gesualdo
  madrigals)
  0.2.0.2 – 4.2.3.0 – strings without dbs
  Boosey

Eight Instrumental Miniatures (1962; after *Les cinq doigts*: *see* 5.2)
  2.2.2.2 – 1.0.0.0 – 2.0.2.2.0
  Chester

Preludes and Fugues in E minor, D minor, B minor and C sharp minor (1969;
  after Bach)
  0.0.3.2 – 0.0.0.0 – strings

2.4 Works for strings

Apollo (1927–8: *see* 1.1)

Concerto in D (1946)
8.8.6.4.4[7]
Boosey

2.5 Works for wind

Chant funèbre op. 5 (1908): lost

Song of the Volga Boatmen (Chant des bateliers du Volga, Hymne à la nouvelle
Russie; 1917; after Russian traditional)
2.2.2.3 – 4.3.3.1 – timp, perc
Chester

Symphonies of Wind Instruments (1920)
3 fl, a fl, 2 ob, cor anglais, cl, a cl, 3 bn (3rd + dbn) – 4.3.3.1
Chorale rev. without cls (1945)
rev. for 3 fl, 2 ob, cor anglais, 3 cl, 3 bn (3rd + dbn) – 4.3.3.1: Boosey

Octet (1922–3)
fl, cl, 2 bn, 2 tpt, 2 trbn
Edition Russe de Musique, Boosey

Concerto (1923–4)
pf solo – pic, 2 fl, ob, cor anglais, 2 cl, 2 bn (2nd + dbn – 4.4.3.1 – timp –
basses
Edition Russe de Musique, Boosey; *see also* 5.1

Pesante (1961: after *Les cinq doigts* no. 8: *see* 5.2)
2 ob, 2 bn, 3 tpt, 3 trbn[8]

2.6 Works for jazz ensemble

Praeludium (1936–7)
2 a sax, t sax, bar sax, 3 tpt, 2 trbn, timp + perc, cel, guitar, 3 vn, va, vc, db
Boosey; *see also* 5.2

Scherzo à la russe (1944)
2 fl, ob, 2 a sax, 2 t sax, bar sax – 1.3.3.1 – timp, perc, pf, harp, guitar – strings
Chappell, Schott; *see also* 2.2

Ebony Concerto (1945)
cl solo – 2 a sax, 2 t sax, bar sax, b cl, hn, 5 tpt, 3 trbn, perc, pf, harp, guitar, db
Charling, Morris

Tango (1953: *see* 5.2)
4 cl, b cl, 4 tpt, 3 trbn, guitar, 3 vn, va, vc, db
Mercury, Schott

3 VOCAL WORKS

3.1 Works with orchestra (= 2.1)

[7]See White, p. 438.   [8]Reproduced in *A Stravinsky Scrapbook*, pp. 103–6.

3.2 Small-scale choral works

Cantata for Rimsky-Korsakov's 60th birthday (1904): lost

Four Russian Peasant Songs (Pod'lyudnïya, Saucers; 1914–17)
SA chorus
Chester
rev. for SA chorus, 4 hn (1954): Chester

Les noces (1914–23: *see* 1.1)

Otche nash' (Pater noster; 1926)
SATB chorus
Edition Russe de Musique, Boosey
rev. with Latin text (1949): Boosey

Simbol' vyerï (Credo; 1932)
SATB chorus
Edition Russe de Musique, Boosey
rev. with Latin text (1949): Boosey

Bogoroditse dyevo (Ave Maria; 1934)
SATB chorus
Edition Russe de Musique, Boosey
rev. with Latin text (1949): Boosey

The Star-Spangled Banner (after John Stafford Smith; 1941)
TTBarB chorus[9]

Mass (1944–8)
SATB chorus (with children in upper parts), 2 ob, cor anglais, 2 bn, 2 tpt, 3 trbn
Boosey

Cantata (English verse of the 15th and 16th centuries; 1951–2)
ST soloists, SSAA chorus, 2 fl, 2 ob (2nd + cor anglais), vc
Boosey; *see also* 3.6

Tres sacrae cantiones (1957–9; by Gesualdo, with replacements of missing parts)
SATTBB, SAATTB, SAATTBB
Boosey

Anthem 'The dove descending breaks the air' (T. S. Eliot;1962)
SATB chorus
Boosey

Introitus (1965)
TB chorus, 2 tam tams (2 players), timp (2 players), pf, harp, va, db
Boosey

[9]Reproduced in ibid., pp. 12–13.

3.3 Works with ensemble

Three Japanese Lyrics (Japanese verse in Russian translation by A. Brandta; 1912–13)
 S, 2 fl (2nd + pic), 2 cl (2nd + b cl), pf, string quartet
 Edition Russe de Musique, Boosey; *see also* 3.5

Pribautki (Pribaoutki; Russian folk verse; 1914)
 Bar, fl, ob + cor anglais, cl, bn, vn, va, vc, db
 Henn, Chester; *see also* 3.5

Cat's Cradle Songs (Berceuses du chat; Russian folk verse; 1915)
 A, 3 cl (1st + E flat, 3rd + b cl)
 Henn, Chester; *see also* 3.5, 5.2

Renard (1915–16: *see* 1.1)

Sektanskaya (1919; later no. 4 of Four Russian Songs)
 S, fl, cimbalom
 see also 3.5. 5.4[10]

Pastorale (1923: *see* 3.5)
 S, ob, cor anglais, cl, bn
 Schott

Three Songs from William Shakespeare (1953)
 Mez, fl, cl, va
 Boosey; *see also* 3.5

Four Songs (1953–4; after Four Russian Songs nos. 1, 4 and Three Tales for Children nos. 2, 1: *see* 3.5)
 Mez, fl, harp, guitar
 Boosey

Two Poems of Balmont (1954: *see* 3.5)
 S, 2 fl, 2 cl, pf, str qt
 Boosey

In memoriam Dylan Thomas (dirge canons and song; Thomas; 1954)
 T, str qt, 4 trbn
 Boosey; *see also* 3.5

Elegy for J.F.K. (W. H. Auden; 1964)
 Bar, 3 cl
 Boosey

Two Sacred Songs (after Hugo Wolf; Paul Heyse, Emanuel Geibel; 1968)
 Mez, 3 cl, 2 hn, str qnt
 Boosey

[10]Reproduced in *SSC I*, pp. 427–9.

3.4 Duos

Petit Ramusianum harmonique (Stravinsky and Cingria; 1937)
  singing and speaking voices[11]

Little Canon (Petit canon; Jean de Meung; 1947)
  TT soloists

3.5 Songs with piano accompaniment

Storm Cloud (Tucha; Pushkin; 1902)
  Soviet State Publishers

How the Mushrooms Prepared for War (Kak' gribï na voynu sobirlis'; Russian
  folk verse; 1904)
  Soviet State Publishers

Conductor and Tarantula (Koz'ma Prutkov; 1906): lost

The Faun and the Shepherdess (1906: *see* 2.1)
  Belaieff, Boosey

Pastorale (1907)
  Jurgenson, Schott; *see also* 3.3, 4.2, 4.4

Two Songs op. 6 (Gorodetzky, 1907–8)
  Jurgenson, Boosey

Two Poems of Verlaine op. 9 (Russian translation by Mitusov; 1910)
  Jurgenson, Boosey; *see also* 2.1

Two Poems of Balmont (1911)
  Edition Russe de Musique, Boosey; *see also* 3.3

Three Japanese Lyrics (1912–13: *see* 3.3)
  Edition Russe de Musique, Boosey

Three Little Songs 'Recollections of My Childhood' (Russian folk verse; 1913)
  Edition Russe de Musique, Boosey; *see also* 2.1

Pribautki (1914: *see* 3.3)
  Henn, Chester

Cat's Cradle Songs (1915: *see* 3.3)
  Henn, Chester

Three Tales for Children (Trois histoires pour enfants; Russian folk verse;
  1915–17)
  Chester; *see also* 2.1, 3.3, 5.4

Berceuse (Stravinsky; 1917)

Four Russian Songs (folk verse; 1918–19)
  Chester; *see also* 3.3, 5.4

[11]Published in *Hommage a C.-F. Ramuz* (Lausanne, 1938) and *Feuilles musicales* (Lausanne,
March–April 1962).

Chanson de Paracha (Parasha's Aria) (1921–2; after *Mavra*: *see* 1.1 and 2.1)
Boosey

Jocasta's Aria with concert ending (?1948; after *Oedipus rex*: *see* 1.1): ?lost[12]

Three Songs from William Shakespeare (1953: *see* 3.3)
Boosey

Song from *In memoriam Dylan Thomas* (1954: *see* 3.3)
Boosey

The Owl and the Pussy-Cat (Edward Lear; 1965–6)
Boosey

3.6 Vocal scores

(Included here are arrangements surely not meant for performance but only for rehearsal use.)

Zvezdoliki (*see* 2.1)

The Nightingale (*see* 1.1): Edition Russe de Musique, Boosey

Renard (*see* 1.1): Henn, Chester

Les noces (see 1.1): Chester

Pulcinella (*see* 1.1): Chester

Mavra (*see* 1.1): Edition Russe de Musique, Boosey

Oedipus rex (*see* 1.1): Edition Russe de Musique, Boosey

Babel (*see* 2.1): Schott

Cantata (*see* 3.2): Boosey

Canticum sacrum (*see* 2.1): Boosey

4 CHAMBER WORKS

4.1 Octets and septets

Histoire du soldat suite (1918: *see* 1.1)
for same instrumental ensemble as the theatre piece
Chester; *see also* 4.2, 5.2

Octet (1922–3: *see* 2.5)

Septet (1952–3)
cl, bn, hn, pf, vn, va, vc
Boosey; *see also* 5.2

Canzonetta (1963; after Sibelius)
cl, b cl, 4 hn, harp, db
Breitkopf

[12]Made for Nell Tangeman. See *SSC I*, p. 348.

4.2 Quintet, quartets and trios

Three Pieces (1914)
  str qt
  Edition Russe de Musique, Boosey; *see also* 5.1

Histoire du solday suite (1919: *see* 1.1)
  vn, cl, pf
  Chester
Concertino (1920)
  str qt
  Hansen; *see also* 2.3, 5.1

Pastorale (1933: *see* 3.3)
  vn, ob, cor anglais, cl, bn
  Schott; *see also* 4.4

Epitaphium (1959)
  fl, cl, harp
  Boosey

Double Canon (1959)
  str qt
  Boosey

4.3 Wind solos and duos

Canons, 2 hn (1917): lost

Three Pieces, cl (1918): Chester

Lied ohne Name, 2 bn (1949, after sketches of 1916)[13]

Lullaby, 2 rec (1960; after Anne's lullaby in *The Rake's Progress*: *see* 1.1):
  Boosey

Fanfare for a New Theatre, 2 tpt (1964): Boosey

4.4 String solos with piano

(For violin and piano except where stated.)

Suite (1925; after *Pulcinella*: *see* 1.1): Edition Russe de Musique

Prélude et Ronde des princesses (1929; after *The Firebird*: *see* 1.1): Schott

Berceuse (1929; after *The Firebird*: *see* 1.1): Schott

Concerto in D (1931: *see* 2.2): Schott

Duo concertant (1931–2): Edition Russe de Musique, Boosey

Danse russe (1932; after *Petrushka*: *see* 1.1): Edition Russe de Musique, Boosey

Chant du rossignol, Marche chinoise (1932; after *The Nightingale*: *see* 1.1):
  Edition Russe de Musique, Boosey

[13]Reproduced in *SSC I*, p. 410.

Stravinsky

Divertimento (1932; after *Le baiser de la fée*: *see* 1.1): Edition Russe de Musique, Boosey

Suite italienne, vc, pf (1932; after *Pulcinella*: *see* 1.1): Edition Russe de Musique, Boosey

Suite italienne (1932; after *Pulcinella*: *see* 1.1): Edition Russe de Musique, Boosey

Berceuse, Scherzo (1933; after *The Firebird*: *see* 1.1): Schott

Pastorale (1933: *see* 3.5): Schott

Chanson russe (1937; after Parasha's aria in *Mavra*: *see* 1.1): Edition Russe de Musique, Boosey

Ballad (1947; after *Le baiser de la fée*: *see* 1.1)

4.5 String solos unaccompanied

La marseillaise, vn (1919; after Rouget de Lisle)

Elégie, va (Elegy; 1944): Chappell, Schott

5 PIANO AND PERCUSSION WORKS

5.1 Piano duets and duos

(Works up to and including the Concertino are for four hands at one keyboard; afterwards Stravinsky wrote for two pianos.)

Petrushka (1910–11: *see* 1.1): Edition Russe de Musique, Boosey

The Rite of Spring (1910–13: *see* 1.1): Edition Russe de Musique, Boosey

Three Pieces (1914: *see* 4.2)

Valse des fleurs (1914)

Three Easy Pieces (1914–15): Henn, Chester; *see also* 2.3, 5.4

Five Easy Pieces (1916–17): Henn, Chester; *see also* 2.3, 5.4

Concertino (1920: *see* 4.2)

Concerto (1923–4: *see* 2.5): Edition Russe de Musique, Boosey

Capriccio (1928–9: *see* 2.2): Edition Russe de Musique, Boosey

Concerto (1931–5): Schott

Concerto in E flat (1937–8: *see* 2.3): Schott

Sonata (1943–4): Chappell, Schott

Septet (1952–3: *see* 4.1): Boosey

Agon (1953–7: *see* 1.1): Boosey

Movements (1958–9: *see* 2.2): Boosey

224

5.2 Piano solos

Tarantella (1898)

Scherzo (1902): Faber

Sonata in F sharp minor (1903–4): Faber

Four Studies op. 7 (1908): Jurgenson

The Firebird (1909–10: *see* 1.1): Jurgenson, Schott

Souvenir d'un marche boche (1915)[14]

Valse pour les enfants (1916–17): in White, p. 248

Chant du rossignol (1917: *see* 2.2): Edition Russe de Musique, Boosey

Rag-time (1918: *see* 2.3): Chester

The Soldier's Tale (1918: *see* 1.1): Chester

Chorus from Prologue to *Boris Godunov* (1918; after Musorgsky)[15]

Piano-Rag-Music (1919): Chester

Chorale from the Symphonies of Wind Instruments (1920: *see* 2.5)[16]

Three Movements from *Petrushka* (1921: *see* 1.1): Edition Russe de Musique, Boosey

Les cinq doigts (The Five Fingers; 1921): Chester; *see* 2.3

Sonata (1924): Edition Russe de Musique, Boosey

Serenade in A (1925): Edition Russe de Musique, Boosey

Apollo (1927–8: *see* 1.1): Edition Russe de Musique, Boosey

Le baiser de la fée (1928: *see* 1.1): Edition Russe de Musique, Boosey

Jeu de cartes (1936: *see* 1.1): Schott

Praeludium (1936–7: *see* 2.6)

Tango (1940): Mercury, Schott; *see also* 2.6

Circus Polka (1942: *see* 2.2): Associated, Schott

Cat's Cradle Song no. 4 (1940: *see* 3.3)[17]

Five Easy Pieces no. 1 (1940: *see* 5.1)[18]

5.3 Cimbalom work

Polka (1915; after Three Easy Pieces no. 3: *see* 5.1)[19]

---

[14]Reproduced in *The Book of the Homeless*, ed. Edith Wharton (London, 1916).
[15]See *SSC I*, p. 414.   [16]Published in the *Revue musicale* (December 1920).
[17]See *SSC I*, p. 414.   [18]Ibid.
[19]Reproduced in *Feuilles musicales* (Lausanne, March–April 1962).

5.4 Pianola works

(*Dates given are those of publication.*)

Four Studies op. 7 (?before 1917: *see* 5.2): Pianola

Etude (1917): Pianola

Pulcinella (1921:*see* 1.1): Pleyel

The Rite of Spring (1921: *see* 1.1): Pleyel, Pianola

Piano-Rag-Music (1921: *see* 5.2): Pleyel

Three Easy Pieces (1921: *see* 5.1): Pleyel

Five Easy Pieces (1921: *see* 5.1): Pleyel

Petrushka (1921: *see* 1.1): Pleyel

Les cinq doigts (1921: *see* 5.2): Pleyel

Rag-time (1921: *see* 2.3): Pleyel

Chant du rossignol (1921: *see* 2.2): Pleyel

Three Tales for Children (1921: *see* 3.5): Pleyel

Four Russian Songs (1921: *see* 3.5): Pleyel

Concertino (1924: *see* 4.2): Pleyel

Les noces (1924–5: *see* 1.1): Pleyel

The Firebird (1926: *see* 1.1): Pleyel, also Duo-Art and Pianola (1927)

Sonata (1927: *see* 5.2): Pleyel, first movement also Duo-Art and Pianola

Concerto, first movement (*see* 2.5): Duo-Art

6 UNFINISHED AND PROJECTED WORKS

David, ballet with scenario by Jean Cocteau, 1914[20]

Koz'ma Prutkov, ?stage piece, 1914[21]

Liturgie, ballet on the mass, ?1914–15[22]

Antoine et Cléopâtre, music for Shakespeare's play in André Gide's translation, 1917[23]

[20]A project initiated by Cocteau, and in which Stravinsky never seems to have been interested. See *SSC I*, pp. 78–84.
[21]Sketches; *see SPD*, p. 133.
[22]An idea of Dyagilev's; see *Memories*, p. 48. Stravinsky says he disapproved of the notion of a balletic mass, but he also says Dyagilev wanted to put vestments on the stage, whereas the Scottish National Gallery of Modern Art has a costume design by Goncharova in nothing like ecclesiastical style.
[23]An Ida Rubinstein project which fell through for financial reasons. Stravinsky had begun the music, and used his material in *Histoire du soldat*. See *SPD*, pp. 161–2.

Batracomiomachia, music for a puppet play, 1919[24]

Dialogue de la Joye et de la Raison (French translation of Petrarch), 2 solo voices and keyboard, 1933[25]

Promethée or *Tobit*, melodrama with words by Paul Claudel, 1938[26]

Ballet after Donizetti, 1942[27]

The Commandos Strike at Dawn, film score, 1942[28]

The Song of Bernadette, film score, 1943[29]

North Star, film score, 1943[30]

Jane Eyre, film score, 1944[31]

String quartet, 1947[32]

Delia, masque with words by Auden and Kallman, 1953[33]

Opera with libretto by Dylan Thomas, 1953[34]

Orchestral piece, 1966–7[35]

7 CHRONOLOGICAL LIST

(Works are entered by year of starting. Titles of arrangements are given in brackets; lesser transcriptions – piano reductions, violin miniatures, pianola rolls – are omitted.)

1898	Tarantella
1899	
1900	
1901	
1902	*Storm Cloud*, Scherzo
1903	Piano Sonata in F sharp minor
1904	Cantata for Rimsky's birthday, *How the Mushrooms*
1905	Symphony in E flat
1906	*The Faun and the Shepherdess, Conductor and Tarantula*
1907	*Scherzo fantastique*, Gorodetzky Songs I, Pastorale

[24]To have been for the Teatro dei Piccoli in Rome; see *SPD*, p. 186.

[25]Sketches reproduced in *SSC 1*, pp. 371–8.

[26]Another Ida Rubinstein project, aborted because of disagreement as to the subject, Stravinsky wanting a Prometheus and Claudel a Tobit. See *SSC III*, pp. 194–6.

[27]See *Dearest Bubushkin*, p. 125.

[28]All these film projects foundered, leaving music which Stravinsky apparently reused in orchestral works: the *Four Norwegian Moods*, the middle movement of the Symphony in Three Movements, the *Scherzo à la russe* and the middle movement of *Ode* respectively.

[29]As for 28.   [30]As for 28.   [31]As for 28.

[32]Invited by William Schuman for the Juilliard Quartet; see *SSC I*, pp. 328–9.

[33]See *SPD*, pp. 204–5.

[34]A work 'about the rediscovery of our planet following an atomic misadventure. There would be a re-creation of language, only the new one would have no abstractions: there would be only people, objects, and words' (*Conversations*, p. 78). Progress was cut off at an early stage by Thomas's death.

[35]Some sketches reproduced in *SPD*, pp. 484–5.

1908   *Fireworks, Chant funèbre*, Gorodetzky Songs II, Piano Studies, *The
        Nightingale* I

(1909)   (Chopin: Nocturne, Valse brillante), (*Two Songs of the Flea*), *The
        Firebird*

1910   (Grieg: 'Kobold'), *The Rite of Spring, Petrushka*, Verlaine Poems

1911   *Zvezdoliki*, Balmont Poems

1912   Japanese Lyrics

1913   (*Khovanshchina*), Three Little Songs, *The Nightingale* II–III

1914   *Les noces*, Three Quartet Pieces, *Pribautki, Valse des fleurs*,
        Three Easy Pieces I, III, Four Russian Peasant Songs III

1915   *Renard*, Four Russian Peasant Songs IV, Three Easy Pieces II,
        Cat's Cradle Songs, Three Tales III, *Souvenir d'un marche boche*

1916   Four Russian Peasant Songs I, *Valse pour les enfants, Chant du
        rossignol*

1917   *Rag-time*, Four Russian Peasant Songs II, Five Easy Pieces,
        (*Song of the Volga Boatmen*), Three Tales I and II,
        Etude for pianola, *Berceuse*, Canons for horns

1918   Four Russian Songs, *Piano-Rag-Music, Histoire du soldat*,
        (*Boris* chorus), (Four Studies I–III), Three Clarinet Pieces

(1919)   (*Firebird* suite), (*Marseillaise*), *Pulcinella*

1920   Symphonies of Wind Instruments, Concertino

1921   *Mavra, Les cinq doigts*, (Three Movements from *Petrushka*), Suite
        no. 2), (*The Sleeping Beauty*: two extracts)

1922   (*Les noces*) Octet

1923   Concerto for piano and wind, (Pastorale), (*Tilimbom*)

1924   Piano Sonata

1925   Serenade in A, (Suite for violin and piano), (Suite no. 1)

1926   *Oedipus rex, Otche nash'*

1927   *Apollo*

1928   *Le baiser de la fée*, (Four Studies: IV), Capriccio

1929   (Three Little Songs)

1930   Symphony of Psalms

1931   *Duo concertant*, Violin Concerto, Concerto for two pianos

1932   (*Suite italienne*), *Simbol' vyerï*

1933   *Perséphone*, (Divertimento)

1934   *Bogoroditse dyevo*

1935

1936   *Jeu de cartes*, Praeludium

1937   *Petit Ramusianum*,   Concerto in E flat 'Dumbarton Oaks'

(1938)   Symphony in C

1939

1940   *Danses concertantes*, Tango

1941   (Bluebird Pas-de-deux), (*The Star-Spangled Banner*)

1942   Symphony in Three Movements, *Circus Polka, Four Norwegian
        Moods*

1943   Sonata for two pianos, *Ode*

1944   *Babel, Scènes de ballet, Scherzo à la russe, Elégie*, Mass

1945   (*Firebird* suite), *Ebony Concerto*

1946   Concerto in D, (*Petrushka*)

1947   *The Rake's Progress, Orpheus*, Little Canon, (Symphonies)

1948	
1949	(*Lied ohne Name*)
1950	
1951	Cantata, (Verlaine Poems)
1952	(Concertino), Septet
1953	Shakespeare Songs, (Tango), (Four Songs), *Agon*
1954	*In memoriam Dylan Thomas*, (Balmont Poems)
1955	*Greeting Prelude, Canticum sacrum*, (*Choral-Variationen*)
1956	
1957	*Threni*, (*Tres sacrae cantiones*: III)
1958	Movements
1959	*Epitaphium*, (*Tres sacrae cantiones*: I–II), Double Canon
1960	(*Monumentum*), *A Sermon, a Narrative and a Prayer*, (Lullaby)
1961	*The Flood*, (*Pesante* for wind)
1962	*Abraham and Isaac, Anthem*, (Eight Instrumental Miniatures)
1963	Variations (Sibelius: Canzonetta)
1964	*Elegy for J.F.K., Fanfare for a New Theatre*
1965	*Introitus, Requiem Canticles*, (Canon), *The Owl and the Pussy-Cat*
1966	
1967	
1968	(Wolf: *Two Sacred Songs*)
1969	
1970	
1971	

Appendix C

List of recordings[1]

(Made for Columbia Records except where stated. Those marked with an asterisk have been reissued by Sony on compact disc, those marked with a dagger by Vogue.)

1 AS CONDUCTOR

Symphony in E flat op. 1: Hollywood 1966*
The Faun and the Shepherdess: Toronto, 1964*
Pastorale (vn, wind qt): Paris, 1933[†]; New York, 1946; Hollywood, 1965*
Scherzo fantastique: Toronto, 1962*
Fireworks: New York, 1946; Moscow, 1962 (Melodiya); New York, 1963*
The Firebird: Paris, 1928 (amalgam of 1911 and 1919 suites[†]); New York, 1946 (1945 suite); Hollywood, 1961 (complete)*; Hollywood, 1967 (1945 suite)*
Two Poems of Verlaine: New York, 1964*
Petrushka: London, 1928 (suite)[†]; New York, 1940 (suite); Hollywood, 1960 (complete rev. version* and suite*); Moscow, 1962 (suite from rev. version, Melodiya)
Two Poems of Balmont: Hollywood, 1955
Zvezdoliki: Toronto, 1962*
The Rite of Spring: Paris, 1929[†], New York, 1940; New York, 1960*
Three Japanese Lyrics: Hollywood, 1955
Three Little Songs: Hollywood, 1955; New York, 1964*
The Nightingale: Washington, 1960*
Four Studies: Toronto, 1962*
Pribautki: New York, 1964*
Cat's Cradle Songs: New York, 1964*
Renard: New York, 1962*
Suites nos. 1–2: Toronto, 1963*
Four Russian Peasant Songs (with hns): Hollywood, 1955; Hollywood, 1965*
Les noces: London, 1934[†]; New York, 1959*
Song of the Volga Boatmen: Moscow, 1962 (Melodiya)
Histoire du soldat (suite): Paris, 1932[†]; New York, 1954; Hollywood 1961*
Rag-time: Paris, 1934[†]; New York, 1962*
Four Songs: Hollywood, 1955
Pulcinella: Paris, 1928, 1932 (4 nos.)[†]; Cleveland, 1953 (complete); Hollywood, 1965 (complete* and suite*)
Concertino (12 insts): Hollywood, 1965*
Symphonies of Wind Instruments: Cologne, 1951*

[1]This list follows Stuart (1990) and is confined to recordings published in the composer's lifetime.

Eight Instrumental Miniatures: Toronto, 1962*
Mavra: Toronto, 1964*
Octet: Paris, 1932[†]; New York 1954; New York, 1961*
Concerto for piano and wind: New York, 1950 (RCA Victor); New York, 1964*
Utche nash': New York, 1949 (Latin version, RCA Victor); Toronto, 1964*
Oedipus rex: Cologne, 1951; Washington, 1962*
Apollo: New York, 1950 (RCA Victor); New York, 1964*
Le baiser de la fée: Mexico City, 1940–41 (Divertimento, RCA Victor); Hollywood, 1947 (Divertimento, RCA Victor); Cleveland, 1955; Hollywood, 1965*
Symphony of Psalms: Paris, 1931[†]; New York, 1946; Toronto, 1963*
Violin Concerto: Paris, 1935 (Polydor)[†]; Hollywood, 1961*
Simbol' vyerï: Hollywood, 1965*
Perséphone: New York, 1957; Hollywood, 1966*
Bogoroditse dyevo: New York, 1949 (Latin version, RCA Victor); Toronto, 1964*
Jeu de cartes: Berlin, 1938 (Telefunken)[†]; Cleveland, 1964*
Praeludium: New York, 1965*
Concerto in E flat: New York, 1947 (Keynote); Hollywood, 1962*
Symphony in C: Cleveland, 1952; Toronto, 1962*
Tango: New York, 1965*
Bluebird Pas-de-deux: New York, 1963*
The Star-Spangled Banner: Toronto, 1964
Danses concertantes: Hollywood, 1947 (RCA Victor)
Circus Polka: New York, 1945; Toronto, 1963*
Four Norwegian Moods: New York, 1945; Toronto, 1963*
Ode: New York, 1945; Moscow, 1962 (Melodiya); Cleveland, 1964*
Babel: Toronto, 1962*
Scherzo à la russe: Hollywood, 1947 (RCA Victor); New York, 1963*
Scènes de ballet: New York, 1945; Toronto, 1963*
Symphony in Three Movements: New York, 1946; Hollywood, 1961*
Ebony Concerto: Hollywood, 1946; New York, 1965*
Concerto in D: New York, 1950 (RCA Victor); New York, 1963*
Orpheus: New York, 1949 (RCA Victor); Moscow, 1962 (Melodiya); Chicago, 1964*
Mass: New York, 1949 (RCA Victor); Hollywood, 1960*
The Rake's Progress: New York, 1953; London, 1964*
Cantata: New York, 1952; Hollywood, 1965–6*
Septet: New York, 1954; Hollywood, 1965*
Three Songs from William Shakespeare: Hollywood, 1954; New York, 1964*
In memoriam Dylan Thomas: Hollywood, 1954; Hollywood, 1965*
Greeting Prelude: New York, 1963*
Canticum sacrum: Hollywood, 1957*
Choral-Variationen: Toronto, 1963*
Agon: Hollywood, 1957*
Threni: New York, 1959*
Movements: Hollywood, 1961*
Monumentum pro Gesualdo: Hollywood, 1960*
A Sermon, a Narrative and a Prayer: Toronto, 1962*
Anthem: Toronto, 1962*

Stravinsky

The Flood: Hollywood, 1962*
Elegy for J.F.K.: New York, 1964*
Introitus: New York, 1966*

2 AS PIANIST

The Firebird (Scherzo, Berceuse): Paris, 1933 (with Dushkin)[†]
Petrushka (Russian Dance): Paris, 1933 (with Dushkin)[†]
The Nightingale (Air, Chinese March): Paris, 1933 (with Dushkin)[†]
Piano-Rag-Music: Paris, 1934*[†]
Suite italienne (2 nos.): Paris, 1933 (with Dushkin)
Mavra (Chanson russe): 1946 (with Szigeti)
Serenade in A: Paris, 1934*[†]
Capriccio: Paris, 1930
Duo concertant: Paris, 1933 (with Dushkin)[†]; New York, 1945 (with Szigeti)*
Concerto for two pianos: Paris, 1938 (with Soulima, plus Mozart: Fugue in C
   minor K. 426 on sixth side)*

Appendix D

Personalia

1 FAMILY

Stravinsky, Anna Kirillovna (née Kholodovskaya) (1854–1935), the composer's mother. She married Fyodor Stravinsky in 1874 and had four sons. In 1922 she left Russia to live with the composer and his family for the rest of her life.

Stravinsky, Catherine (Ekaterina) Gavrilovna (née Nossenko) (1881–1939), the composer's cousin and first wife. They married in 1906 and had four children. After the birth of the last, in 1914, she was often in poor health. She also appears, from several reports and from her letters, to have been something of a saint, deeply religious and unworried by her husband's longstanding affair with Vera de Bosset. Stravinsky dedicated to her *The Faun and the Shepherdess*, the *Pribautki* and the Serenade in A.[1]

Stravinsky, Fyodor Ignat'yevich (1843–1902), the composer's father. After law studies he trained at the St Petersburg Conservatory as a bass, and sang at the Mariinsky from 1876 until his death, creating roles for Tchaikovsky and Rimsky-Korsakov.

Stravinsky, Gury Fyodorovich (1884–1917), the composer's younger brother. He was a baritone, and dedicatee of the Verlaine songs. The *Pribautki* were also intended for him.

Stravinsky, Lyudmila Igorevna (1908–38), the composer's elder daughter. She married Yuri Mandelstamm in 1935, and had a daughter Catherine, born in 1937.

Stravinsky, Maria Milena Igorevna (1914–), the composer's younger daughter. She married André Marion in 1944.

Stravinsky, Svyatoslav Soulima Igorevich (1910–), the composer's younger son. In the 1930s he performed at his father's concerts, notably in the first performance of the Concerto for two pianos; he also made the vocal scores of the Symphony of Psalms and *Perséphone*. In 1946 he married Françoise Blandlat; their son John had been born the year before.

Stravinsky, Theodore (Fyodor) Igorevich (1907–89), the composer's elder son. His designs appeared on the published scores of *Oedipus rex*, the *Duo concertant* and *Perséphone*. He also published a book, *Le message d'Igor Strawinsky* (Lausanne, 1948).

Stravinsky, Vera Arturovna (née de Bosset, formerly Sudeikina) (1888–1983), the composer's second wife. Born wealthy, she had a rich early life on the fringes of Moscow theatre. She married Sergey Sudeikin, already her third husband, in 1918: he was an artist, one of whose jobs had been painting scenery for *The Rite of Spring*. They moved to Paris in 1920 and separated in 1922, the year after the start of her affair with Stravinsky. Thereafter she was

---

[1]See *SSC* I, pp. 3–19.

his usual travelling companion, and in 1940 became his wife. He dedicated his last original work, *The Owl and the Pussy-Cat* to her, and also said she was the secret dedicatee of the Octet. After his death she flowered as a painter.[2]

2 WRITERS

Andersen, Hans Christian (1805–75), Danish writer of fairy stories, including the sources of *The Nightingale* and *Le baiser de la fée.*

Auden, Wystan Hugh (1907–73), English poet, living largely in the United States after 1939. He collaborated with Britten on various works – songs, films, radio features, plays, an opera – between 1935 and 1941. Later, with his partner Chester Kallman, he wrote and translated librettos, including that of *The Rake's Progress.* He also wrote the words for Stravinsky's *Elegy for J.F.K.* and suggested the poems to be set in the Cantata.[3]

Balmont, Konstantin (1867–1942), Russian poet, author of abundant symbolist lyrics. Stravinsky set three of them in *Zvezdoliki* and a pair of songs, both works written at the time of *The Rite of Spring.*

Cingria, Charles-Albert (1883–1954), Swiss writer of Dalmatian origin. Stravinsky knew him from his early years in Switzerland, and originally dedicated the Three Quartet Pieces to him. In *An Autobiography* he wrote warmly of Cingria's recent book on Petrarch, and a little later they collaborated on a sixtieth birthday tribute to Ramuz.[4]

Claudel, Paul (1868–1955), French writer, never close to Stravinsky though there was some correspondence in 1938 about an abortive project for Ida Rubinstein.[5]

Cocteau, Jean (1889–1963), French poet and artist. Quickly attracted to the Ballets Russes, he apparently knew Stravinsky from the time of *Petrushka,* and dedicated his verse collection *Le Potomak* (1913–14) to the composer, whom in 1914 he tried to involve in a collaboration on a David ballet. His interests then turned to Satie and Les Six, but in 1925 Stravinsky invited him to write the libretto for what became *Oedipus rex,* and in 1935–6 there seems to have been some contact preparatory to *Jeu de cartes.* In 1952 they worked together again on a production of the opera–oratorio, designed as well as narrated by Cocteau.[6]

Dekker, Thomas (*c.*1570–*c.*1632), English playwright, whose words Stravinsky set in the final part of *A Sermon, a Narrative and a Prayer.*

Eliot, Thomas Stearns (1885–1965), American poet, living largely in England. He and Stravinsky did not meet until 1956, but for the next few years they were regularly in contact. Eliot became Stravinsky's publisher in respect of his conversation books, and Stravinsky tried to engage the poet as librettist of a Noah play for television in 1959, a project eventually achieved with Craft's help in 1961–2, during which time he set lines from Eliot's 'Little Gidding' as an anthem. Eliot's death provoked the *Introitus.*[7]

Gide, André (1869–1951), French writer. He met Stravinsky in 1917 to talk about working together on a version of *Antony and Cleopatra* for Ida Rubinstein, on whose behalf they came together again in 1933 to produce *Perséphone.*[8]

---

[2]See *Dearest Bubushkin.*
[3]See *SSC I,* pp. 299–324.
[4]See *SSC III,* pp. 111–32.
[5]See *SSC III,* pp. 194–6.
[6]See *SSC I,* pp. 73–125.
[7]See *SPD,* pp. 537–44.
[8]See *SSC III,* pp. 184–93.

Gorodetzky, Sergey (1884–1967), Russian poet, two of whose poems, a cloister scene and a 'mystic song of the ancient Russian flagellants', Stravinsky set in 1907–8. His evocations of old Russia may also have been among the compost from which *The Rite of Spring* grew. He remained in the Soviet Union.

Huxley, Aldous (1894–1963), English writer, one of Stravinsky's closest friends in Los Angeles in the late 1940s and 1950s. The Variations were dedicated to his memory.

Kallman, Chester (1921–75), American poet, joint librettist with Auden of *The Rake's Progress*.

Kochno, Boris (1904–), Russian writer, acting as Dyagilev's secretary and as librettist of *Mavra*.

Lear, Edward (1812–88), English poet, whose 'The Owl and the Pussy-Cat' Stravinsky set.

Mitusov, Stepan Stepanovich (1878–1942), Russian musician and writer. A fellow member with Stravinsky of Rimsky-Korsakov's circle, he wrote the libretto of *The Nightingale*, which is dedicated to him, and the translations of two Verlaine poems Stravinsky set. He remained in the Soviet Union as a working musician.

Pushkin, Alexander Sergeyevich (1799–1837), Russian poet. An early song, the orchestral cycle *The Faun and the Shepherdess* and *Mavra* were all based on works of his.

Ramuz, Charles-Ferdinand (1878–1947), Swiss writer. He and Stravinsky met in 1915, and the next year he made a French translation of *Renard* at the composer's request. He also translated *Les noces* and all the Russian songs of this period, besides working directly with Stravinsky on *Histoire du soldat*. They remained in occasional contact thereafter. Ramuz published a volume of *Souvenirs sur Igor Stravinsky* (Lausanne, 1929), and Stravinsky honoured him with a musical tribute on his sixtieth birthday.[9]

Roerich, Nicolas (Rerikh, Nikolay Konstantinovich) (1874–1947), Russian ethnologist, writer and painter, the scenarist and first designer of *The Rite of Spring*, which Stravinsky dedicated to him.

Shakespeare, William (1564–1623). Nothing came of World War I projects based on *A Midsummer Night's Dream* and *Antony and Cleopatra*, but in 1953 Stravinsky set a sonnet and two songs.

Thomas, Dylan (1914–53), Welsh poet. He and Stravinsky met in May 1953 to discuss an operatic project, which was cut short by the poet's death a few months later. Stravinsky wrote *In memoriam Dylan Thomas* early the next year.

Verlaine, Paul (1844–96), French poet. Stravinsky set two of his poems in Mitusov's translation in 1910.

3 BALLET PEOPLE

Balanchine, George (Balanchivadze, Gyorgy Melitonovich) (1904–83), Georgian–American choreographer. He joined the Dyagilev company in 1924, and for them choreographed Stravinsky's *Chant du rossignol* and *Apollon musagète*. In 1934 he moved to New York, where he formed successively the American Ballet, the Ballet Society and the New York City Ballet. His artistic relationship with Stravinsky remained close. He was responsible for the first productions of *Jeu de cartes*, *Orpheus*, *Agon* and *The Flood*, for the first New

[9]See *SSC III*, pp. 25–110.

York production of *The Rake's Progress*, and for choreographed versions of concert works including the Violin Concerto, *Danses concertantes, Monumentum pro Gesualdo*, Movements, Variations, *Duo concertant*, Capriccio and Symphony in Three Movements.

Benois, Alexander Nikolayevich (1870–1960), Russian artist, associated with the Ballets Russes from the first. He worked with Stravinsky on the scenario for *Petrushka*, besides producing designs that have frequently been copied; the score is dedicated to him. He also designed the first *Baiser de la fée*.

Bolm, Adolph (1884–1951), Russian–American choreographer. He danced with the Ballets Russes, and then settled in the United States, where he choreographed, and took the leading role in, the first *Apollon musagète*.

Dolin, Anton (1904–83), English dancer and choreographer, a member of the Ballets Russes in the 1920s. During the war he was in New York, where he choreographed the first production of *Scènes de ballet*.

Dyagilev, Sergey Pavlovich (Diaghilev, Serge) (1872–1929), Russian impresario, founder of the Ballets Russes, which began as an export from the Mariinsky Theatre in St Petersburg but soon became an independent company based in the West. Stravinsky's music was included in his first Paris season, in 1909, and thenceforth for twenty years most of the composer's larger works were written for Dyagilev: *The Firebird, Petrushka, The Rite of Spring, The Nightingale, Les noces, Pulcinella, Mavra* and *Oedipus rex. Les noces* was dedicated to him, as was a polka for piano duet. The personal relationship had its ups and down, but Stravinsky evidently had warm feelings for the man, of a kind somewhere between friendship and filiality.[10]

Fokine, Michel (Fokin, Mikhail Mikhailovich) (1880–1942), Russian choreographer. He was Dyagilev's first principal choreographer, responsible for the first *Firebird* and *Petrushka*. After breaking with Dyagilev during the First World War, he pursued an independent career in Western Europe and North America, reviving his Stravinsky productions for various companies but not working again with the composer directly.

Jooss, Kurt (1901–), German choreographer. Working in Essen he created versions of *Petrushka* and *Pulcinella*, then moved to England in 1933. He choreographed *Perséphone* for Ida Rubinstein. In 1949 he returned to Germany.

Karsavina, Tamara Patonovna (1885–1978), Russian dancer. Described by Stravinsky in *An Autobiography* as 'that beautiful and gracious artist', she was principal ballerina of the Ballets Russes from the first, and created leading roles in *The Firebird, Petrushka, Chant du rossignol* and *Pulcinella*. In later years she lived in London.

Kirstein, Lincoln (1907–), American ballet director, associate of Balanchine. Stravinsky dedicated his *Fanfare to a New Theatre* 'to Lincoln and George'. *Agon* too is dedicated to them.[11]

Lifar, Serge (1905–86), Russian–French dancer and choreographer. He joined the Ballets Russes in 1923 and was the first Apollo in Balanchine's version for the company. He was also Dyagilev's heir, and as such the inheritor of important Stravinsky manuscripts which came on to the market after his death.

Massine, Leonid Fyodorovich (1895–1979), Russian–American choreographer. He was with the Ballets Russes from 1914, and choreographed *Chant du rossignol, Pulcinella* and a new *Rite of Spring*, all in 1920. He later worked with various companies in Europe and New York.

[10]See *SSC II*, pp. 3–45.   [11]See *SSC I*, pp. 265–95.

Nijinska, Bronislava Fominichna (1891–1972), Russian–American choreographer. With her brother she was one of the original members of Dyagilev's company, dancing in the first *Petrushka*. Her choreographic creations, admired by Stravinsky, included the first *Renard, Noces* and *Baiser de la fée*. In later years she worked with various companies in Europe and the United States.

Nijinsky, Vaslav Fomich (1889–1950), Russian dancer and choreographer. One of the original members of Dyagilev's company, he created the role of Petrushka and choreographed *The Rite of Spring*. He danced for the last time in 1919, and spent most of his later life in mental institutions.[12]

Pitoëff, Georges and Ludmila, Russian dancers, fellow exiles with Stravinsky in Switzerland, where they staged and danced the first *Histoire du soldat*.

Romanov, Boris Georgyevich (1891–1957), Russian–American choreographer, working with the Ballets Russes, for whom he choreographed *The Nightingale*. He later worked as a ballet master on both sides of the Atlantic.

Rubinstein, Ida Lvovna (*c.* 1885–1960), Russian dancer. With Dyagilev in his first Paris seasons, she then formed companies of her own to put on specially commissioned works, including *Le baiser de la fée* and *Perséphone*.

4 PAINTERS

Auberjonois, René (1872–1957), Swiss painter, one of Stravinsky's friends in Switzerland and the designer of the first *Histoire du soldat*.

Balla, Giacomo (1871–1958), Italian futurist painter who devised a dancer-less light show for *Fireworks* in 1917.

Berman, Eugene (1899–1971), Russian–American designer. He was one of Stravinsky's close friends in Los Angeles, and the designer of the first production of *Danses concertantes*.

Depero, Fortunato (1892–1960), Italian futurist painter whose designs for *Chant du rossignol* in 1917 were not used.

Goncharova, Natalya Sergeyevna (1881–1962), Russian painter, married to Larionov. Both worked for Dyagilev: together on *Renard*, she alone on *Les noces* and the 1926 revival of *The Firebird*. They settled in France. Stravinsky dedicated the *Cat's Cradle Songs* to them.

Larionov, Mikhail Fyodorovich (1881–1969), Russian painter, married to Goncharova (q.v.)

Matisse, Henri (1869–1954), French painter. *Chant du rossignol*, which he designed for both Massine in 1920 and Balanchine in 1925, was one of his few theatrical productions.

Noguchi, Isamu (1904–), Japanese–American sculptor and designer, associated particularly with Martha Graham, though he also designed the first *Orpheus*.

Picasso, Pablo (1881–1973) Spanish painter. He and Stravinsky met in 1917, but seemingly not often after the time when they were brought together by Dyagilev. Picasso provided a drawing for the front cover of the piano version of *Histoire du soldat* and designed the first *Pulcinella*.

Tchelitchev, Pavel (1898–1957) Russian–American painter, designer of *Balustrade*.

5 MUSICIANS

Akimenko, Fyodor Stepanovich (1876–1945) Ukrainian composer, a pupil of

[12]See *SSC II*, pp. 46–9.

Rimsky-Korsakov and teacher of Stravinsky. He wrote an opera, *The Snow Fairy* (1914), songs, instrumental pieces, etc.

Ansermet, Ernest (1883–1969), Swiss conductor. He knew Stravinsky from the time of *The Nightingale*, received the definitive dedication of the Three Quartet Pieces, and on Stravinsky's recommendation became principal conductor of the Ballets Russes in 1915. In 1918 he formed the Orchestre de la Suisse Romande. He was responsible for several Stravinsky first performances, but in 1937 there was a split over his wish to make cuts in *Jeu de cartes*.[13]

Bach, Johann Sebastian (1685–1750), German composer, whose late chorale variations on *Vom Himmel hoch* Stravinsky arranged.

Boulanger, Nadia (1887–1979), French teacher and conductor, a champion of Stravinskian neo-classicism and the first conductor of the 'Dumbarton Oaks' Concerto. Stravinsky wrote a canon for her sixtieth birthday.[14]

Casella, Alfredo (1883–1947), Italian composer and organizer. He met Stravinsky in Paris, where he was resident until 1915; thereafter he was the composer's chief ally in Italy. Stravinsky dedicated to him a march for piano duet.[15]

Chávez, Carlos (1899–1978), Mexican composer and conductor, responsible for Stravinsky's visits to Mexico in the 1940s and, a quarter of a century later one of the last to see him.

Craft, Robert (1923–), American conductor and writer. His close relationship with Stravinsky moved from regular correspondence in 1947 through a first meeting in 1948 to his joining the composer's household in 1949. His enthusiasm for Schoenberg and Webern, as well as Stravinsky, provided an opportunity for Stravinsky to reconsider those composers in the 1950s. Later he was responsible for eliciting several volumes of conversations with the composer, for assisting in his conducting work, and for preparing the libretto of *The Flood*; Stravinsky dedicated his arrangement of Bach's *Vom Himmel hoch* variations to Craft. After the composer's death Craft edited his selected correspondence and other documents for publication.[16]

Dahl, Ingolf (1912–70), German–American composer, one of Stravinsky's closest musical associates in Los Angeles in the 1940s. His works, echoing the relationship, are mostly instrumental.

Debussy, Claude (1862–1918), French composer, acquainted with, and impressed by, Stravinsky, from the time of *The Firebird*: indeed the impression may have gone as deep as the music, in *Jeux* and the last piano Etude, for example. Complementarily, Debussyism is frequent in Stravinsky's early music, not least in the choral icon *Zvezdoliki* which he dedicated to Debussy. Another work, the Symphonies of Wind Instruments, was dedicated to Debussy's memory.[17]

Delage, Maurice (1879–1961), French composer, one of Stravinsky's first and closest friends in Paris: he was the dedicatee of the first Japanese Lyric. But he disapproved of Stravinsky's neo-classicism, and there was little contact after 1923.[18]

Dushkin, Samuel (1891–1976), Polish–American violinist, with whom Stravinsky gave concerts between 1931 and 1937, and for whom he wrote the

[13]See *SSC I*, pp. 129–233.   [14]See *SSC I*, pp. 237–61.
[15]See *SSC II*, pp. 125–34.   [16]See *SSC I*, pp. 327–70.
[17]See *SSC III*, pp. 3–9.   [18]See *SSC I*, pp. 23–39.

Violin Concerto, the *Duo concertant* and several transcriptions.[19]

Gesualdo, Carlo, Prince of Venosa (*c*.1561–1613), Italian composer, subject of Stravinsky's intense interest during his seventies, when he supplied missing parts for three motets and made an instrumental version of three madrigals.

Herman, Woody (Woodrow Charles) (1913–87), American jazz clarinettist, for whom the *Ebony Concerto* was written.

Kalafati, Vasily Pavlovich (1869–1942), Greek–Russian composer, pupil of Rimsky-Korsakov and teacher of Stravinsky (and Prokofiev). He wrote an opera, *The Gypsies* (1939–41), orchestral works, chamber music, etc.

Klemperer, Otto (1885–1973), German conductor. According to Craft, 'Stravinsky respected Klemperer more than almost any other conductor'.[20] Klemperer conducted and produced *Mavra* and *Oedipus rex* at the Kroll Opera in Berlin in 1928.

Koussevitzky, Sergey Alexandrovich (1874–1951), Russian–American conductor and publisher. His marriage to a tea heiress enabled him to found the Edition Russe de Musique, which published much of Stravinsky's music during the decade and a half after the First World War. He conducted the first concert performance of *The Rite* (Moscow, 1914) and the premières of the Symphonies of Wind Instruments, the Concerto for piano and wind, the Symphony of Psalms and *Ode*, the last two with the Boston Symphony Orchestra, of which he was principal conductor from 1924 to 1949.

Lourié, Arthur Vincent (1892–1966), Russian composer. Early experimental works were followed by a period as music commissar immediately after the Revolution. He arrived in Paris in 1924 and became one of Stravinsky's closest friends, until a quarrel before the latter's departure for the United States. He also moved there in 1941. Much of his music is religious, and may have helped urge Stravinsky towards the Symphony of Psalms.

Monteux, Pierre (1875–1964), French conductor. As Dyagilev's principal conductor in the pre-war years, he gave the first performances of *Petrushka*, *The Rite* and *The Nightingale*. Much of his later career was spent in the United States, notably with the San Francisco Symphony (1936–52), which he several times invited Stravinsky to conduct. Stravinsky wrote the *Greeting Prelude* for his eightieth birthday.[21]

Morton, Lawrence (1904–87), American concert director, notably of the Monday Evening Concerts in Los Angeles in the 1950s and 1960s. Several of Stravinsky's smaller works had their first performances at these concerts, including the Eight Instrumental Miniatures dedicated to Morton.

Musorgsky, Modest Petrovich (1839–81), Russian composer. Stravinsky was less public in his admiration of Musorgsky than of Tchaikovsky – except musically, in arrangements of three works.

Nabokov, Nicolas (1903–78), Russian–American composer, cousin of the writer. He had known Stravinsky at least since 1928, when he had a piece presented by Dyagilev, and was one of the composer's closest friends in his last years. His own works include an opera, *Love's Labour's Lost* (1973), to an adaptation by Auden and Kallman.[22]

Pergolesi, Giovanni Battista (1710–36), Italian composer and pseudonym, whose music Stravinsky adapted in *Pulcinella*.

---

[19]See *SSC II*, pp. 293–311.   [20]*SPD*, p. 283.
[21]See *SSC II*, pp. 49–76.   [22]See *SSC II*, pp. 364–420.

Rácz, Aladár (1886–1958), Hungarian cimbalomist, responsible for introducing Stravinsky to the instrument while he was playing at Maxim's in Geneva.

Ravel, Maurice (1875–1937), French composer, one of Stravinsky's first and closest friends in Paris: he was the dedicatee of the third Japanese Lyric, and worked with Stravinsky on *Khovanshchina*. But the relationship seems to have ended after 1923.[23]

Rimsky-Korsakov, Nikolay Andreyevich (1844–1908), Russian composer. Stravinsky had lessons with him from 1902 and wrote a lost *Chant funébre* in his memory. He remained in contact with the family (*The Firebird* was dedicated to Andrey Nikolayevich), at least until his *Khovanshchina* edition, implicitly displacing Rimsky's.

Roland-Manuel (Lévy, Roland Alexis Manuel) (1891–1966), French composer. Introduced to Stravinsky by Ravel, he played a large part in writing the *Poétique musicale*.

Rubinstein, Artur (1887–1982), Polish–American pianist, for whom Stravinsky wrote the *Piano-Rag-Music* and Three Movements from *Petrushka*.

Sacher, Paul (1906–), Swiss conductor, commissioner of, among much else, Stravinsky's Concerto in D and *A Sermon, a Narrative and a Prayer*, both of which are dedicated to him. His Sacher Foundation in Basle has by far the largest collection of Stravinsky manuscripts.

Satie, Erik (1866–1925), French composer, a friend of Stravinsky's and dedicatee of a waltz for piano duet.[24]

Schmitt, Florent (1870–1958), French composer, one of Stravinsky's first and closest friends in Paris: he was the dedicatee of the second Japanese Lyric. There appears, however, to have been no contact after 1921.[25]

Schoenberg, Arnold (1874–1951), Austrian–American composer. Stravinsky attended an early performance of *Pierrot lunaire*, conducted by Schoenberg, and in 1919 his *Pribautki* and *Cat's Cradle Songs* were performed by Schoenberg's concert society. But thereafter there was no musical contact, and seemingly no personal contact either, even though they were both living in Los Angeles.

Tchaikovsky, Pyotr Il'yich (1840–93), Russian composer, Stravinsky's chosen musical godfather. One of Stravinsky's childhood memories was of seeing Tchaikovsky at the Mariinsky. He orchestrated parts of *The Sleeping Beauty* for Dyagilev (and another number later for Balanchine), based *Le baiser de la fée* on music by Tchaikovsky, and included Tchaikovsky's works in his concert programmes in the 1940s and 1950s.

Ziloti, Alexander Il'yich (1863–1945), Ukrainian conductor, active in St Petersburg from 1903 until the Revolution. He gave the first performances of the *Scherzo fantastique* and *Fireworks*. From 1922 he lived in New York, though there seems to have been no contact with Stravinsky during this period.

6 PATRONS AND PUBLISHERS

Bliss, Mildred (Mrs Robert Woods Bliss), American patroness, responsible for

---

[23]See *SSC III*, pp. 15–22. [24]See *SSC III*, pp. 10–14.
[25]See *SSC II*, pp. 104–14.

commissioning the Concerto in E flat, which was first performed at her house, Dumbarton Oaks, in Washington, DC: hence the work's soubriquet.

Chanel, Gabrielle ('Coco') (1883–1971), French couturière. She provided Stravinsky with a Paris home in 1920–21, and was his mistress.

Errazuriz, Eugenia, Chilean patroness, who supported Stravinsky with a monthly stipend from 1916 and was the dedicatee of the Five Easy Pieces, the Etude for pianola and *Rag-time*.[26]

Kling, Otto Marius (1870–1924), German publisher, director of the London firm of Chester from 1915 until his death. He dealt with much of Stravinsky's music from that period.

Païchadze, Gavril Grigoryevich (1881–1976), Russian publisher, Paris director of the Edition Russe de Musique, which was acquired by Boosey & Hawkes in 1946. Much of Stravinsky's music from *Petrushka* to *Perséphone* appeared under the ERM imprint.

Polignac, Princesse Edmond de (Singer, Winnaretta) (1865–1943), American–French patroness, commissioner of *Renard*, which is dedicated to her, as is the Piano Sonata.

Reinhart, Werner (1884–1951), Swiss patron, who subsidized *Histoire du soldat*. Stravinsky dedicated that work to him, and also the Three Pieces for clarinet.[27]

Strecker, Willy (1884–1958), German publisher, director of Schott, Stravinsky's principal publisher during the 1930s.[28]

[26]See *SSC II*, pp. 182–4.   [27]See *SSC III*, pp. 139–83.
[28]See *SSC III*, pp. 217–72.

Appendix E

Bibliography

Titles commonly mentioned in footnotes are there abbreviated, as indicated here inside square brackets at the end of relevant entries.

1 PRIMARY SOURCES AND PICTURE BOOKS

Igor Stravinsky: *Chroniques de ma vie* (Paris, 1935–6), English translation as *An Autobiography* (London, 1936; New York, 1936) [*An Autobiography*]

Igor Stravinsky: *Poétique musicale* (Cambridge, Mass., 1942), English translation as *Poetics of Music* (Cambridge, Mass., 1947), bilingual edition (Cambridge, Mass., 1970)

Igor Stravinsky and Robert Craft: *Conversations with Igor Stravinsky* (London, 1959; New York, 1959) [*Conversations*]

Igor Stravinsky and Robert Craft: *Memories and Commentaries* (London, 1960; New York, 1960) [*Memories*]

Igor Stravinsky and Robert Craft: *Expositions and Developments* (London, 1962; New York, 1962) [*Expositions*]

Igor Stravinsky and Robert Craft: *Dialogues and a Diary* (London, 1968; New York, 1963), reissued as *Dialogues* without the diary (London, 1982) [*Dialogues*]

Igor Stravinsky and Robert Craft: *Themes and Episodes* (New York, 1966)

Arnold Newman and Robert Craft: *Bravo Stravinsky* (Cleveland and New York, 1967)

Igor Stravinsky and Robert Craft: *Retrospectives and Conclusions* (New York, 1969), combined with preceding as *Themes and Conclusions* (London, 1972)

Robert Craft: *Stravinsky: The Chronicle of a Friendship 1948–1971* (London, 1972; New York, 1972)

L. Kutateladse, ed.: *Statï, pisma, vospominaniya* (Leningrad, 1972)

L. S. Dyachkova, ed.: *I. F. Stravinsky: Statï i materiali* (Moscow, 1973)

Theodore Stravinsky: *Catherine & Igor Stravinsky: A Family Album* (London, 1973)

Vera Stravinsky and Robert Craft: *Stravinsky in Pictures and Documents* (London, 1979; New York, 1978) [*SPD*]

Igor Stravinsky: La carrière européenne, Bibliothèque Nationale exhibition catalogue (Paris, 1980)

Robert Craft: *Igor and Vera Stravinsky: A Photograph Album* (London, 1982)

Alexander Schouvaloff and Victor Borovsky: *Stravinsky on Stage* (London, 1982)

Robert Craft, ed.: *Stravinsky: Selected Correspondence*, three volumes (London, 1982, 1984 and 1985) [*SSC I–III*]

Robert Craft: *A Stravinsky Scrapbook* (London, 1983)

Strawinsky: Sein Nachlass, Sein Bild, Kunstmuseum Basel exhibition catalogue (Basle, 1984)
Robert Craft, ed.: *Dearest Bubushkin: Selected Letters and Diaries of Vera and Igor Stravinsky* (London, 1985)

2 SECONDARY LITERATURE

C. F. Ramuz: *Souvenirs sur Igor Strawinsky* (Lausanne, 1929)
Merle Armitage, ed.: *Igor Strawinsky* (New York, 1936)
Théodore Strawinsky: *Le message d'Igor Strawinsky* (Lausanne, 1948), English translation as *The Message of Igor Stravinsky* (London, 1953)
Edwin Corle, ed.: *Igor Stravinsky* (New York, 1949)
Minna Lederman, ed.: *Stravinsky in the Theatre* (London, 1951; New York, 1949)
Roman Vlad: *Strawinsky* (Rome, 1958), English translation as *Stravinsky* (London, 1960, third edition 1979)
Milein Cosman and Hans Keller: *Stravinsky at Rehearsal* (London, 1962)
Paul Henry Lang, ed.: *Stravinsky: a New Appraisal of his Work* (New York, 1963)
Eric Walter White: *Stravinsky: The Composer and his Works* (London, 1966, second edition 1979) [White]
Benjamin Boretz and Edward T. Cone, ed.: *Perspectives on Schoenberg and Stravinsky* (Princeton, 1968)
Paul Horgan: *Encounters with Stravinsky: A Personal Record* (London, 1972; New York, 1972)
Lillian Libman: *And Music at the Close: Stravinsky's Last Years* (London, 1972; New York, 1972)
Allen Forte: *The Harmonic Organization of 'The Rite of Spring'* (New Haven, 1978)
François Lesure, ed.: *Igor Stravinsky: Le sacre du printemps: Dossier de presse* (Geneva, 1980)
Boris Asafev: *A Book about Stravinsky* (Ann Arbor, 1982)
François Lesure, ed.: *Stravinsky: Etudes et témoignages* (Paris, 1982)
Paul Griffiths: *Igor Stravinsky: The Rake's Progress* (Cambridge, 1982)
Mikhail Druskin: *Igor Stravinsky: His Life, Works and Views* (Cambridge, 1983)
Charles M. Joseph: *Stravinsky and the Piano* (Ann Arbor, 1983)
Pieter C. van den Toorn: *The Music of Igor Stravinsky* (New Haven, 1983)
Jann Pasler, ed.: *Confronting Stravinsky* (Berkeley, 1986)
Ethan Haimo and Paul Johnson, eds: *Stravinsky Retrospectives* (Lincoln, Nebraska, 1987)
Pieter C. van den Toorn: *Stravinsky and The Rite of Spring: The Beginnings of a Musical Language* (Oxford, 1987)
Stephen Walsh: *The Music of Stravinsky* (London, 1988)
Louis Andriessen and Elmer Schönberger: *The Apollonian Clockwork: On Stravinsky* (Oxford, 1989)
Philip Stuart: *Igor Stravinsky: The Composer in the Recording Studio: A Comprehensive Discography* (London, 1991)
Robert Craft: *Stravinsky: Glimpses of a Life* (London, 1992 [*Glimpses*])

Index

BILLERICAY MUSIC STUDY GROUP

THE 'RITE' AND THE RIOT

FOR INFORMATION:
TEL. 01277 653466.